Lecture Notes in Computer Science   11391

Commenced Publication in 1973
Founding and Former Series Editors:
Gerhard Goos, Juris Hartmanis, and Jan van Leeuwen

More information about this series at http://www.springer.com/series/7409

Akka Zemmari · Mohamed Mosbah
Nora Cuppens-Boulahia · Frédéric Cuppens (Eds.)

Risks and Security of Internet and Systems

13th International Conference, CRiSIS 2018
Arcachon, France, October 16–18, 2018
Revised Selected Papers

 Springer

Editors
Akka Zemmari
University of Bordeaux
Talence, France

Nora Cuppens-Boulahia
IMT Atlantique
Brest, France

Mohamed Mosbah
University of Bordeaux
Talence, France

Frédéric Cuppens
IMT Atlantique
Brest, France

ISSN 0302-9743   ISSN 1611-3349   (electronic)
Lecture Notes in Computer Science
ISBN 978-3-030-12142-6   ISBN 978-3-030-12143-3   (eBook)
https://doi.org/10.1007/978-3-030-12143-3

Library of Congress Control Number: 2018968326

LNCS Sublibrary: SL3 – Information Systems and Applications, incl. Internet/Web, and HCI

This Springer imprint is published by the registered company Springer Nature Switzerland AG
The registered company address is: Gewerbestrasse 11, 6330 Cham, Switzerland

Preface

The 13th International Conference on Risks and Security of Internet and Systems (CRiSIS 2018) took place during October 16–18, 2018 in Arcachon, France. It continued a tradition of successful conferences: Bourges (2005), Marrakech (2007), Tozeur (2008), Toulouse (2009), Montréal (2010), Timisoara (2011), Cork (2012), La Rochelle (2013), Trento (2014), Mytilene (2015), Roscoff (2016), and Dinard (2017).

The CRiSIS conference constitutes an open forum for the exchange of state-of-the-art knowledge on security issues in Internet-related applications, networks, and systems. Following the tradition of the previous events, the program was composed of high-quality contributed papers. The program call for papers looked for original and significant research contributions to the following topics:

- Analysis and management of risk
- Attacks and defenses
- Attack data acquisition and network monitoring
- Cryptography, biometrics, watermarking
- Dependability and fault tolerance of Internet applications
- Distributed and embedded systems security
- Empirical methods for security and risk evaluation
- Hardware-based security and physical security
- Intrusion detection and prevention systems
- Privacy protection and anonymization
- Risk-aware access and usage control
- Security and risk assessment and metrics
- Security and dependability of operating systems
- Security and safety of critical infrastructures
- Security and privacy of peer-to-peer system and wireless networks
- Security models and security policies
- Security of new generation networks, security of VoIP and multimedia
- Security of e-commerce, electronic voting, and database systems
- Security of social networks
- Security of industrial control systems
- Smartphone security and privacy
- Traceability, metrology and forensics
- Trust management
- Use of smart cards and personal devices for Internet applications
- Web and cloud security.

In response to this call for papers, 34 papers were submitted. Each paper was reviewed by at least three reviewers, and judged according to scientific and presentation quality, originality, and relevance to the conference topics. The Program Committee selected 12 regular papers and six short papers. The program was completed with excellent invited talks given by Dominique Mery (University of Nancy, France), Manoj Singh Gaur (IIT Jammu, India), and Vijay Laxmi (MNIT Jaipur, India). Finally, the conference included two tutorials given by Tayssir Touili (University of Paris 13, France) and Romain Laborde (University of Toulouse, France).

It is impossible to organize a successful program without the help of many individuals. We would like to express our appreciation to the authors of the submitted papers, the Program Committee members, and the external referees. We owe special thanks to the Organizing Committee for the hard work they did locally in Arcachon.

November 2018

Akka Zemmari
Mohamed Mosbah
Nora Cuppens-Boulahia
Frédéric Cuppens

Organization

General Chairs

Jean Louis Lanet	LHS, Inria, France
Mohamed Mosbah	LaBRI, Bordeaux INP, France

Program Co-chairs

Nora Cuppens-Boulahia	IMT Atlantique, France
Akka Zemmari	LaBRI, University Bordeaux, France

Publicity Chairs

Mohamed Mosbah	Bordeaux INP, France
Reda Yaich	IRT SystemX, France

Sponsorship and Publication Chair

Frédéric Cuppens	IMT Atlantique, France Axel Legay, UCL, Belgium

Organization Co-chairs

Mohamed Mosbah	LaBRI, Bordeaux INP, France
Akka Zemmari	LaBRI, University of Bordeaux, France

Local Organization

Auriane Dantes	LaBRI, University of Bordeaux, France
Katel Guerin	LaBRI, University of Bordeaux, France
Sofian Maabout	LaBRI, University of Bordeaux, France
Nadia Chaabouni	LaBRI, University of Bordeaux, France
Charazed Ksouri	LaBRI, University of Bordeaux, France
Ghislaine Le Gall	IMT Atlantique, France

Program Committee

Esma Aimeur	University of Montreal, Canada
Luca Allodi	Eindhoven University of Technology, The Netherlands
Jocelyn Aubert	Luxembourg Institute of Science and Technology, Luxembourg
Fabrizio Biondi	Inria Rennes, France
Anis Bkakria	IMT Atlantique, France

Contents

An Empirical Study
on the Comprehensibility of Graphical
Security Risk Models Based
on Sequence Diagrams

Vetle Volden-Freberg[(✉)] and Gencer Erdogan

SINTEF Digital, Oslo, Norway
{vetle.volden-freberg,gencer.erdogan}@sintef.no

Abstract. We report on an empirical study in which we evaluate the comprehensibility of graphical versus textual risk annotations in threat models based on sequence diagrams. The experiment was carried out on two separate groups where each group solved tasks related to either graphical or textual annotations. We also examined the efficiency of using these two annotations in terms of the average time each group spent per task. Our study reports that threat models with textual risk annotations are equally comprehensible to corresponding threat models with graphical risk annotations. With respect to efficiency, however, we found out that participants solving tasks related to the graphical annotations spent on average 23% less time per task.

Keywords: Security risk models · Empirical study · Comprehensibility

1 Introduction

Security risk models based on sequence diagrams are useful to design and select tests focusing on security risks the system under test is exposed to [4,25]. This testing strategy is referred to as risk-driven security testing [8]. The field of risk-driven testing needs more formality and proper tool support [5]. To address this need, we developed a tool to help security testers design and select security tests based on the available risk picture by making use of risk-annotated sequence diagrams. The tool is freely available as a plugin [2] for Eclipse Papyrus [23].

We specifically developed the tool to support the CORAL approach, which is a model-based approach to risk-driven security testing [4]. The CORAL approach provides a domain specific modeling language that captures security risks in terms of sequence diagrams annotated with graphical icons representing risk constructs. However, as part of the development of the tool, we conducted an empirical study to evaluate the comprehensibility of the graphical icons representing risk constructs in the CORAL language versus corresponding textual representation of the risk constructs in terms of UML stereotypes [22].

© Springer Nature Switzerland AG 2019
A. Zemmari et al. (Eds.): CRiSIS 2018, LNCS 11391, pp. 1–17, 2019.
https://doi.org/10.1007/978-3-030-12143-3_1

The contribution of this paper is the empirical study. We believe the study is useful for the security risk community to better understand the effectiveness of security risk models based on sequence diagrams. The study may also be useful for others who wish to conduct similar empirical studies, as well as for tool developers who consider to develop similar tools.

The overall goal of our empirical study was to investigate, from the perspective of comprehensibility, whether it is better to use the graphical icons provided by the CORAL language to represent risk constructs or if it is better to use corresponding textual representation in terms of UML stereotypes. Throughout this paper, by graphical annotations, we mean representing risk constructs using graphical icons provided by the CORAL language [4], and by textual annotations, we mean representing risk constructs using UML stereotype annotations [22]. Based on this overall goal, we defined two research questions:

RQ1. Will the use of either graphical or textual annotations to represent risk constructs in threat models based on sequence diagrams affect the objective performance of comprehensibility?

RQ2. Will the use of either graphical or textual annotations to represent risk constructs in threat models based on sequence diagrams affect the participants' efficiency in solving the provided tasks?

In Sect. 2, we present the kind of threat models considered in our empirical study. In Sect. 3, we present an overview of our research method which consists of three main steps: experiment design, experiment execution, and experiment data analysis. Sections 4–6 present our empirical study with respect to the aforementioned steps of our research method. In Sect. 7, we discuss our results in relation to research questions RQ1 and RQ2 as well as threats to validity. In Sect. 8, we discuss related work. Finally, in Sect. 9, we provide our conclusions.

2   Threat Models Considered in the Empirical Study

It is beyond the scope of this paper to explain in detail the CORAL language [4] as well as UML sequence diagrams and stereotypes [22]. However, it is necessary to illustrate the kind of threat models considered in our empirical study.

Figures 1(a) and (b) illustrate two semantically identical threat models using graphical and textual risk annotations, respectively. Figure 1(a) is developed using the CORAL language, while in Fig. 1(b) we have replaced the graphical risk annotations with corresponding textual risk annotations using UML stereotypes. The graphical icons representing risk constructs in the CORAL language are inspired by corresponding graphical icons in CORAS, which is a model-driven approach to risk analysis [17].

Both threat models in Figs. 1(a) and (b) illustrate a stored cross-site scripting attack [32] on an example web application that stores feedback from users, such as an online forum. The *hacker* first clicks on a button on the web application to add new feedback (*clickAddNewFeedback*), and then updates the feedback with malicious script (*updateFeedbackText(script)*). This causes the unwanted

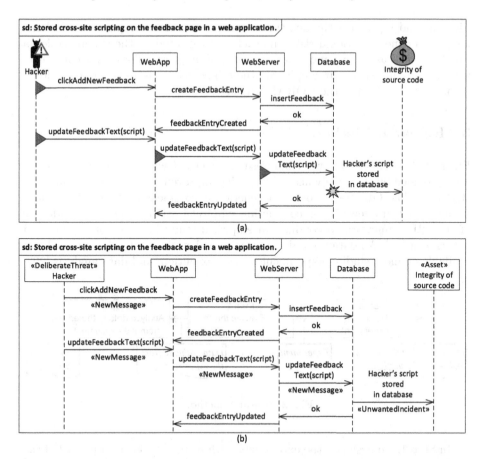

Fig. 1. (a) Threat model with graphical risk annotations based on the CORAL language. (b) Threat model with corresponding textual risk annotations using stereotypes. (Color figure online)

incident *Hacker's script stored in database*, which in turn has an impact on the asset *Integrity of source code* because the script may be executed by the browser when accessed by a user, which modifies the content of the web page.

From a conceptual point of view, the graphical icon representing a hacker in Fig. 1(a) is referred to as a *deliberate threat* in CORAL [4]. A deliberate threat is a human threat that has malicious intents. During risk assessment, we assess security risks that may harm certain security *assets* we want to protect. In CORAL, an asset is illustrated by a moneybag icon. Messages initiated by a threat with the intention of manipulating system behavior are referred to as *new messages*. A new message is represented by a red triangle which is placed at the transmitting end of the message. An *unwanted incident* is represented by a message with a yellow explosion sign at the transmitting end and conveys that an asset is harmed or its value is reduced. As already mentioned, Fig. 1(b) "mirrors"

Fig. 1(a) and represents the above risk constructs as stereotypes. The CORAL language defines additional risk constructs not captured by the threat model in Fig. 1(a), such as *altered messages* and *deleted messages*. These risk constructs were also included in our empirical study. The reader is referred to [4] for a detailed explanation of the CORAL language.

3   Research Method

Figure 2 shows an overview of our research method which is based on guidelines provided by the widely accepted quality improvement paradigm framework (QIP) [1]. The QIP framework is a generic improvement cycle which can also be used as a framework for conducting empirical studies [30]. We made use of the QIP framework to conduct an empirical study in terms of a controlled experiment [30]. All data related to our empirical study is fully documented and available online including experiment design, execution, and data analysis [29].

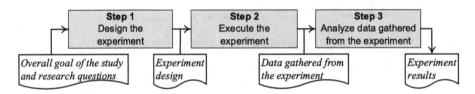

Fig. 2. Research method.

In Step 1, we designed the experiment with respect to the overall goal of the study and research questions defined in Sect. 1. The experiment was designed in terms of formulating the hypothesis, identifying independent and dependent variables, defining the experiment process, and preparing experiment material.

Based on the experiment process defined in Step 1, we executed the experiment in Step 2 as follows. First, we identified the subjects of the experiment and then conducted a demographic survey and based on that divided the participants fairly into groups A and B. Then, we provided Group A and Group B training material for the graphical and textual annotations, respectively. Finally, we conducted a questionnaire focusing on the graphical and textual annotations answered by Group A and Group B, respectively. The demographic survey and the questionnaire were carried out using the online survey tool Eval&Go [6]. The training material was provided via email subsequent to the demographic survey, but prior to the questionnaire.

In Step 3, we analyzed the data gathered from the online questionnaire in terms of visualizing data, using descriptive statistics, and carrying out hypothesis testing of the hypothesis defined in Step 1.

4 Experiment Design

In this section, we first formulate the hypothesis and identify the independent and dependent variables before presenting the experiment material. The process of the experiment is already described in Sect. 3.

4.1 Formulate Hypothesis and Identify Variables of the Experiment

Following the goal and research questions in Sect. 1, we devised hypothesis H_0.

H_0: Threat models with textual annotations are equally comprehensible in comparison to threat models with graphical annotations.

There exists no empirical evidence to support that either annotation is superior to the other. For this reason, we formulate alternative hypotheses H_1 and H_2.

H_1: Threat models with textual annotations are more comprehensible than threat models with graphical annotations.

H_2: Threat models with graphical annotations are more comprehensible than threat models with textual annotations.

In order to assess and compare the two different annotations with respect to the hypothesis, we need to identify independent and dependent variables for our experiment. Independent variables are considered to be the input to an experiment. In effect, the motivation for an experiment is to investigate whether variations in the independent variables have an effect on the dependent variables (output of the experiment) [30].

The independent variable in our experiment is the threat model representation whose notation can hold two different values: graphical or textual risk annotations. The dependent variables are comprehensibility and efficiency.

Comprehensibility refers to the ability of the participant to develop and comprehend models [24]. This is measured by effectiveness, which in our case is the degree to which the participant is able to reach successful task accomplishment, taking into account the task scores in the questionnaire.

Efficiency refers to the ability of the participant to develop and comprehend a model relatively quickly according to the syntax and semantics of the modeling language [24]. Having in mind that there currently is no empirical evidence to suggest what is a relatively quick comprehension of the threat models considered in our experiment, comparison between the two populations (Group A and Group B) with respect to efficiency is necessary.

4.2 Experiment Material

We prepared the experiment material in terms of a letter of consent to be signed by the participants, a demographic survey, training material, and a questionnaire with tasks to solve.

In order to communicate with the participants and divide the participants fairly into two groups, names and corresponding email addresses were recorded and associated with their respective response to the demographic survey. With respect to training material, we prepared one document for each group explaining the experiment. Group A received training material for the graphical annotations, while Group B received training material for the textual annotations. Due to space limitations, we will not go into further details of the training material. However, this is thoroughly documented and available online [29].

As mentioned in Sect. 3, we used the tool Eval&Go to conduct the online demographic survey and questionnaire. In addition to Eval&Go, we considered the tools SurveyGizmo, SurveyMonkey, Zoho Survey, Google Forms, Survey-Planet, LimeSurvey, and QuestionPro [29]. We selected Eval&Go because it was the only tool fulfilling most of our requirements (two out of three): (1) provide a timer functionality to enforce a time limit per question and (2) not store e-mail/IP addresses, browser information or cookies, as well as prevent the possibility to trace a response to a particular participant. Point (2) was important to take into account the anonymity of the participants. Our third requirement was a time stamp feature to record the individual time *each participant spent per task*. None of the tools provided this feature. However, Eval&Go did record the average time *each group spent per task*.

The demographic survey consists of 22 questions (Q) and were grouped into the following categories to best help us divide the participants fairly into two groups: occupation (Q1–Q4), work experience within IT or engineering (Q5–Q6), academic degree (Q7–Q12), knowledge of UML modeling (Q13), knowledge of sequence diagrams (Q14), work experience within model-driven engineering (Q15–Q16), knowledge and work experience within risk assessment or risk analysis (Q17–Q19), knowledge and work experience within user interface design or usability (Q20–Q22). The questions related to "knowledge" were answered using a Likert scale with the following five values {no knowledge, minor knowledge, some knowledge, good knowledge, expert}.

The tasks in our experiment address comprehensibility and are therefore focused on model-reading [10,28]. To observe noticable difference in comprehensibility between the two control groups, it is important to have a mixture of easy and difficult tasks [11,12]. For this reason, we divided the questionnaire in two parts. Part 1 consists of 6 less complicated tasks concerned with identifying different risk constructs in a threat model, for example, *How many altered messages are modeled in the threat model?* Part 2 consists of 7 more complex tasks focusing on model interpretation, for example, *According to the model, describe how the hacker causes the unwanted incident to occur.* Developing tasks with an appropriate level of complexity is not trivial. The tasks were therefore developed in several iterations where for each iteration a third researcher reviewed the tasks and provided feedback to the authors. In total, there were seven iterations until the task set for the questionnaire was finalized. With respect to task scores, a participant can obtain a maximum score of 12 points in Part 1, and a maximum of 15 points in Part 2. This is because in some of the tasks it is possible to obtain more than one point. Wrong or no answer to a question results in zero points. The complete task set for the questionnaire as well as the questions for the demographic survey are available online [29].

To avoid potential situations where a participant overestimates the amount of time required for a given task or that the easier tasks are correctly answered by most of the participants, we enforced a time limit per question. These time limits were also reviewed in the iterative process of developing the tasks. Each task in Part 1 has a time limit of 60 s. The last six out of the seven tasks in Part 2 were presented to the participant as three separate pairs of tasks because each pair addresses one threat model. The first out of the seven tasks in Part 2 has a time limit of 180 s, while each pair of tasks in Part 2 has a time limit of 300 s. This means that Part 1 has a total time limit of 6 min (6 tasks × 60 s = 360 s), while Part 2 has a total time limit of 18 min (180 s + 3 pairs of tasks × 300 s = 1080 s). Thus, the total allocated time for all 13 tasks is 360 s + 1080 s = 24 min.

5   Experiment Execution

The participants were recruited through our network and selected based on two criteria: (1) hold or being in pursuit of a degree within computer science and (2) have knowledge of programming and/or have technical experience within ICT. This type of sampling is referred to as purposive sampling [26]. We recruited in total 16 participants of which 10 were graduates and 6 were undergraduates within the field of computer science.

On June 14th 2017, the invitations for the demographic survey were sent to all participants by email. By June 18th 2017, all participants had submitted their answers. We identified four groups of participants based on their occupation: five students, eight working, two studying and working, and one specified as other. The participants were divided fairly in two groups with respect to their academic degree, years of work experience, and knowledge profiles. Table 1 shows the participants in Groups A and B, where Group A represents the participants solving tasks related to graphical annotations, while Group B represents the participants solving tasks related to textual annotations. With respect to academic degree (AD), both groups have three participants with a bachelor's degree and five participants with a master's degree.

Group A has on average 2 years of work experience (WE), while Group B has on average 5 years of work experience. This difference is because Group B has one participant with 20 years of work experience. However, to keep the groups balanced, we placed five participants with work experience in each group. None of the participants had work experience with model-driven engineering (MDE-WE). One participant had two years of work experience with risk assessment or analysis (R-WE). Finally, four participants had work experience with user interface design or usability (UI-WE), with one, two, four and eight years of experience, respectively.

The columns UML (UML modeling), SD (sequence diagrams), R (risk assessment or analysis), and UI (user interface design or usability) show the participants' assessment of their own knowledge within these domains. The digits in these columns correspond to the steps in the Likert scale defined in Sect. 4. That is, the digit 0 corresponds to "no knowledge", 1 corresponds to "minor knowledge", and so on. As shown in Table 1, the average level of knowledge (with respect to UML, SD, R, and UI) are similar for both groups, except for UML modeling, where Group A has a slightly better score (2.12) compared to Group B (2).

Table 1. Participants of Groups A and B. B = Bachelor's degree, M = Master's degree.

	Participant	AD	WE	UML	SD	MDE-WE	R	R-WE	UI	UI-WE
Group A	**P1**	B	0	2	2	0	2	0	2	0
(graphical)	**P2**	B	2	1	1	0	1	0	0	0
	P3	B	1	3	3	0	2	0	0	0
	P4	M	1	2	2	0	0	0	2	0
	P5	M	0	2	2	0	1	0	2	0
	P6	M	4	2	1	0	1	0	2	2
	P7	M	8	2	2	0	2	0	4	8
	P8	M	0	3	3	0	3	0	0	0
	Average	**M**	**2**	**2.12**	**2**	**0**	**1.5**	**0**	**1.5**	**1.25**
Group B	**P9**	B	1	2	2	0	0	0	1	1
(textual)	**P10**	B	20	2	2	0	1	0	2	0
	P11	B	5	2	2	0	1	0	1	0
	P12	M	0	2	2	0	2	0	2	0
	P13	M	5	1	1	0	1	0	2	0
	P14	M	9	2	2	0	3	2	2	4
	P15	M	0	2	2	0	2	0	1	0
	P16	M	0	3	3	0	2	0	1	0
	Average	**M**	**5**	**2**	**2**	**0**	**1.5**	**0.25**	**1.5**	**0.62**

Having divided the participants fairly in two groups, we distributed the questionnaire containing the tasks on June 18th 2017 via email where we included an anonymous link to the survey. All answers were submitted by June 25th 2017. Table 2 shows the complete task scores. The tasks T1–T6 belong to Part 1 of the questionnaire, while tasks T7–T13 belong to Part 2 of the questionnaire.

With respect to time usage, we recorded via the tool Eval&Go the average time *per group* spent for each task in the questionnaire (see Table 3). The column $\bar{x}(t_A)$ shows the average time (seconds) Group A spent for each task, while column $\bar{x}(t_B)$ shows the average time Group B spent for each task. Recall that the last six out of the seven tasks in Part 2 of the questionnaire were presented to the participant as three pairs of tasks. The column Δt shows the difference in average time Group B spent compared to Group A, i.e., $\Delta t = \bar{x}(t_B) - \bar{x}(t_A)$. The column % shows this difference in terms of percentage. Finally, a positive value for Δt and % indicates that Group B spent more time than Group A, while a negative value indicates that Group B spent less time than Group A.

Table 2. Task scores for Group A and Group B. T = Task, P = Participant.

	Group A									Group B								
	P1	P2	P3	P4	P5	P6	P7	P8	Avg.	P9	P10	P11	P12	P13	P14	P15	P16	Avg.
T1	1	1	1	0	0	1	1	1	0.75	1	0	1	1	1	1	0	1	0.75
T2	1	1	1	0	1	1	1	1	0.875	1	0	1	1	1	1	0	1	0.75
T3	1	1	1	0	1	1	1	1	0.875	1	1	1	1	1	1	0	1	0.875
T4	3	1	2	0	2	3	0	2	1.625	3	2	0	3	3	3	1	3	2.25
T5	2	0	2	1	2	2	2	2	1.625	2	2	1	2	2	2	1	2	1.75
T6	4	4	4	2	4	4	3	4	3.625	4	4	4	4	3	4	4	3	3.75
T7	0	2	0	0	0	2	1	0	0.625	0	0	0	0	0	0	0	0	0
T8	1	1	0	1	1	1	1	0	0.75	1	1	1	1	1	0	1	1	0.875
T9	1	3	0	0	3	2	1	3	1.625	2	2	0	2	2	0	0	2	1.25
T10	1	1	0	1	1	1	1	1	0.875	1	1	1	1	0	1	1	1	0.875
T11	2	0	0	0	0	0	3	3	1	2	2	0	3	3	0	0	2	1.5
T12	2	3	2	0	0	1	0	2	1.25	3	3	1	3	2	0	0	2	1.75
T13	1	2	2	0	2	2	2	2	1.625	2	2	0	2	2	2	0	2	1.5
Total	20	20	15	5	17	21	17	22	17.125	23	20	11	24	21	15	8	21	17.875

Table 3. The average time per group spent for each task.

Task #	$\bar{x}(t_A)$	$\bar{x}(t_B)$	Δt	%
1	22	31	9	40.91%
2	22	24	2	9.09%
3	13	21	8	61.54%
4	49	46	−3	−6.12%
5	36	41	5	13.89%
6	44	51	7	15.91%
7	119	145	26	21.85%
8+9	156	233	77	49.36%
10+11	167	205	38	22.75%
12+13	232	232	0	0.00%
Total	**860**	**1029**	**169**	

6 Experiment Data Analysis

Figure 3 shows box plots of the total score for Group A and Group B produced by IBM SPSS [9], which is the tool we used for statistical analysis. The box plot on the left hand side in Fig. 3 represents the distribution of Group A, while the box plot on the right hand side in Fig. 3 represents the distribution of Group B. The box plot for Group A reports an outlier of record 4 (i.e., Participant 4), having a total score of 5 (see Table 2). This record has a low score because the

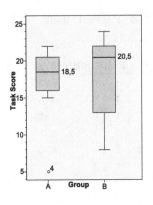
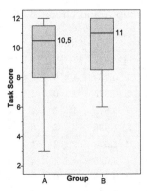
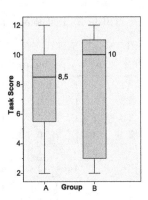

Fig. 3. Total score.   **Fig. 4.** Total score Part 1.   **Fig. 5.** Total score Part 2.

participant gave several blank answers. This might be because the participant did not know how to solve the tasks. It can also be because the participant was not interested in participating. For this reason, throughout this section, we analyze both situations; one where the outlier is included, and one where it is excluded. In addition, we analyze the data from three perspectives with respect to the task scores: total score, total score Part 1 only, total score Part 2 only.

In general, the box plots of the three different perspectives (Figs. 3, 4 and 5) do not give any clear indication whether there is any significant difference between the two groups. It may seem, however, that Group B has a slight improvement over Group A. If we in the total score (Fig. 3) exclude the outlier from Group A, the distributions of both groups seem to be approximately normally distributed. However, if we look at the total score for Part 1 (Fig. 4) and the total score for Part 2 (Fig. 5) individually, the distributions are not as normally distributed. We therefore proceed to apply additional descriptive statistics to investigate further whether there is any significant difference between the two groups.

Table 4 shows additional descriptive statistics of the three different perspectives in terms of mean, variance, standard deviation, standard error, skewness, and kurtosis [7,18]. The columns A and B show descriptive statistics of the total score for Group A and Group B, respectively, while the column A* shows descriptive statistics of the total score for Group A excluding the outlier.

The high mean scores for "Total score Part 1" compared to "Total score Part 2" indicate that the participants had a good understanding of the tasks in Part 1, while the lower mean scores for "Total score Part 2" indicate that the participants struggled more with the tasks in Part 2, as expected. Moreover, Table 4 shows that Group B is less skewed and more normally distributed compared to Group A. Skewness and kurtosis are measures used to check whether the data follow a normal distribution [18]. A skewness value close to zero indicates a symmetrical distribution, positive and negative values indicate a right-skewed and left-skewed distribution, respectively. Both groups have negative skewness in all

Table 4. Descriptive statistics of the total task scores.

	Total score			Total score Part 1			Total score Part 2		
	A	B	A*	A	B	A*	A	B	A*
Mean (Avg.)	17.13	17.88	18.86	9.38	10.13	10.29	7.75	7.75	8.57
Variance	29.554	34.411	6.476	9.125	4.982	2.905	11.357	18.214	6.952
Std. deviation	5.436	5.866	2.545	3.021	2.232	1.704	3.370	4.268	2.637
Std. error	1.922	2.074	0.962	1.068	0.789	0.644	1.191	1.509	0.997
Skewness	−1.862	−0.827	−0.373	−1.515	−1.029	−0.618	−0.638	−0.579	−0.570
Kurtosis	3.956	−0.812	−1.314	2.279	−0.069	−1.396	−0.291	−2.097	0.547

perspectives included in Table 4. This confirms our observation from the box plots in Figs. 3, 4 and 5.

The kurtosis gives an indication of how big the *tails* (distance from the mean) of the distribution are [18]. A normal distribution has a kurtosis value of 0, while positive and negative values indicate larger and smaller tails, respectively. A distribution with a positive kurtosis implies a distribution that is more steep towards the top than a normal distribution. A negative kurtosis implies a distribution that is more flat towards the top than a normal distribution. The values for kurtosis that fall within an acceptable range to be classified as acceptable for a normal distribution is (for a sample size $n = 25$) minimum −1.2 and maximum 2.3 [18]. Note that for our sample sizes (which are $n = 8$) the ranges do not cover this size. For this reason, the kurtosis may be biased, however, it does give an indication whether the distribution is approximately normally distributed or not. The kurtosis values for Group A and Group B differ from each other by some margin. For example, looking at the values for "Total score" in Table 4, we see that the kurtosis for Group B is well within the acceptable range (−0.812). Group A is outside the acceptable range with a difference of $3.956 - 2.3 = 1.656$. Group A is also outside the range when excluding the outlier (−1.314).

In general, the descriptive statistics in Table 4 shows that the two groups are similar, with Group B having a slightly better score than Group A (mean). With the exclusion of the outlier (column A*), however, Group A seems to have a better mean score with a smaller median than Group B. Further, this yields a higher precision of measurement for Group A than Group B, with a lower standard deviation and standard error. Additionally, Group A gains a smaller skewness value, indicating an approximately normal distribution. Thus, we argue that Group B has performed better than Group A. However, the exclusion of Group A's outlier suggests that Group A performed better than Group B. It is important to note, however, that the differences are small and we cannot conclude whether there is a significant difference between the groups only by comparing their descriptive statistics for either of the three perspectives. For this reason, we proceed to hypothesis testing to answer our null hypothesis H_0.

In our experiment we applied two conditions (graphical versus textual annotations) with different participants taking part in each condition. For this reason, an appropriate hypothesis testing method is the independent samples t-test, also called an unpaired t-test [9,27]. There are two variants of this t-test, one assuming equal variances, and one assuming unequal variances. To determine which variant to use, we carried out Levene's test for equality of variances for each of the three perspectives (including and excluding the outlier in Group A). Moreover, for the t-test, we used a 95% confidence interval and degrees of freedom given by $df = n_1 + n_2 - 2$, which in our case is $df = 8 + 8 - 2 = 14$. Table 5 summarizes the results from the t-tests for testing the null hypothesis H_0 (defined in Sect. 4) for all the perspectives mentioned above. The symbol * in Table 5 denotes the t-tests in which we have excluded the outlier in Group A from the total score. The column "Statistically significant?" provides a yes/no value depending on whether the t-statistics indicate a significant effect between Group A and Group B.

Table 5. Summary of the independent samples t-tests.

	T-statistics	Statistically significant?	Accept H_0?
Total score	$t = -0.265, p = 0.795$	No	Yes
Total score*	$t = 0.430, p = 0.677$	No	Yes
Total score Part 1	$t = -0.565, p = 0.581$	No	Yes
Total score Part 1*	$t = -0.265, p = 0.795$	No	Yes
Total score Part 2	$t = 0.000, p = 1.000$	No	Yes
Total score Part 2*	$t = 0.454, p = 0.658$	No	Yes

7   Discussion

As shown in Table 5, the independent samples t-tests for all perspectives, including the perspectives in which the outlier in Group A is excluded, report on the acceptance of our null hypothesis. This means that the comprehensibility of threat models with either graphical or textual annotations with respect to the given task set is equally comprehensible. Thus, to answer **RQ1**, the use of either graphical or textual annotations seem not to affect the objective performance of comprehensibility. That is, there is no evidence indicating that graphical annotations are more effective than textual annotations or vice versa, in terms of comprehension, with respect to the threat models considered in our study.

With respect to **RQ2**, we examine the average time each group spent per task and note that Group B spent considerably more time than Group A for the whole task set (see Table 3). Furthermore, eight out of the ten reported differences seen from column Δt in Table 3 are in favour of Group A. On average, Group B spent approximately 23% more time *per task* compared to Group A. Thus, to answer RQ2, this indicates that graphical annotations aid the participant in more efficient task solving, compared to textual annotations. This claim is further substantiated by Moody [20], who argues that visual representations are more efficient than textual because they are processed in parallel by the visual system, while textual representations are processed serially by the auditory system. This is because textual representations are one-dimensional (linear), while graphical are two-dimensional (spatial) [20].

However, it is important to note, since we lack individual time, we cannot ascertain that there were participants who contributed heavily to the average time statistic. This statistic could for example be affected by a participant either having skipped many questions, or spent all/most of the available time for a task. However, we note that there is a difference in time as described above, and that having a more precise measurement of individual time may be of interest in future experiments to further answer RQ2.

In the following, we discuss threats to validity in terms of conclusion validity, internal validity, construct validity, and external validity [30,31].

Conclusion Validity. For our hypothesis test we chose to use the independent samples t-test, which assumes a normal distribution and independent control groups. This choice was motivated by our findings during the data visualisation and use of descriptive statistics. In addition, the two control groups were completely independent, and each group were only subject to a single treatment. If the data was not normally distributed, we could have performed a non-parametric test such as the Mann-Whitney u-test [9]. Although parametric tests (such as the independent t-test carried out in our study) generally has higher power than non-parametric test, i.e., less data is needed to get significant results [30], the t-tests were in addition carried out from multiple perspectives to mitigate arriving at a false conclusion when rejecting or accepting our null hypothesis. Moreover, we acknowledge that by having a larger sample size, our conclusions would be more robust.

Internal Validity. A threat to internal validity is introduced by not having randomized assignment of the treatment for our control groups. This threat is mitigated by dividing the participants fairly in two groups based on competence as explained in Sect. 5. The fair division of groups ensures to some extent that the groups are even in terms of level of knowledge. The fair division could have been further strengthened in the study by, for example, adding an additional step in which the roles of Groups A and B are swapped in terms of solving tasks for the textual and graphical annotations, respectively. However, the measurement of knowledge based on the Likert scale can be imprecise. Imprecision may be due to the Dunning-Kruger effect [3]. This is an effect wherein less competent people tend to overestimate their skills and knowledge, while more competent people tend to underestimate their skills and knowledge. Another threat to internal validity concerns the introductory material since the participants have to go through it on their own. As a consequence, we cannot control the degree to which the participant learns the given material. This uncertainty leads to two different situations in which a participant either spends more or less time learning the material than others. Finally, since we could not control the environment in which the participant answered the questionnaire, there was no way to ensure that the participant did not carry out internet searches to look for clues. In an attempt to mitigate this, the tasks had timers enforcing time restrictions.

Construct Validity. A threat to construct validity is introduced by the theoretical constructs comprehensibility and efficiency and the manner in which they are measured in the study. Comprehensibility is measured with respect to task scores, while efficiency is measured with respect to average time. However, these measurement types for comprehensibility and efficiency are often used in similar studies [13,19,21]. Furthermore, to prevent bias, all experiment material are the same for both groups with the only difference being the graphical or textual annotations. Finally, as mentioned in Sect. 4, the experiment material was reviewed and improved by a third researcher in seven iterations.

External Validity. Our sample of participants does not fully represent the target group of CORAL, which are professionals within security testing and risk assessment, who ultimately are the stakeholders likely to use the CORAL approach. The focus of the study, however, was concerned with the comprehensibility and efficiency when interpreting *predefined* threat models with either graphical or textual annotations. Thus, the study was not concerned with testing nor assessing risks and therefore did not require participants with high expertise in these fields. The sample does, however, consist of developers at different levels, which is also a relevant target group. It can be argued, that developers are most familiar with textual notation used in programming languages. Yet, all participants stated they had experience in using UML in some form. Although the time limitations per task were carefully identified in seven iterations (see Sect. 4.2), the time limitations may have had a potential impact on the results. However, evaluating this would require a separate study.

8   Related Work

Hogganvik et al. [14] empirically investigated the comprehensibility of a domain specific modeling language (DSML) for security risk analysis based on the UML use-case notation [22]. In particular, they investigated the comprehensibility of two versions of their DSML. One version using only stereotypes to capture security risk constructs versus the other version using graphical annotations to capture security risk constructs. This study involved both professionals and students. Their findings, which are similar to ours, report that the participants using graphical risk annotations were able to conclude faster, however, not reaching a higher correctness of interpreting the models.

Meliá et al. [19] compared graphical and textual notations for the maintainability of model-driven engineering domain models in a pilot study. The study was performed with students as participants, and showed that the participants using textual notation performed better with regard to analyzability coverage and modifiability efficiency. This study compares pure textual models against graphical models, and employ metrics different from our study. Furthermore, the graphical models are represented by UML class diagrams, while in our study we address threat models based on sequence diagrams.

Labunets et al. [15, 16] report on an empirical study in which they investigate the comprehensibility of security risk models in terms of tabular versus graphical representations. They conclude that tabular risk models are more effective than graphical ones with respect to extracting certain information about security risks, while graphical risk models are better in terms of solving tasks involving different information cues, different relationships and different judgments. While they evaluate the comprehensibility of tabular risk models versus graphical risk models, we evaluate the comprehensibility of graphical versus textual *risk annotations* on sequence diagrams.

9 Conclusion

We have carried out an empirical study in which we evaluate the comprehensibility of two different annotations representing risk constructs in threat models based on sequence diagrams. The two being either graphical icons provided by the CORAL language [4] or textual UML stereotype annotations [22]. The experiment was carried out on two separate groups A and B, where Group A solved tasks related to the graphical annotations, while Group B solved tasks related to the textual annotations. We also examined the efficiency of these two annotations in terms of the average time each group spent per task.

With respect to comprehensibility, our study reports that threat models using textual risk annotations to support risk assessment are equally comprehensible to corresponding threat models using graphical risk annotations. With respect to efficiency, our study reports that the use of graphical annotations leads to more efficient task solving in comparison to textual annotations. Participants receiving tasks related to the graphical annotations spent on average 23% less time per task compared to the participants receiving tasks related to the textual annotations. Although Group A was able to conclude faster, they did not reach a higher correctness of interpreting the threat models. Note that our evaluation on efficiency is based on the average time each group spent per task, and not based on the individual time each participant spent per task. Thus, as future work, further studies should evaluate the efficiency using individual time. However, our findings are in line with and substantiated by similar studies [14].

Acknowledgments. This work has been conducted within the AGRA project (236657) funded by the Research Council of Norway.

References

1. Basili, V.R., Caldiera, G., Rombach, H.D.: Experience Factory. Wiley, Hoboken (2002)
2. CORAL Plugin for Eclipse Papyrus. https://bitbucket.org/vetlevo/no.uio.ifi.coral. profile/. Accessed 6 July 2018

3. Dunning, D., Johnson, K., Ehrlinger, J., Kruger, J.: Why people fail to recognize their own incompetence. Curr. Dir. Psychol. Sci. **12**(3), 83–87 (2003)
4. Erdogan, G.: CORAL: a model-based approach to risk-driven security testing. Ph.D. thesis, University of Oslo (2016)
5. Erdogan, G., Li, Y., Runde, R.K., Seehusen, F., Stølen, K.: Approaches for the combined use of risk analysis and testing: a systematic literature review. Int. J. Softw. Tools Technol. Transfer **16**(5), 627–642 (2014)
6. Eval&Go. http://www.evalandgo.com/. Accessed 6 July 2018
7. Everitt, B.S., Skrondal, A.: The Cambridge Dictionary of Statistics. Cambridge University Press, Cambridge (2010)
8. Felderer, M., Schieferdecker, I.: A taxonomy of risk-based testing. Int. J. Softw. Tools Technol. Transfer **16**(5), 559–568 (2014)
9. Field, A.: Discovering Statistics Using IBM SPSS Statistics. SAGE Publications, Newcastle upon Tyne (2013)
10. Hadar, I., Reinhartz-Berger, I., Kuflik, T., Perini, A., Ricca, F., Susi, A.: Comparing the comprehensibility of requirements models expressed in use case and Tropos: results from a family of experiments. Inf. Softw. Technol. **55**(10), 1823–1843 (2013)
11. Halford, G.S., Baker, R., McCredden, J.E., Bain, J.D.: How many variables can humans process? Psychol. Sci. **16**(1), 70–76 (2005)
12. Halford, G.S., Wilson, W.H., Phillips, S.: Processing capacity defined by relational complexity: implications for comparative, developmental, and cognitive psychology. Behav. Brain Sci. **21**(6), 803–831 (1998)
13. Hogganvik, I., Stølen, K.: Empirical investigations of the CORAS language for structured brainstorming. Technical report A05041, SINTEF Information and Communication Technology (2005)
14. Hogganvik, I., Stølen, K.: On the comprehension of security risk scenarios. In: Proceedings of the 13th International Workshop on Program Comprehension (IWPC 2005), pp. 115–124. IEEE (2005)
15. Labunets, K., Massacci, F., Paci, F., Marczak, S., de Oliveira, F.M.: Model comprehension for security risk assessment: an empirical comparison of tabular vs. graphical representations. Empir. Softw. Eng. **22**(6), 3017–3056 (2017)
16. Labunets, K., Massacci, F., Tedeschi, A.: Graphical vs. tabular notations for risk models: on the role of textual labels and complexity. In: Proceedings of the 11th International Symposium on Empirical Software Engineering and Measurement (ESEM 2017), pp. 267–276. IEEE (2017)
17. Lund, M.S., Solhaug, B., Stølen, K.: Model-Driven Risk Analysis: The CORAS Approach. Springer, Heidelberg (2011). https://doi.org/10.1007/978-3-642-12323-8
18. Madsen, B.S.: Statistics for Non-Statisticians. Springer, Heidelberg (2016). https://doi.org/10.1007/978-3-662-49349-6
19. Meliá, S., Cachero, C., Hermida, J.M., Aparicio, E.: Comparison of a textual versus a graphical notation for the maintainability of MDE domain models: an empirical pilot study. Softw. Qual. J. **24**(3), 709–735 (2016)
20. Moody, D.L.: The "physics" of notations: toward a scientific basis for constructing visual notations in software engineering. Trans. Softw. Eng. IEEE **35**(6), 756–779 (2009)
21. Nilsson, E.G., Stølen, K.: The FLUIDE framework for specifying emergency response user interfaces employed to a search and rescue case. Technical report A27575, SINTEF Information and Communication Technology (2016)
22. Object Management Group. Unified Modeling Language (UML), Version 2.5.1, 2017. OMG Document Number: formal/2017-12-05

23. Papyrus Modeling Environment. https://www.eclipse.org/papyrus/. Accessed 6 July 2018
24. Schalles, C.: Usability Evaluation of Modeling Languages. Springer, Heidelberg (2012). https://doi.org/10.1007/978-3-658-00051-6
25. Schieferdecker, I., Großmann, J., Schneider, M.: Model-based security testing. In: Proceedings of the 7th Workshop on Model-Based Testing (MBT 2012). Electronic Proceedings in Theoretical Computer Science (EPTCS), vol. 80, pp. 1–12 (2012)
26. Shull, F., Singer, J., Sjøberg, D.I.K.: Guide to Advanced Empirical Software Engineering. Springer, London (2007). https://doi.org/10.1007/978-1-84800-044-5
27. Singh, K.: Quantitative Social Research Methods. SAGE Publications, Newcastle upon Tyne (2007)
28. Staron, M., Kuzniarz, L., Wohlin, C.: Empirical assessment of using stereotypes to improve comprehension of UML models: a set of experiments. J. Syst. Softw. **79**(5), 727–742 (2006)
29. Volden-Freberg, V.: Development of tool support within the domain of risk-driven security testing. Master's thesis, University of Oslo (2017)
30. Wohlin, C., Höst, M., Henningsson, K.: Empirical research methods in software engineering. In: Conradi, R., Wang, A.I. (eds.) Empirical Methods and Studies in Software Engineering. LNCS, vol. 2765, pp. 7–23. Springer, Heidelberg (2003). https://doi.org/10.1007/978-3-540-45143-3_2
31. Wohlin, C., Runeson, P., Höst, M., Ohlsson, M.C., Regnell, B., Wesslén, A.: Experimentation in Software Engineering. Springer, Heidelberg (2012). https://doi.org/10.1007/978-3-642-29044-2
32. Cross-Site Scripting (XSS). https://www.owasp.org/index.php/Cross-site_Scripting_(XSS). Accessed 6 July 2018

Are Third-Party Libraries Secure?
A Software Library Checker for Java

Fabien Patrick Viertel$^{(\boxtimes)}$, Fabian Kortum, Leif Wagner, and Kurt Schneider

Software Engineering Group, Leibniz Universität Hannover, Hannover, Germany
{f.viertel,f.kortum,l.wagner,k.schneider}@se.uni-hannover.de

Abstract. Nowadays, there are many software libraries for different purposes that are used by various projects. An application is only as secure as its weakest component; thus if an imported library includes a certain vulnerability, an application could get insecure. Therefore a widespread search for existing security flaws within used libraries is necessary. Big databases like the National Vulnerability Database (NVD) comprise reported security incidents and can be utilized to determine whether a software library is secure or not. This classification is a very time-consuming and exhausting task.

We have developed a tool-based automated approach for supporting developers in this complex task through heuristics embedded in an eclipse plugin. Documented vulnerabilities stored in databases will be taken into consideration for the security classification of libraries. Weaknesses do not always entail the same consequences; a scoring that identifies the criticality oriented on their potential consequences is applied. In this paper, a method for the enrichment of knowledge containing vulnerability databases is considered.

Our approach is focussing on the scope of software weaknesses, which are library reasoned and documented in vulnerability databases. The Java Library Checker was implemented as eclipse plugin for supporting developers to make potential insecure third-party libraries visible to them.

Keywords: Software library · Vulnerability database · Metadata

1 Introduction

Only few software engineers take care of security during the software development process. After all they have no security experience because they are never getting in touch with security [1]. In the software development, code reuse through off-the-shelf libraries is a common practice. By design, many third-party libraries are insecure [11]. The Maven library repository lists now around 25.000 Java software libraries[1]. If developers are looking for libraries, usually they only focus on their functional needs and they do not care about security [1]. Like the own written source code, libraries can contain vulnerabilities too. They will be

---

[1] Maven Repository: https://mvnrepository.com/popular (06.2018).

© Springer Nature Switzerland AG 2019
A. Zemmari et al. (Eds.): CRiSIS 2018, LNCS 11391, pp. 18–34, 2019.
https://doi.org/10.1007/978-3-030-12143-3_2

defined by the MITRE Corporation, which operates the Common Vulnerabilities and Exposures (CVE)[2] database, as follows: "A 'vulnerability' is a weakness in the computational logic (e.g., code) found in software and some hardware components (e.g., firmware) that, when exploited, results in a negative impact to confidentiality, integrity, OR availability..."

One example for the impact of security flaws in libraries is the Apache Commons Collection. This library is imported by several projects, specifically the JBoss application server. Almost all projects which used this library became insecure through the vulnerabilities CVE-2015-6420, CVE-2015-7450 and CVE-2017-15708[3]. They affect the Apache Commons Collection under a specific library version as well with Java versions below or equals Java Runtime Environment 1.7. A potential consequence of them may arise in attackers' attempt to execute remote code. This is enabled through deserialization without type checking of the received serialized object. The default *ObjectInputStream* deserializes any serializable class [3].

The Open Web Application Security Project (OWASP), name the use of libraries with known vulnerabilities as one of the ten most significant risks for web projects [4]. The statement of the US-Cert that a system is only as secure as its weakest component[4] implies that a single weakness within a library can make a whole system insecure. To prevent applications to use vulnerable versions or completely insecure libraries a security check for any imported library in a project would be a possible task to improve the security of software projects.

The major aspect for libraries is that they distribute very fast including their vulnerabilities. To permit the propagation of known vulnerabilities in the early software development phases, a possible operation is to prevent the use of insecure software libraries. Supporting developers with this task and applying security proactively and not just in the late maintenance phases, we investigate the following research questions:

- **RQ1: Is it possible to automatically check whether a software code library contains a known vulnerability?**
  By the means of this research question we investigate whether the available metadata of software libraries are sufficient to uniquely identify them.
- **RQ2: Can the top 20 Maven libraries be checked for weaknesses automatically?**
  Not all libraries can be identified with the approach described in this work. Sometimes there are no metadata available. Therefore we take into consideration - among others - the top 20 used Maven libraries for the evaluation.
- **RQ3: Which scope and limitations exist for the automated software library check regarding to known vulnerabilities?**
  We want to check whether the approach is transferable from Java to other programming languages. Furthermore, the necessary modifications for applying our procedure to other languages will be considered.

---

[2] Common Vulnerabilities and Exposures: https://cve.mitre.org/about/ (10.2017).

[3] CVE-Search: https://nvd.nist.gov/vuln/search/ (06.2018).

[4] US-Cert Security the Weakest Link: https://goo.gl/ZCuCc8 (06.2018).

For the decision, whether a library containing a security flaw or not, much information has to be considered. This includes checking known vulnerabilities, which were already reported in the past and documented somehow. One source containing this knowledge is the public free accessible vulnerability databases CVE and NVD. The content of these databases is fully synchronized and count as one of the biggest databases for vulnerabilities [7]. The difference between the two databases is that the NVD is augmented with additional analysis and contains a fine-grained search engine. Both databases contain documentation of found weaknesses identified by a unique identifier, the CVE-ID. The security knowledge about existing security flaws changes rapidly over time and is soon getting obsolete on account of new attack vectors, changing technologies, innovations and many more. The security community continuously reports weaknesses, which are investigated afterwards by security experts to enrich the database with proper content. Developers need to check iteratively the knowledge of already found weaknesses to decide on the security relevance of libraries. For security content databases like the NVD, it is possible to search for a user input string which displays a list of results. Not just any found entry affects our library. Therefore, developers have to check them all for the relevance of their search. Developers could easily get overwhelmed by the number of entries in their search. Furthermore, for professional developers, company internal vulnerability databases have to be checked too. Whenever a weakness for a library is found, the developer has to decide whether to use the library or to look for another one with similar functionality. For supporting this decision they can take advantage of the security scoring system introduced by the NVD. To handle this continual increasing knowledge, a good management is inevitable. The previously described procedure is shown in Fig. 1.

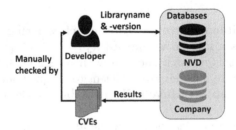

Fig. 1. Manual security check of libraries

With the aim of supporting developers to solve these problems, we have developed a metric-based approach for determining whether an imported software library has security flaws in it based on already reported vulnerabilities. This knowledge will be accessed with the use of the NVD. Our approach is implemented in an eclipse plugin in order to directly support developers in their common integrated development environment. Furthermore, a semi-automated knowledge acquisition procedure with user interaction of developers is considered.

The remainder of this paper is structured as follows. In Sect. 2 the related work will be mentioned, and their main purpose will shortly be described. An overview of our approach will be given in Sect. 3. Section 4 describes the knowledge sources for Java metadata and challenges that occur for the identification of libraries based on them. Furthermore, the applied search including metrics will be introduced. The approaches' scope and limitations in context with the transferability to other programming languages will be presented in Sect. 5. In Sect. 6 the experimental setup including the test set is introduced. The evaluation results and discussion regarding our research questions are presented in Sect. 7. Threats to validity will be viewed in Sect. 8. In Sect. 9, we concludes our work and gives an insight into future work.

2 Related Work

This study relates to previous work and research results with the major focus on static library and code inspections, metrics comparison for valid security determination, as well as on the fundamental idea of an active risk exposures support at software development progress.

Hovemeyer et al. [8] implemented an automatic detector for a variety of bug patterns found in Java applications and libraries. The authors show, that the effort required to implement a bug pattern detector tends to be low and that even extremely simple detectors find bugs in real applications. Since security fragments and exposures rely on code idioms, we aim for an adapted solution that inspects libraries before compilation and supports the developer in writing more secure software.

Hoepman et al. [6] investigated that giving access to open source security fragments might seem counterintuitive, but in fact, it presents the highest security. The authors discovered, that opening the source code of existing systems will at first increase their exposure, due to the fact that information about vulnerabilities becomes available to attackers. Since the code is publicly available, any interested person can exposure the system, try for bugs, thus increasing the security opportunities of the system. Besides, fixes will quickly be available so that the period of increased exposure becomes shortened. This is especially beneficial in case open source libraries that can help with extension methods to identify weakening spots within new development projects.

Software metrics can help developers to choose the libraries most appropriate for their needs. De la Mora et al. [3] established a library comparison based on several metrics extracted from multiple sources such as software repositories, issue tracking systems, and Q&A websites. The authors consolidate all information within a single website, upon which developers can make informed decisions by comparing metric data belonging to libraries from several domains. De la Mora's methodology in combination with security approaches, e.g., the Open Web Application Security Project (OWASP) [4], provides the necessary base for establishing proactive development support for anyone interested in security improved development.

Likewise, we actively consider static code and library analyzes within our research, as previous studies by Giffhorn et al. [5] and Louridas et al. [9] did before. Their primary focus is solely on static code checking in action. Louridas created an Eclipse plugin, which contains a wide range of analysis techniques such as dependence graph computation, slicing, and chopping for sequential and concurrent programs, computation of path conditions and algorithms for software security. The author's plugin analyzes Java programs with a broad range of slicing and chopping algorithms, and use accurate algorithms for language-based security to check applications for information leaks. Such processing in combination with the metrics comparison strategy will make coding more secure.

To distinguish between our approach and the approaches mentioned above, we concentrate on the support of the software developer while using secure libraries with the use of public and private available vulnerability databases like the NVD, CVE, and company internal Databases. Libraries metadata is broken down into meaningful attributes which are used to identify libraries uniquely.

3   Approach Overview

To classify source code libraries semi-automatically regarding their security properties, our approach is separated into five major steps: identification of library, search for vulnerabilities, report results, enrichment and use of knowledge. If developers are looking for off-the-shelf libraries, they select them often only with the focus on their functional need and do not take care of security, which could be implied by the less security background of developers [1]. So developers import an external software library into a software project to enhance its functionality. At this point, the software might become insecure. Regarding our approach, at first, libraries are identified by the relevant attributes of their metadata like the library version, -name and vendor.

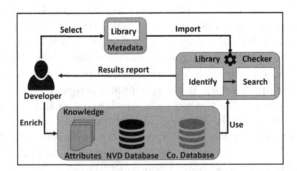

Fig. 2. Approach overview

If knowledge about the attributes is missing, it can be enriched by user interaction. The recognised meta information is used with the aim to search for weaknesses of a library inside of vulnerability databases like the NVD or other databases like company internal. If a database contains at least one entry, which matches to the metadata, a security flaw is found. Thus results including scoring of criticality are displayed to the developer. Similarity metrics support the mentioned search process to receive a highly specified outcome. Figure 2 gives a compact overview of the described approach.

4   Challenges: Identification of Libraries

For identifying a particular Java library imported into a project, much information has to be considered. Sometimes it could be challenging to identify a library through the availability of their metadata uniquely. For Java there exist name conventions and recommendations for setting metadata into a manifest file but these are voluntary guidelines which do not have to be implemented. Therefore, the availability of metadata itself is optional, and it is possible that there is no meta information neither in the library name nor the manifest file. In the following, the containing meta information of library name and the manifest file will be analyzed concerning the purpose of library identification.

The *library filename* is one source for identifying the library name as well as the version number, which is used within a project. The 20 most used Java libraries of the Maven repository confirm this statement. Filenames of libraries are in the format of *Libraryname-Version.jar* whereby the library name can consist of more than one word, and they will be separated in the filename by dashes. One example for a particular library filename is *slf4j-api-1.7.25.jar*. In this example the library name is *slf4j-api* which is followed by its version *1.7.25* and ends with the datatype *.jar*. The prefix of the datatype is the library version number that is separated by dots. Preston-Werner described the division of the version number into major-, minor-, and patch-version[5]. This segmentation is common for the most filenames of software libraries. However, the filename is not enough to get sufficient results for the identification. Sometimes library files have names, which are not identifying the library itself. They can be abbreviated to short forms f. e. containing only the initial letters of words. This could lead to ambiguous results, which makes the identification of libraries imprecise. To improve the identification of libraries, further metadata could be considered.

There is, for example, the *JAR-Manifest* as an additional knowledge source as a unique file inside of a library. It contains information about the Java library itself. The official JAR file specification describes the structure of the manifest. It has a main section which declares attributes that are relevant for the whole jar file[6]. For custom file entries new sections can be created separately by empty lines. Figure 3 compresses example content of a manifest file of the *Jetty* library. The main part is visible within the lines 1–11 of the figure. Furthermore, the manifest contains three custom sections covered in the parts 13–15, 17–18 and 20–21.

---

[5] Semantic Versioning: http://semver.org/ (10.2017).
[6] ORACLE: JAR File Specification: https://goo.gl/dTR3xr (10.2017).

For our approach, we focus on the main part of the manifest file. It includes the *version number*, *ant version*, *the company* or *group*, which developed the library, *sealed state*, *specification version*, *implementation version*, *package title*, *implementation vendor* and *URL*, as well as the *main class*. Through a manual audit, we recognize *vendor*, *product* and *version* as useful attributes for the identification of software libraries. The values could be part of the filename as well as the manifest file. These are optional values, which are not set in every filename or manifest file. In some cases, only one or two values are set in arbitrary combinations. For identifying pre-release versions of libraries, like alpha or beta, a further attribute named update version is needed. We checked the occurrence of these attributes within the manifest file for a set of 38 software libraries, which is presented in Fig. 3.

In conclusion, 14 libraries do not have any metadata inside the manifest, and the other 24 libraries contain at least one of the attributes. The most often occurred attribute is the *implementation-version* with an amount of 23, followed by the *implementation-title* with an amount of 22 and the *implementation-vendor* attribute occurred 19 times. These results implicate the necessity of further steps to take care of distinct cases that partly do and do not have any metadata.

One additional problem is the inconsistency of manifest files in libraries. For example, if we view the three libraries *Struts*, *Commons HttpClient* and *Axis* of the Apache company, the attribute implementation-vendor has a different allocation for the same vendor. The allocation is seen in the following enumeration. Each line starts with the vendor and ends with the library name in brackets.

- **The Apache Software Foundation** (Struts)
- **Apache Sofware Foundation** (Commons HttpClient)
- **Apache Web Services** (Axis)

These are long forms of the vendor. On the opposite, there is the *Common Platform Enumeration* (CPE) standard for the documentation of vulnerabilities that is used in the CVE and NVD database [2].

The CPE defines the CPE-Vendor-Attribute, as a short and concise representation of the vendor. In the case of the three considered libraries, the CPE-Vendor-Attribute is named *Apache*. Therefore, a simple string comparison is not possible for the search of weaknesses regarding software libraries. If we consider for example the filename of the *axis2* library of Table 1, resulting tokens are *axis2* and *kernel* as the potential product name. However, the matching product name of the CPE is *axis2*, which only fits the first token. A similar problem occurs in the case of the *Struts Framework* library and their opposed CPE product name *struts*. The only difference, in this case, is the usage of capital letters in the token "Struts" of the meta information of the library. Another problem occurs for the comparison of the *Commons FileUpload* library and their corresponding CPE product name of *commons_fileupload*. In the last case, a further problem arises with the *xalan-2.7.0* library and their corresponding CPE product name of *xalan-java*.

The difference of the CPE product name is the substitution of the single space with an underscore and the case sensitivity of letters. In the last case, a

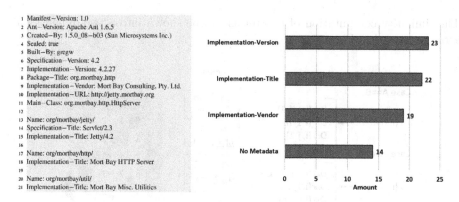

```
 1  Manifest—Version: 1.0
 2  Ant—Version: Apache Ant 1.6.5
 3  Created—By: 1.5.0_08—b03 (Sun Microsystems Inc.)
 4  Sealed: true
 5  Built—By: gregw
 6  Specification—Version: 4.2
 7  Implementation—Version: 4.2.27
 8  Package—Title: org.mortbay.http
 9  Implementation—Vendor: Mort Bay Consulting, Pty. Ltd.
10  Implementation—URL: http://jetty.mortbay.org
11  Main—Class: org.mortbay.http.HttpServer
12
13  Name: org/mortbay/jetty/
14  Specification—Title: Servlet/2.3
15  Implementation—Title: Jetty/4.2
16
17  Name: org/mortbay/http/
18  Implementation—Title: Mort Bay HTTP Server
19
20  Name: org/mortbay/util/
21  Implementation—Title: Mort Bay Misc. Utilities
```

Fig. 3. Manifest example and distribution of attributes

further problem arises with the *xalan-2.7.0* library and their corresponding CPE product name of *xalan-java*. Inside of the CPE product name is an additional token *java*, that is not part of the metadata of that library.

Table 1. Example: comparison of metadata and CPEs

Metadata-Type	Value	CPE-Product
Filename	axis2-kernel-1.4.1	axis2
Implementation-Title	Struts Framework	struts
Implementation-Title	Commons FileUpload	commons_fileupload
Filename	xalan-2.7.0	xalan-java

4.1 Search and Metrics

To find a match between the libraries metadata, included in the filename and manifest file, and a vulnerability entry in the database, called CPE-Product in the following, is not an easy task. Trivial string comparison is not valid. None of the beforehand viewed libraries would be found by simple string comparison. Therefore, a similarity metric is needed.

The *Levenshtein-Distance* is a metric, coming from the field of information retrieval, which is used for our approach [10]. It is defined as a metric that measures the amount of minimum insert, substitution and delete operations which are necessary for transforming a string A into a string B. It is also called *edit distance*. If the edit distance equals zero, then two strings are equals. Furthermore, it is possible to add a weight to the different types of operations. To differentiate between the two cases of substitutions for two letters a with m and a with b the distance between them in the alphabet could be taken as a possible weight. However, for our approach, an equal weighting for every transformation is considered.

The similarity computation of two terms can be shown into a two-dimensional array presented in Fig. 4.

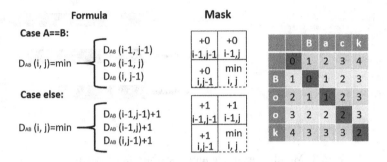

Fig. 4. Levenshstein formula and example

The first row and column represent the values of the case if each character of a term has to be deleted for the transformation. Every cell contains the value of operations, which are needed to transform the substring of string A into a substring of string B. If there is the same letter in the same position of the two substrings, the amount of operations is zero, which misleads to an incensement of the previously needed transformations. In this case, two characters are different so that an action is required, the weight of that operation will be allocated to the cell with respect to the minimum of the previously needed transformations. For a better understanding, a mask which can put over the two-dimensional array is attached to the formula.

The diagonal of the matrix displays the value of operations which are needed to transform the two terms. Therefore the lowest value in the lower right corner is the result of actions which are required to convert string A into string B. In other words: this is the value of the Levenshtein-Distance.

For example, the transformation of the word A as *Book* to another word B as *Back* is displayed in the right part of Fig. 4. The first letter for the transformation is the *a* of string B which has to be replaced by an *o*. Furthermore, the letter *c* of string B has to be replaced again by an *o*, so that the two strings A and B are equal *Book*. This results in a value of two for the Levenshtein-Distance. It is not a sufficient strategy to use only the Levenshtein-Distance. For example, the calculation of the Levenshtein-Distance of the metadata library name *Framework struts* and the CPE library name *struts* results in 10, which is not a sufficient threshold for this distance metric. For the library search, a lot of wrong results will occur with such a high threshold. Therefore, a deeper concentration on the tokens is necessary. If we focus on the same library concerning tokens, the Levenshtein-Distance of the two tokens *Struts* and *struts* results in one through a single substitution of the capital letter *S* to the small letter *s*, which results into a sufficient threshold.

For an automated creation and classification of tokens, regular expressions (regex) will be used. This means it is possible to distinguish between *version numbers* and terms that can be the *vendor* attribute as well as the *title* of the library itself. With the regex `.*/d+.*` it is possible to recognize version numbers containing the structure of the beforehand explained version hierarchy. For identifying terms like library names and the vendor attribute the regex `*/p{L}.*` is used. Terms like the *implementation title* can also include a number; therefore, a simple string check for numbers is not valid. An example of this is the library name *axis2*.

User interaction is necessary for missing or irrelevant attributes. The developer has to set manually the three attributes title, vendor and version number, which enriches the knowledge of the library checker to make future library classifications more valuable.

Furthermore, redundant tokens of product, version, and vendor will be cleared through the transformation into a set. After the tokens are identified, the power set $\mathcal{P}(X) := \{U \mid U \subseteq X\}$ excluded the empty set is calculated, where X is a list of the tokens *vendor*, *title*, and *version number*. This increases the probability for a library matching classification. For example, we could have the tokens {apache, commons, fileupload} which results into a power set of {{apache}, {commons}, {fileupload}, {apache, commons}, {apache, fileupload}, {commons, fileupload}, {apache, commons, fileupload}}. The described procedure of the token building, power set generation and the knowledge enrichment is visualized in Fig. 5.

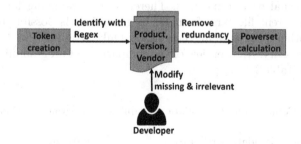

Fig. 5. Knowledge enrichment and tokenization

For identifying whether a library is insecure or not, vulnerability databases can be checked with the previously created power set of tokens. To get sufficient results for the search the entries of the subsets inside of the power set will be concatenated. The subset of {commons, fileupload} leads to a string of *commonsfileupload* for the search of libraries.

5 Scope and Limitations

Programming languages can differ concerning the availability and stored destination of metadata. Metadata could be automatically generated for projects such as manually set or enriched by developers. Some languages distinguish between optional and mandatory attributes, other do not have a distinction for them. Regulations and specifications of programming languages define this information. The missing annotation whether attributes are optional or mandatory makes a comparison of metadata availability difficult. Generally attributes like Name and Version are set as mandatory attributes. No of the supposed specifications define one of them as optional. Therefore, we considered these attributes for languages with missing type annotation as compulsory. To answer research question *RQ3* the library metadata management for the most demand programming languages[7] in work life will be investigated.

All of these languages have in common that they share a mandatory subset of available attributes; the *product name* and *version number*. For *PHP* and *JavaScript* exists no separate mandatory *vendor* attribute. In their specification is defined that the vendor name could be part of the product name. Python has an optional attribute named Author, which could contain the vendor name as well. The other mentioned programming languages contain the vendor as a mandatory attribute or at least not defined as optional. To answer our research question regarding the availability of metadata, the adaption of our approach to languages other than Java is possible. All of these attributes could be part of the library file- and folder names as well as stored into separate metadata sources. Maybe, the results can differ if the partially optional vendor attribute is not set.

Some languages contain all metadata in the library source code, some store the data in the library and partially in other files, further languages store them entirely in external or internal files. Therefore, programming languages store metadata in different files and formats. In general, it is possible to apply our approach to other programming languages. Only wrappers for the metadata content are necessary. An overview of the comparison of programming languages is presented in Table 2.

Table 2. Comparison of metadata availability of programming languages

Language	Metadata attributes	Destination
Java	Name, Version, Vendor	Inside Library, Manifest
C++	Name, Version, Vendor	Library
C#	Name, Version, Vendor	Library
JavaScript	Name, Version, Author, Hompage	Fileheader, package.json
Perl	Name, Version, Author	META.json, META.yml
PHP	Name, Vendor, Version	Composer.json
Python	Metadata-version, Name, Version	pkg-info file

---

[7] Most Demand Programming Languages: https://goo.gl/XiWcMw (06.2018).

6 Experimental Setup

As the test set for our evaluation 38 Java software libraries were considered. All of these libraries are divided into two classes; 17 libraries with known vulnerabilities and 21 other frequently used libraries. The test set include the popular *JUnit*, *Mojito*, and several *Apache* libraries such as various other libraries. We obtained the libraries from downloading them from the Maven repository. They were selected through the top 20 most popular libraries of the repository, and the NVD-data feeds identified the vulnerable libraries using for the evaluation. For one of the 20 most used libraries exists a CVE; the *Jackson Databind* library. A listing of all considered libraries is seen in Table 3.

Table 3. Test-libraries

With CVE-Entry	Without CVE-Entry
Apache Axis 1.4	JUnit 4.12
Apache Axis2 1.4.1	Scala Library 2.13.0-M2
Apache Commons Fileupload 1.2.1	SLF4J API Module 1.7.25
Apache Commons HttpClient 3.1	Guava 23.0
Jetty 4.2.27	Apache Log4j 1.2.17
Jetty 6.1.0	Apache Commons IO 2.5
javax.mail 1.4	javax.mailapi 1.5.6
Apache OpenJPA 2.0.1	Apache Commons Logging 1.2
Apache Struts 1.2.7	Logback Classic Module 1.2.3
Apache Struts2 Core 2.1.2	Clojure 1.8.0
Apache Xalan-Java 2.7.0	SLF4J LOG4J 12 Binding 1.7.25
XStream 1.4.8	Mockito All 1.10.19
OpenSymphony XWork 2.1.1	Mockito Core 2.10.0
Spring Security Core 4.2.0	Servlet API 2.5
Elasticsearch 1.4.2	Apache Commons Lang 2.6
Apache Commons Collection 3.2.1	Apache Commons Lang3 3.6
Jackson Databind 2.9.1	javax.servlet-api 4.0.0
	Clojure Tools.nrepl 0.2.13
	Apache HttpClient 4.5.3
	Daytrader-EJB 2.1.7
	Clojure Complete 0.2.4

For each Java library, we assigned manually a list of CPEs which represent the libraries metadata. A CPE applies to a library if their *vendor*, *product name*, and *version number* correlate with each other. The *version number* has to be equals to the library version, or the CPE has to be valid for all prior software versions.

For each CPE the concluding CVEs were investigated and assigned. These data were considered as reference values for the evaluation. The classification based on the data of the CVE database containing around 94.785 reported vulnerabilities and 214.955 CPEs of September 18th, 2017.

The right assignment of CPEs and the finding of their related CVEs identifies the critical parts of our approach. If a CPE is falsely assigned, no CVE will be found for it. Therefore, the evaluation is split into three steps. Firstly, the precision and recall for the found CPEs is calculated. Secondly, the recall and precision will be calculated for the finding of the correct CVEs regarding found CPEs. Thirdly, an overall evaluation of the classification of libraries as secure or insecure will be computed.

For our evaluation, we focus on methods of the information retrieval introduced by Manning et al. in "Introduction to Information Retrieval" [10]. These methods based on the results of the confusion matrix with respect to metrics like *recall*, *precision*, and *F1-measure*. The goal of a high recall and precision is always a drawback. With a high recall of 100%, everything that is security related can be found if it is part of the data. However, with high recall, it often takes a loss of precision, which leads to wrong security error notifications. A secure library could be classified as insecure, something that might confuse the developer. Therefore we created three configurations with distinct goals: High recall for finding the most vulnerable libraries, high precision for mitigating the number of incorrect error notifications and a combination of both which takes as a consequence the mitigation of both recall and precision to receive an overall higher combination of that values. These configurations will be compared to each other, and the reasons for classifications will be regarded.

7   Results and Discussion

The high recall configuration was designed to find as many vulnerabilities as possible. 96% of the CPEs of our reference set were found and assigned to the corresponding library. The result set missed out two CPEs. Different vendor names between CPE and library lead to this mismatch. A reason for that is the changed ownership of libraries. Both of the mismatches reference newer software version of libraries but they are tagged to be valid for previous versions. If the vendor changes during a product life-cycle, this affects our approach negatively. Furthermore, by using the resulting CPE set 95% of all vulnerabilities were found.

The overall precision of the result set is 47.57% for CPEs and 54.44% for CVEs. We consider two main reasons for a mismatch between libraries and CPEs. On the one hand the most frequent error is an inappropriate update component of a CPE. The update component usually describes a pre release version like *alpha*, *beta* or *release-candidate*. If the given library has not the same update level as the CPE it will be classified as false positive. On the other hand we have to deal with broad version declarations. Instead of having a precise version number, the version component could identify the abscence of a version restriction. These CPEs are valid for all library versions, which implies that the version filter criteria could not be applied. Similar problems will arise with the previous version tag. The higher the version number with previous version tag the more error-prone is the result set.

Table 4. Comparison of the configurations according to CVE & CPE

Configuration	Goal	Average recall	Average precision	F1
Recall	CPE	**96.27**	47.57	63.67
Recall	CVE	**95.1**	54.44	69.24
Precision	CPE	57.74	**100**	73.21
Precision	CVE	65.54	**100**	**79.18**
Combined	CPE	72.96	74.91	**73.92**
Combined	CVE	72.57	76.44	74.46

To gain a better precision while having a high recall we introduce the so-called combined configuration. Here we tackle the problems with the update component and too broad version fields by using stricter filter rules. To match with CPE updates, the update value have to be also part of the library's filename. As a result the average precision rises to 74.91% for CPEs and 76.44% for CVEs while decreasing the recall to 72.96% for CPEs and 72.57% for CVEs.

In order to get a result set with a minimum of false positives we designed the precision configuration. Therefore, we created additionally filter rules for the version field such that CPEs with no available version information will be discarded. Another rule affects the previous version tag. The examination of the false positive CPEs that includes the previous version tag, identified that the library's major version number and the CPEs major version number differ. We suppose that a change in a major version number is related to big changes in source code and consequently the previous version tag of the CPE may be not applicable in most cases. After applying all rules, we retrieve a 100% precision on both CPE and CVE. On the downside our recall decreases to 57.74% for CPEs and 65.54% for CVEs.

When applying the F1 measure which is the harmonic mean of precision and recall, the precision configuration performs best for CVEs and the combined configuration for CPEs. This test setup was performed without a manually pre processing of the libraries vendor, product name and version. With user interaction the low precision on the recall configuration can be mitigated while finding the most vulnerabilities. The results of the CPE assignment and the corresponding CVE finding are presented in Table 4.

If the results considering precision, recall, F1 measure of Table 5 will be focused, we can see that each configuration solves the predefined research questions *RQ1* and *RQ2*.

With the described approach it is possible to automatically detect known vulnerabilities for libraries including the top 20 used Maven libraries. Our library

Table 5. The performance of the configurations

Configuration	Recall	Precision	F1
Recall	**100**	68	80.95
Combined	94	84.21	88.89
Precision	82.35	**100**	**90.32**

checker performs a binary classification into secure and vulnerable JAR files. If at least one CVE was found for a given library, it would be classified as vulnerable. Otherwise, this library will be regarded as secure. The recall configuration correctly classifies all vulnerable libraries. Eight secure libraries were falsely rated as vulnerable which yields in a precision of 68%. All libraries without weaknesses were correctly classified as secure. The combined configuration reduces the number of false positives for the classification of secure libraries as vulnerable to three but also misclassifies a vulnerable library as secure. The precision configuration has no false positives; this means that no secure library was falsely classified as vulnerable. On the other hand, there are three false negatives which means that a vulnerable library was classified as secure.

8 Threats to Validity

Wohlin et al. define types of threats to validity for empirical software engineering research [12]. We consider the types of threats conclusion, internal, construct, and external relevant to our work.

Conclusion: The imbalanced nature of the test set can influence the recall and precision. Considering the occurrence of software in the real world, the ratio of vulnerable libraries and secure libraries is not reflected in our test set. However, it is imaginable that there are other metrics, which tackles the problem of imbalanced test sets better than recall and precision.

Internal: The test set with 44.73% vulnerable and 55.26% of secure libraries potentially influence the received evaluation results. Maybe they would differ if the test set would be changed. The used Java Runtime Environment version is not considered. Some libraries are insecure in specific Java versions and are secure in other versions. This could result in false positives.

Construct: Levenshtein metric configuration is remarkable for the results of the comparison of library metadata. There are different approaches to comparing the similarity of files: usage of fingerprints would be an alternative. It is possible to create a fingerprint of a file and compare it to the fingerprint of another file.

External: Our approach is not applicable to other programming languages without small adaptions. The availability of metadata attributes and storage location differs among languages. Therefore, wrappers to other languages are necessary to apply our approach. Maybe other available meta information of libraries within other languages than Java are more suitable to improve the library classification results.

9 Conclusion and Future Perspectives

The use of third-party software code libraries can make a system insecure through their containing weaknesses. Within this paper, we introduce an approach for supporting developers by recognizing insecure libraries based on already documented vulnerabilities in the early software development phase. The metadata of libraries is used to fulfil this detection. We present three different configurations with respect to high recall, high precision and a combination of both for detecting reported vulnerabilities for Java software code libraries based on vulnerability databases. The approach uses metrics like the Levenshtein-Distance for finding a match between a libraries metadata and an entry of a vulnerability database. The results show that the identification of libraries through metadata using the described metrics worked fairly well. Furthermore, our work provides a practical tool for supporting Java software developers as well as the investigation of transferability to other programming languages.

Our future research is striving towards fingerprint generation for libraries and compare them to each other to identify a library and compare these results to the approach described in this paper. To solve the problem of our internal validity, we want to enhance the results of our approach regarding the used JRE Version for the software project in which the library is imported. Furthermore, we plan to do an empirical study considering as to how to display security notifications efficiently to developers without any disturbance.

References

1. Acar, Y., Stransky, C., Wermke, D., Mazurek, M.L., Fahl, S.: Security developer studies with GitHub users: exploring a convenience sample. In: Symposium on Usable Privacy and Security (SOUPS) (2017)
2. Cheikes, B.A., Waltermire, D., Scarfone, K.: Common platform enumeration: naming specification version 2.3. NIST Interagency Report 7695, NIST-IR 7695 (2011)
3. de la Mora, F.L., Nadi, S.: Which library should I use? A metric-based comparison of software libraries (2018)
4. Fox, D.: Open web application security project. Datenschutz und Datensicherheit - DuD 30(10), 636 (2006)
5. Giffhorn, D., Hammer, C.: Precise analysis of Java programs using JOANA. In: Cordy, J.R. (ed.) Eighth IEEE International Working Conference on Source Code Analysis and Manipulation, pp. 267–268. IEEE, Piscataway (2008)
6. Hoepman, J.H., Jacobs, B.: Increased security through open source. Commun. ACM 50(1), 79–83 (2007)
7. Homaei, H., Shahriari, H.R.: Seven years of software vulnerabilities: The ebb and flow. IEEE Secur. Priv. 1, 58–65 (2017)
8. Hovemeyer, D., Pugh, W.: Finding bugs is easy. ACM SIGPLAN Not. 39(12), 92–106 (2004)
9. Louridas, P.: Static code analysis. IEEE Softw. 23(4), 58–61 (2006)
10. Manning, C.D., Raghavan, P., Schütze, H.: Introduction to Information Retrieval. Cambridge University Press, Cambridge (2009). Reprinted edn

11. Watanabe, T., et al.: Understanding the origins of mobile app vulnerabilities: a large-scale measurement study of free and paid apps. In: 2017 IEEE/ACM 14th International Conference on Mining Software Repositories, pp. 14–24. IEEE, Piscataway (2017)
12. Wohlin, C., Runeson, P., Höst, M., Ohlsson, M.C., Regnell, B., Wesslén, A.: Experimentation in Software Engineering. Springer, Heidelberg (2012). https://doi.org/10.1007/978-3-642-29044-2

A Prediction-Based Method for False Data Injection Attacks Detection in Industrial Control Systems

Lyes Bayou[1]([✉]), David Espes[2], Nora Cuppens-Boulahia[1],
and Frédéric Cuppens[1]

[1] IMT-Atlantique - LabSTICC, 2 Rue de la Châtaigneraie, Césson Sévigné, France
`lyes.bayou@telecom-bretagne.eu`
[2] University of Western Brittany - LabSTICC, Brest, France

Abstract. False data Injection attacks is an important security issue in Industrial Control Systems (ICS). Indeed, this kind of attack based on the manipulation and the transmission of corrupted sensing data, can lead to harmful consequences such as disturbing the infrastructure functioning, interrupting it or more again causing its destruction (overheating of a nuclear reactor). In this paper, we propose an unsupervised machine learning approach for false data injection attack detection. It uses a Recurrent Neural Network (RNN) for building a prediction model of expected sensing data. These latter are compared to received values and an alert security is raised if these values differ significantly.

1 Introduction

False data Injection attacks is one of the most important security issue for Industrial Control Systems (ICS). Indeed, this kind of attack can lead to harmful consequences such as disturbing the infrastructure functioning, interrupting it or more again causing its destruction (overheating of a nuclear reactor). Furthermore, targeting ICS can lead not only to economical losses but can also threaten human lives [1].

We describe in this paper an unsupervised learning approach using a Recurrent Neural Network (RNN) which is a time series predictor for building our model. Based on the previous received sensing data, the RNN is used for predicting the next expected sensing values. These latter are compared to the received ones. An alert is raised if received values differ significantly for the predicted values.

Tests performed on a real life industrial dataset show that the proposed method is able to detect a wide range of attacks.

The rest of the paper is organized as follows. In Sect. 2 we present related work. In Sect. 3, we describe the false data injection attack issue and its impact on industrial installations. Section 4 describes our proposed solution based on the LSTM technique. In Sect. 5, we describe the dataset that we use for testing our proposition. Section 6 presents results of conducting tests and the evaluation of our solution. Finally, we present the conclusion of our work in Sect. 7.

© Springer Nature Switzerland AG 2019
A. Zemmari et al. (Eds.): CRiSIS 2018, LNCS 11391, pp. 35–40, 2019.
https://doi.org/10.1007/978-3-030-12143-3_3

2   Related Works

In the literature, several techniques have been proposed to solve false data injection issue. This include watermarking [2], correlation entropy [3] and physical process invariants [4].

In [5], an ANN-based (recurrent) Anomaly detection system is proposed. It is a Windows based attributes extraction techniques, and it applies a combination of Error-back propagation, Levenberg-Marquardt, clustering of normal behavior and classification classification.

In [3] a process-aware approach is proposed to detect when a sensor signal is maliciously manipulated. It is based on 2 kinds of correlation entropy: plant wide entropy and sensor entropy.

In [4] propose a system that is implemented into the PLC. It uses of physical invariants: conditions that must holds whenever the ICS is in a given state.

3   False Data Injection Detection Issue

This paper aims to address the false data injection issue. Indeed, an attacker can inject into the network false sensing data which could lead to harmful effects to the installation. Thus, in [6], the author propose that additionally to the *confidentiality*, *integrity* and *availability* proprieties, *the veracity* should also considered as a relevant security property. Indeed, authentication and non-repudiation verify the claimed origin of an assertion but the assertion itself may be true or false. Thus, veracity property ensures that an assertion truthfully reflects the aspect it makes a statement about [3,6].

If a sensor sends wrong sensing data, these latter will be normally processed as only the identity of the sender is checked. To achieve such an action, an attacker can either measled the target sensor about its environment or by taking the control over it.

Security mechanisms like Intrusion detection systems, ensure the identity of the sender and the packet delivery without being modified, delayed or deleted. They can also detect if a sensor usurps the identity of another sensor. However, they cannot detect if a sensor sends deliberately false sensing data.

One solution that mitigates this kind of attacks and ensures sensing data veracity is to perform consistency checks. This means comparing sensing data sent by each sensors to a prediction model [6].

4   Proposed Solution

We aim to apply machine learning techniques to detect false data injection. Among available techniques, we choose to apply the Long Short Term Memory Networks (LSTM) neural networks [7]. The LSTM is a recurrent neural network that uses "memory cells" that allow the network to learn when to forget previous memory states or when to update the hidden states when new information is provided. Recurrent Neural Networks can learn and train long temporal sequences.

Our idea is to train an LSTM network on the information provided by each sensor. Then, the trained network is used to predict the next value to be returned by the sensor. Finally, the returned value is compared to the predicted one. An alert is raised if the two values differ significantly.

4.1 The Long Short Term Memory Networks (LSTM) Recurrent Neural Networks (RNN)

Although Recurrent Neural Networks (RNN) have proven to be successful in many tasks such as text generation and speech recognition, it is difficult for RNNs to learn and train on long temporal sequence [8]. This is due to the vanishing and exploding gradient problem that propagates through the multiple layers of the RNN.

LSTM solves above mentioned limitation by containing "memory cells" that allow the network to learn when to forget previous memory states or when to update the hidden states when new information are provided [7].

The memory blocks are memory cells that stores the temporal state of the network in addition to special multiplicative units called gates used to control the flow of information. In each memory block, there is an input, an output gate as well as the forget gate. The input gate controls the flow of input activations into the memory cell while the output gate controls the output flow of cell activations into the rest of the network. The forget gate modulates the cell's self-recurrent connections. Using the LSTM architecture, we calculate function H using the following equations:

$$i_t = \sigma(W_{xi}x_t + W_{hi}h_{t-1} + W_{ci}c_{t-1} + b_i)$$
$$f_t = \sigma(W_{xf}x_t + W_{hf}h_{t-1} + W_{cf}c_{t-1} + b_f)$$
$$c_t = f_t c_{t-1} + i_t \tanh(W_{xc}x_t + W_{hc}h_{t-1} + b_c)$$
$$o_t = \sigma(W_{xo}x_t + W_{ho}h_{t-1} + W_{co}c_t + b_o)$$
$$h_t = o_t \tanh(c_t)$$

where σ is the logistic sigmoid function, i_t is the input gate, f_t is the forget gate, ot is the output gate, c_t is the cell activation vector, h_t being the hidden vector and W being the weight matrices from the cell to get vectors. The additional cells enables the LSTM to learn long-term temporals which traditional RNNs are not capable of learning. In addition, stacking multiple layers of LSTM allows for the modelling of complex temporal sequences.

5 Case Study: The Secure Water Treatment Testbed (SWaT) Dataset

The Secure Water Treatment Testbed (SWaT) [4] is a fully operational scaled down water treatment plant for IC security studies.

It consists of a modern six-stage process. Stage P1 controls the inflow of water to be treated, by opening or closing a motorized valve that connects the inlet pipe to the raw water tank. The SWaT Dataset is generated from the Secure Water Treatment Testbed. The data collected from the testbed consists of 11 days of continuous operation. 7 days of data was collected under normal operation while 4 days of data was collected with attack scenarios.

5.1 Attack Scenarios

Table 1 describes some of attacks launched against process P1. Attack's duration are indicated in minutes (and second).

Table 1. P1 attack's description

Attack	Type	Duration	Attacker's intents	Start state	Attack	Impact
A1	SSSP	15:39 (939 s)	Overflow tank	MV-101 is closed	Open MV-101	Tank overflow
A2	SSSP	7:22 (442 s)	Burst the pipe that sends water between process P1 and process P2	P-101 is on P-102 is off	P-101 is on, P-102 is on	Pipe bursts
A3	SSSP	6:22 (382 s)	Underflow the tank and damage P-101	LIT-101 Water level between L and H	Increase by 1 mm every second	NO
A4	SSMP	12:00 (720 s)	Tank overflow	MV-101 is ON; LIT-101 between L and H	Keep MV-101 on continuously; LIT-101 700 mm	Tank overflow
A5	MSSP	24:02 (1444 s)	Underflow tank in P1; Overflow tank in P3	P-101 is off; P102 is on; LIT-301 is between L and H	P-101 on continuously; Set value of LIT-301 as 801 mm	Tank 101 underflow; Tank 301 overflow

6   Tests and Evaluation

Tests were conducted using python and machine learning libraries such as Numpy, Keras and Tensoflow.

6.1 Pre-processing

Sensor's values were processed as time series. Each time series was pre-processed by centering and reducing it.

6.2 Training

In the training phase, we used records of 04 days of normal functioning. This allows us to build our prediction model. For that we apply the following steps:

- Applying deep learning to ICS measurements used as time series.
- Use of LSTM with 2 hidden layers (100, 50) and ReLu as activation function.
- Use of a time window of 5 mn (300 rows).

The obtained LSTM-network shows more than 99% of prediction accuracy (regression).

6.3   Results

Graphs in Fig. 1 indicates sensor's received values in red and predicted values in blue. Thus, from Fig. 1, we can clearly see that before launching each attack, red and blue curves are merged together. This indicates that our model predict successfully the next expected sensors values. On the other hand, during attacks, curves of the targeted sensors differ significantly. This indicates an anomaly in received sensing data.

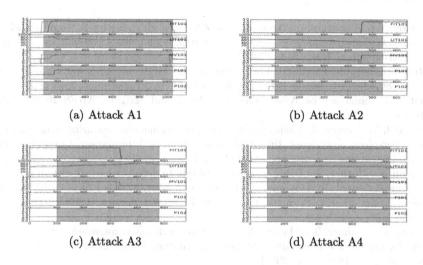

(a) Attack A1   (b) Attack A2

(c) Attack A3   (d) Attack A4

Fig. 1. Attack's detection (Color figure online)

6.4   Attacks Detection

Attacks detection is implemented using 2 metrics, the Root Mean Square Error (RMSE) and the Mean Square Error (MSE). Results are represented in Fig. 2. Indeed, peaks in each graph correspond to an attack.

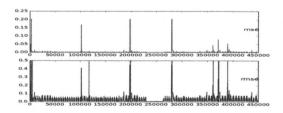

Fig. 2. MSE and RMSE values

7   Conclusion and Future Works

In this paper, we proposed an unsupervised learning approach for false data injection attacks against Industrial Control Systems. The conducted experiments demonstrated the ability of this techniques to detect a wide kind of attacks. As future work, we aim to automatize attack's detection.

References

1. Huang, Y.L., Cárdenas, A., Amin, S., Lin, Z.S., Tsai, H.Y., Sastry, S.: Understanding the physical and economic consequences of attacks on control systems. Int. J. Crit. Infrastruct. Prot. **2**(3), 73–83 (2009)
2. Rubio-Hernán, J., De Cicco, L., García-Alfaro, J.: Revisiting a watermark-based detection scheme to handle cyber-physical attacks. In: Proceedings - 2016 11th International Conference on Availability, Reliability and Security, ARES 2016 (2016) 21–28
3. Krotofil, M., Larsen, J., Gollmann, D.: The process matters : ensuring data veracity in cyber-physical systems. In: ACM Symposium on Information, Computer and Communications Security, pp. 133–144 (2015)
4. Adepu, S., Mathur, A.: Using process invariants to detect cyber attacks on a water treatment system. In: Hoepman, J.-H., Katzenbeisser, S. (eds.) SEC 2016. IAICT, vol. 471, pp. 91–104. Springer, Cham (2016). https://doi.org/10.1007/978-3-319-33630-5_7
5. Linda, O., Vollmer, T., Manic, M.: Neural network based intrusion detection system for critical infrastructures. In: 2009 International Joint Conference on Neural Networks, pp. 1827–1834 (2009)
6. Gollmann, D.: Veracity, plausibility, and reputation. In: Askoxylakis, I., Pöhls, H.C., Posegga, J. (eds.) WISTP 2012. LNCS, vol. 7322, pp. 20–28. Springer, Heidelberg (2012). https://doi.org/10.1007/978-3-642-30955-7_3
7. Hochreiter, S., Schmidhuber, J.: Long short-term memory. Neural Comput. **9**(8), 1735–1780 (1997)
8. Malhotra, P., Ramakrishnan, A., Anand, G., Vig, L., Agarwal, P., Shroff, G.: LSTM-based encoder-decoder for multi-sensor anomaly detection (2016)

Outsourcing Signatures of Confidential Documents

Hervé Chabanne[1,2(✉)], Julien Keuffer[1,3], and Emmanuel Prouff[4]

[1] Idemia, Paris, France
{herve.chabanne,julien.keuffer}@idemia.com
[2] Télécom Paristech, Paris, France
[3] Eurecom, Biot, France
[4] ANSSI, Paris, France
emmanuel.prouff@ssi.gouv.fr

Abstract. We describe an industrial case study of the application of zero-knowledge Succinct Non-interactive Argument of Knowledge techniques to enable a client to securely outsource the signature of a confidential document he owns to a digital signature provider. On the one hand, the client gets a valid standard signature of his confidential document while the signature provider learns nothing more from the document than its digest. On the other hand, the signature provider has the guarantee that the client was in possession of his message. We report implementation results to show the practicability of our ideas.

1 Introduction

1.1 Motivation

As an example of application of our proposal consider e-tendering Systems. On the one hand, quoting [8] "Submitted tenders are highly confidential documents, which are always the target for business collusion" (see also [7]). On the other hand, quoting [8] again "In the e-tendering process, non-repudiation is required .... Non-repudiation is usually implemented trough the use of a digitally signed message. Digitally signed messages are often as legally binding as traditional signatures". A trusted-third party is envisaged here to sign the tenders but its impartiality is also questioned [3].

More generally, companies may rely today on a Digital Signature Provider (DSP), who manages and automates the entire workflow to produce electronic signatures of documents. Within this outsourced signature framework, the client may want an additional property, namely confidentiality-preserving of the message to be signed, while the DSP may require guarantees that the client is indeed

E. Prouff—This work has been done when the author was working at Safran Identity and Security (now Idemia).

This work was partly supported by the TREDISEC project, funded by the European Union under the ICT theme of the H2020 research and innovation programme.

in possession of the message for legal reasons. For instance, the European Regulation eIDAS states in Article 13 that "trust service providers shall be liable for damage caused intentionally or negligently to any natural or legal person due to a failure to comply with the obligations under this Regulation" [19].

Message confidentiality is usually not provided by DSPs since it is frequently mandatory to upload the message before signature. A straightforward solution to preserve the confidentiality of the message would be to first run an authentication protocol between the client and the DSP and afterward to outsource only the message digest to get a signature. Indeed, the vast majority of standard signature with appendix protocols only need the hash of the message as input to build the signature [18]. However, this solution implies that the DSP does no longer have guarantees that the client is in possession of the original document.

Blind signature schemes [5] provide message confidentiality for the client: the signer gets neither information about the message he signs nor about its signature. However the existing schemes do not end today with a signature in a standard [18]. As far as we are aware of, no blind signature scheme has been standardized. As we seek applications where the digital signature can have legal repercussions, this seems paramount.

1.2 Our Contribution

We leverage on a current trend developed in the domain of cryptocurrencies to address our solution using zero-knowledge Succinct Non-interactive Argument of Knowledge (zk-SNARK). Consider a hash function H and a password pwd such that $H(pwd) = h$. One may want to prove without revealing it that he knows a pre-image of h. He uses a zk-SNARK for this. This proof will not reveal the value of pwd thanks to zero-knowledge property.

To the best of our knowledge, this problem of a proof of knowledge of a pre-image for a hash function has been first formulated at Crypto 1998 Rump Session with the SHA-1 function. Until recently, no progress have been reported. The situation changes with the arrival of new cryptocurrencies. [1] provides for Zero-Cash a hand-optimized SHA-256 compression function zk-SNARK to prove the knowledge of a pre-image. [17] also gives a manually optimized implementation of this function. This application seems to become popular as it is benchmarked in [9] and, then, very recently, in [16].

It should be noted that this popularity exceeds zk-SNARKs as Secure Multiparty Computations also bring efficient provers. [15] requires interactions to produce the proof and [11] outputs a non-interactive proof using the Fiat-Shamir heuristic, which results in a proof of non-negligible length. Both papers provide implementation results for the knowledge of a hash pre-image, the hash function being SHA-1 for [15] and SHA-1 and SHA-256 for [11]. However, only the compression function of these hash functions have been benchmarked. In both cases, the amount of communication (resp. the size of the proof) scales linearly with the size of the circuit used to produce the ZK proof. Thus, using results of [11], proving knowledge of a SHA-256 pre-image of a 1 KB message will produce a proof whose size is at least 13 MB (see Sect. 3 for results on zk-SNARKs).

2 Verifiable Computing Schemes

With the advent of cloud computing, efficient schemes for delegation of computation have been proposed [12,14], building on the PCP theorem. Despite the improvements made, these schemes were either lacking expressiveness (only a restricted class of computation could be delegated) or concrete efficiency (constants too high in the asymptotic). Few constructions aiming practicality have been proposed by Groth [13] or Setty et al. [21] but the breakthrough of Gennaro et al. [10] really opened the way to near practical and general purpose verifiable computation schemes by introducing quadratic arithmetic programs (QAPs), an efficient way of encoding the arithmetic circuit satisfiability problem. Parno et al. [20] embedded QAPs into a bilinear group, producing a Succinct Non-interactive ARGument (SNARG) that can be turned into a zk-SNARK with almost no additional costs. Their system, called Pinocchio, is also publicly verifiable: public evaluation and verification keys (see below Sect. 2.1) are computed from the QAPs and anyone with access to the verification key can validate the proof. Note that in order to have an efficient verifier, SNARKs built on QAPs requires a preprocessing phase where the evaluation and verification keys are computed, enabling to produce a constant size proof and to get a constant verification time.

There exists several zk-SNARK implemented systems, all building on QAPs. They compile a program written with a high-level language into a circuit, turning the latter into a QAP and then applying a cryptographic machinery to get a SNARK [2,6,16,20,22]. These systems make different trade-offs between efficiency for the prover and expressivity of the computations to be verified, comparisons can be found in the survey [23].

2.1 Public Verifiability

We first recall the definitions of non-interactive publicly Verifiable Computing (VC) schemes (see for instance [10]). Let f be a function and λ be a security parameter. The Setup procedure produces two public keys, an evaluation key EK_f and a verification key VK_f. These keys depend on the function f, but not on the inputs. The setup phase might be done once for all, and the keys are reusable for all future inputs: $(EK_f, VK_f) \leftarrow \text{Setup}(1^\lambda, f)$. Then a prover, given some input x and the evaluation key EK_f, computes $y = f(x)$ and generates a proof of correctness π for this result: $(y, \pi) \leftarrow \text{Prove}(EK_f, x)$. Anyone, given the input/output (x, y), the proof π and the verification key VK_f can check the proof: $d \in \{0, 1\} \leftarrow \text{Verify}(VK_f, x, y, \pi)$. Regarding the security properties such a scheme should satisfy, honestly generated proofs should be accepted (correctness), and a cheating prover should not convince a verifier of a false computation (soundness). Formal definitions and security proofs can be found in [20].

An extended setting for VC scheme where the function f has two inputs $f(x, w)$, and where the zero-knowledge property ensures that the verifier learns nothing about the second input w, can also be defined. This is, for instance, the case for the Pinocchio system which supports it.

2.2 Our Proposal to Sign Confidential Documents

We only consider signatures where only a hash of a document is needed to produce a signature of this document.

In our idea, the DPS (see Sect. 1.1) plays the role of verifier while the client is the prover. The DSP computes the public keys for evaluation EK_f and verification VK_f where f is defined as $f(h, pwd) = (\text{SHA-256}(pwd) == h)$ when the underlying hash function is SHA-256. It provides the key EK_f to the client. We can imagine that there is a different evaluation key for each client, or even, an evaluation key per document to be signed.

Whenever, a client wants a confidential document to be signed by the DPS, he computes thanks to the evaluation key, a zk-SNARK proof establishing that he knows a pre-image of a given hash h, this proof together with h are sent to the DSP. With his key VK_f, the DSP verifies the validity of the proof and, in this case, computes a signature of the confidential document using its sole hash.

3 Implementation Details

On the one hand, practical zk-SNARKs end up with proof of constant and short size: less than 300 bytes. Their verification is therefore really fast, usually tens of milliseconds. On the other hand, all the state of the art protocols computing zk-SNARKs demand an overhead for the prover. For instance, [1] reports 27100 multiplicative gates for their SHA-256 compression function circuit, which results in 1.25 s to prove knowledge of a pre-image and 17 ms to verify the proof. The Setup phase needed to generate public evaluation and verification keys, lasts 4.58 s. [17] reports 26100 multiplicative gates for their solution, while [16] tends to the same performances in an automated way.

[9] reports for SHA-1 function and for a message of length: 4-bytes (resp. 96 bytes, resp.159 bytes), the following timings for Setup: 25.82 s (resp. 26.33 s, resp. 32.56 s) and Prove: 49.75 s (resp. 32.98 s, resp. 49.83 s). The verification time of Verify is constant at 11 ms.

Recently, [4] working on Zero Knowledge Contingent Payments over the Bitcoin network – which also relies on a proof of pre-image for a hash function – introduced two new protocols based on zk-SNARKs. To that end, Campanelli *et al.* built an optimized circuit for representing SHA-256.

We implement our protocol with zk-SNARKs, using the Libsnark library [2]. For our experiments, we test the case where three computations of the compression function of SHA-256 have to be done to process the proof. The tests were run on two different machines. The first one is running at 3:6 GHz with 4 GB of RAM, with no parallelisation. The second one is more powerful: it has 8 cores running at 2:9 GHz with 16 GB of RAM and uses parallelisation. As shown in the first two rows of Table 1, for a security level of 128 bits, using three circuits instead of one decreases approximately the proving time by a factor 3 without modifying the verification time, which is due to the use of zk-SNARKs and their constant size proofs. However, this comes at the cost of a slower key generation time and a verification key size which is approximately three times larger.

We also benchmark our protocol instantiated with zk-SNARKs on the first machine at a lower security level of 80 bits (i.e. the security of the proof of knowledge property), the results are shown in the last row of Table 1.

Table 1. Benchmark of our solution.

	Setup	EK_f Size	VK_f Size	Prove	Verify
One circuit	30 s	55 MB	23 kB	14 s	7 ms
Three circuits	36 s	57 MB	60 kB	5.5 s	7 ms
80 bits	33 s	45 MB	54 kB	3.8 s	16 ms

4 Conclusion

After two decades with no significant progress, there are today a lot of proposals to build a proof of knowledge of a pre- image for a hash function [4,9,11,15,16]. This renewed interest is, partly, related to cryptocurrencies. We here give a new scope of application, apart of this domain, namely, the outsourcing signatures of confidential documents where a client delegates the signature of his documents to a Digital Signature Provider (DSP). For comparability, we report our own implementation with the Libsnark library [2] (Sect. 3).

As an open issue related to our proposal, we want to mention the ability for the DSP to add freshness to the proof required before its signature. We address this problem in Sect. 2.2 at the cost of renewing the evaluation keys. For instance, consider that a nonce is sent by the DSP to be included to the proof. I.e. the prover receives a nonce ν from the verifier and computes a hash of the original message m concatenated with ν. At the end, the prover computes $H(m), H(m||\nu)$ and a proof that these two hashes are related. After reception of the proof, the verifier checks consistency of the value computed from the nonce and verifies the proof. Dealing with a hash function designed using the Merkle-Damgard construction, as for SHA-256, we then have to take care of different cases for the padding considering the fact that the message together with the nonce belongs to the same block or not. At first glance, the design of a proof of knowledge for a relation between $H(m)$ and $H(m||\nu)$ seems intricate.

References

1. Ben-Sasson, E., et al.: Zerocash: decentralized anonymous payments from Bitcoin. In: 2014 IEEE Symposium on Security and Privacy, pp. 459–474 (2014)
2. Ben-Sasson, E., Chiesa, A., Genkin, D., Tromer, E., Virza, M.: SNARKs for C: verifying program executions succinctly and in zero knowledge. In: Canetti, R., Garay, J.A. (eds.) CRYPTO 2013. LNCS, vol. 8043, pp. 90–108. Springer, Heidelberg (2013). https://doi.org/10.1007/978-3-642-40084-1_6

3. Betts, M., et al.: Towards secure and legal e-tendering. J. Inf. Technol. Constr. **11**, 89–102 (2006)
4. Campanelli, M., Gennaro, R., Goldfeder, S., Nizzardo, L.: Zero-knowledge contingent payments revisited: attacks and payments for services. In: Proceedings of the 2017 ACM SIGSAC, Conference on Computer and Communications Security, pp. 229–243
5. Chaum, D.: Blind signatures for untraceable payments. In: Chaum, D., Rivest, R.L., Sherman, A.T. (eds.) Advances in Cryptology, pp. 199–203. Springer, Boston (1982). https://doi.org/10.1007/978-1-4757-0602-4_18
6. Costello, C., et al.: Geppetto: versatile verifiable computation. In: IEEE Symposium on Security and Privacy, SP 2015, pp. 253–270 (2015)
7. Du, R., Foo, E., Boyd, C., Fitzgerald, B.: Defining security services for electronic tendering. In: ACSW Frontiers 2004, Workshops, pp. 43–52 (2004)
8. Du, R., Foo, E., Nieto, J.G., Boyd, C.: Designing secure e-tendering systems. In: Katsikas, S., López, J., Pernul, G. (eds.) TrustBus 2005. LNCS, vol. 3592, pp. 70–79. Springer, Heidelberg (2005). https://doi.org/10.1007/11537878_8
9. Fournet, C., Keller, C., Laporte, V.: A certified compiler for verifiable computing. In: IEEE 29th Computer Security Foundations Symposium, CSF 2016, pp. 268–280 (2016)
10. Gennaro, R., Gentry, C., Parno, B., Raykova, M.: Quadratic span programs and succinct NIZKs without PCPs. In: Johansson, T., Nguyen, P.Q. (eds.) EURO-CRYPT 2013. LNCS, vol. 7881, pp. 626–645. Springer, Heidelberg (2013). https://doi.org/10.1007/978-3-642-38348-9_37
11. Giacomelli, I., Madsen, J., Orlandi, C.: Zkboo: Faster zero-knowledge for boolean circuits. In: 25th USENIX Security Symposium, pp. 1069–1083 (2016)
12. Goldwasser, S., Kalai, Y.T., Rothblum, G.N.: Delegating computation: interactive proofs for muggles. In: Proceedings of the 40th Annual ACM Symposium on Theory of Computing, pp. 113–122 (2008)
13. Groth, J.: Short pairing-based non-interactive zero-knowledge arguments. In: Abe, M. (ed.) ASIACRYPT 2010. LNCS, vol. 6477, pp. 321–340. Springer, Heidelberg (2010). https://doi.org/10.1007/978-3-642-17373-8_19
14. Ishai, Y., Kushilevitz, E., Ostrovsky, R.: Efficient arguments without short PCPs. In: 22nd Annual IEEE Conference on Computational Complexity, CCC 2007, pp. 278–291
15. Jawurek, M., Kerschbaum, F., Orlandi, C.: Zero-knowledge using garbled circuits: how to prove non-algebraic statements efficiently. In: 2013 ACM SIGSAC Conference on Computer and Communications Security, CCS 2013 (2013)
16. Kosba, A., Papamanthou, C., Shi, E.: xJsnark: a framework for efficient verifiable computation. In: 2018 IEEE Symposium on Security and Privacy (SP) (2018)
17. Kosba, A.E., Miller, A., Shi, E., Wen, Z., Papamanthou, C.: Hawk: the blockchain model of cryptography and privacy-preserving smart contracts. In: IEEE Symposium on Security and Privacy, pp. 839–858 (2016)
18. Digital signature standard (DSS): Federal Information Processing Standard 186-4, National Institute of Standards and Technology (2013)
19. Regulation No 910/2014 L257. Official Journal of the European Union (2014)
20. Parno, B., Howell, J., Gentry, C., Raykova, M.: Pinocchio: nearly practical verifiable computation. In: 2013 IEEE Symposium on Security and Privacy, pp. 238–252 (2013)
21. Setty, S.T.V., McPherson, R., Blumberg, A.J., Walfish, M.: Making argument systems for outsourced computation practical (sometimes). In: 19th Annual Network and Distributed System Security Symposium, NDSS 2012 (2012)

22. Wahby, R.S., Setty, S.T.V., Ren, Z., Blumberg, A.J., Walfish, M.: Efficient RAM and control flow in verifiable outsourced computation. In: 22nd Annual Network and Distributed System Security Symposium, NDSS 2015 (2015)
23. Walfish, M., Blumberg, A.J.: Verifying computations without reexecuting them. Commun. ACM **58**(2), 74–84 (2015)

Trust Evaluation Model for Attack Detection in Social Internet of Things

Wafa Abdelghani[1,2(⊠)], Corinne Amel Zayani[2], Ikram Amous[2],
and Florence Sèdes[1]

[1] IRIT Laboratory, Paul Sabatier University, Toulouse, France
{abdelghani.wafa,sedes}@irit.fr
[2] Miracl Laboratory, Sfax University, Sfax, Tunisia
{corinne.zayani,ikram.amous}@isecs.rnu.tn

Abstract. Social Internet of Things (SIoT) is a paradigm in which the Internet of Things (IoT) concept is fused with Social Networks for allowing both people and objects to interact in order to offer a variety of attractive services and applications. However, with this emerging paradigm, people feel wary and cautious. They worry about revealing their data and violating their privacy. Without trustworthy mechanisms to guarantee the reliability of user's communications and interactions, the SIoT will not reach enough popularity to be considered as a cutting-edge technology. Accordingly, trust management becomes a major challenge to provide qualified services and improved security.

Several works in the literature have dealt with this problem and have proposed different trust-models. Nevertheless, proposed models aim to rank the best nodes in the SIoT network. This does not allow to detect different types of attack or malicious nodes.

Hence, we overcome these issues through proposing a new trust-evaluation model, able to detect malicious nodes, block and isolate them, in order to obtain a reliable and resilient system. For this, we propose new features to describe and quantify the different behaviors that operate in such system. We formalized and implemented a new function learned and built based on supervised learning, to analyze different features and distinguish malicious behavior from benign ones. Experimentation made on a real data set prove the resilience and the performance of our trust model.

Keywords: Social Internet of Things · Social networks ·
Trust management · Trust attacks · Resilience

This work was financially supported by the PHC Utique program of the French Ministry of Foreign Affairs and Ministry of higher education and research and the Tunisian Ministry of higher education and scientific research in the CMCU project number 18G1431.

A. Zemmari et al. (Eds.): CRiSIS 2018, LNCS 11391, pp. 48–64, 2019.
https://doi.org/10.1007/978-3-030-12143-3_5

1   Introduction

The Internet of Things is expected to be dominated by a huge number of inter-actions between billions of persons and heterogeneous communications among hosts, smart objects and among smart objects themselves. It provides a variety of data that can be aggregated, fused, processed, analyzed and mined in order to extract useful information [6]. Unquestionably, the main strength of the IoT vision is the high impact on several aspects of every-day life and behavior of potential users. However, many challenging issues prevent the vision of IoT to become a reality, such as interoperability, navigability, trust, privacy and secu-rity management and resource discovery in such heterogeneous and decentralized network. To resolve some of the cited issues, a new paradigm called Social Inter-net of Things (SIoT) is born.

Integrating social networking concepts into the Internet of Things has led to the Social Internet of Things paradigm, enabling people and connected devices to interact with offering a variety of attractive applications. SIoT appeared as a result of an evolutionary process that affected modern communication by the advent of IoT in telecommunication scenarios [3]. The first step of this process consists in making objects smart. The next step consists in the evolution of objects with a degree of smartness to pseudo-social objects [3] which can interact with the surrounding environment and perform a pseudo-social behavior with other objects. The last step consists of the appearance of social objects includes being able to autonomously establish relationships with other objects, to join communities and build their own social networks whose can differ from their owner's ones [3]. Adopting such vision is, therefore, a promising new trend, with numerous advantages. First, navigability and resources discovery are improved by narrowing down their scopes to a manageable social network of everything [2]. Second, the scalability is guaranteed like in the human social networks [4]. Third, the heterogeneity of devices, networks and communication protocols is resolved by the use of social networks [2]. And a larger data source becomes available as it comes from a set of users. The continuous feeding of data from communities gives us big data [10]. Quantity and variety of contextual data have increased allowing improved services intelligence and adaptability to users' situational needs [2].

However, the SIoT paradigm does not allow to fix trust, security and privacy issues. Furthermore, the numerous advantages of SIoT such as improving nav-igability, and increasing quantity and variety of contextual data, make privacy and security of IoT users more compromised.

In the literature, trust mechanisms have been widely studied in various fields. Several works in the literature have dealt with this problem. They have pro-posed different trust-models, based on different features and measures, aiming to rank the best nodes in the SIoT network. Regarding the existing related works, our contribution in this paper are summarized as follow:

1. Unlike most existing reputation and trust management schemes in the litera-ture, our goal is to detect malicious nodes. This allows us to isolate (or block)

the malicious nodes, limit the interactions made with them, and obtain a trustworthy system (network). Classifying trustworthy nodes would not prevent malicious ones from performing their malicious behaviors that could break the basic functionality of the given system.

2. To achieve the goals of ensuring a reliable and trustworthy system, we first present an informal description of each kind of trust-related attack. Then, we propose a new trust model based on new features derived from the description of each type of trust-related attack. Works in the literature use more global features such as the centrality of the node or the number of friends in common between two nodes. These features have no relation (from a semantic point of view) with the mentioned trust-related attacks.

3. To combine the proposed features, the majority of related works use the weighted mean. However, the performed behaviors for each type of trust attack are different. A weighted mean cannot detect all types of attacks since the features considered and the weights assigned to each feature may differ from one type of attack to another. We propose new features in our work and a new way to combine them using machine learning techniques, in order, to classify nodes into benevolent nodes and malicious nodes.

The rest of the paper is organized as follows. In Sect. 2, we present background about main concepts. In Sect. 3, we analyze and compare related works. In Sect. 4, We give a formal presentation of the proposed trust evaluation model. In Sect. 5, we detail the design of the proposed features. In Sect. 6, we detail the proposed classification function which allows to aggregate proposed feature in order to distinguish malicious behavior from benign ones. In Sect. 7, we present evaluations that enabled us to validate the resilience our trust evaluation model. Finally, we conclude in Sect. 8 with providing future insights.

2   Background

The Social Internet of Things paradigm allows people and objects to interact within a social framework to support a new kind of social navigation. The structure of the SIoT network can be shaped as required to facilitate the navigability, perform objects and services discovery, and guarantee the scalability like in human social networks. However, trust must be ensured for leveraging the degree of interaction among things.

Trust is a complicated concept used in various contexts and influenced by many measurable and non-measurable properties such as confidence, belief, and expectation on the reliability, integrity, security, dependability, ability, and other characters of an entity [20]. There is no definitive consensus about the trust concept in the scientific literature. Indeed, although its importance is widely recognized, the multiple approaches towards trust definition do not lend themselves to the establishment of metrics and evaluation methodologies.

Trust can be defined as a belief of a trustor in a trustee that the trustee will provide or accomplish a trust goal as trustor's expectation. In SIoT environment, trustors and trustees can be humans, devices, systems, applications, and services.

Measurement of trust can be absolute (e.g., probability) or relative (e.g., level of trust). The trust goal is in a broad understanding. It could be an action that the trustee is going to perform; it could also be an information that the trustee provides.

Trust management mechanisms and trust evaluation models are proposed to ensure trust in different types of systems. Their roles consist of providing (computing) a trust score, which will help nodes to take decision about invoking or not, services provided by other nodes. There are several varieties of attacks that are designed to specifically break this functionality. We present in this section the main trust-related attacks cited in the literature [1,5,7]. We also explain the differences between trust management mechanisms and trust evaluation models.

2.1 Trust Attacks in SIOT Networks

An attack is a malicious behavior established by a malicious node launched to break the basic functionality of a given system and to achieve a variety of malicious ends. A malicious node, in general, can perform communication protocol attacks to disrupt network operations. We assume such attack is handled by intrusion detection techniques [9,16] and is not addressed in our work.

In the context of SIoT, we are concerned about trust-related attacks that can disrupt the trust system. In this kind of attacks, a malicious node could boost its own reputation to gain access to higher functions or generally be disruptive in a manner that brings down the overall efficiency of the system. Thus, a malicious IoT device (because its owner is malicious) can perform the following trust-related attacks. We assume that there are some others attacks which can be autonomously launched by devices. We will consider them in future works. In this paper, we focus on attacks performed by IoT devices under the control of them malicious owners.

- **Self Promoting attacks (SPA):** is an attack where malicious nodes, provide bad-quality service, try to boost their reputation (by giving good rates for themselves) in order to be selected as service providers.
- **Bad Mouthing Attacks (BMA):** is an attack where malicious nodes try to destroy the reputation of well-behaved nodes (by giving them bad rates) in order to decrease their chance to be selected as service providers.
- **Ballot Stuffing Attacks (BSA):** is an attack where malicious nodes try to promote the reputation of other malicious nodes in order to increase their chance to be selected as service providers.
- **Discriminatory Attacks (DA):** is an attack where malicious nodes attack discriminatory other nodes, without a strong social relationship with them, because of human propensity towards strangers.

In Table 1, we propose an informal specification of the malicious behavior for each type of trust-related attack.

Table 1. An informal description of malicious behavior for each type of trust attacks.

	Invoker (u_i)	Provider (u_j)	Interactions $I(u_i, u_j)$
BMA	Malicious node: - Provides poor quality services - Provides bad votes that do not reflect his actual opinion to destroy the reputation of u_j	Benign node: - Has a good reputation - Provides good quality services	- A lot of interaction - The majority of votes provided by u_i to u_j are negative
BSA	Malicious node: - It has a good reputation - It gives high scores that do not reflect his actual opinion in u_j in order to promote his reputation	Malicious node: - Provides good quality services - Has a bad reputation in the network	- A lot of interaction - The majority of votes provided by u_i to u_j are positive
SPA	Malicious node: - Provides services of poor quality - Has a bad reputation in the network - Provides high ratings that do not reflect his opinion to u_j in order to promote reputation	Malicious node: - Provides poor quality services	- A lot of interaction - The majority of votes provided by u_i to u_j are positive - u_i and u_j are often nearby - They have same interests - They provide same services
DA	Malicious node: - Provides bad votes to the majority of other users	Malicious/benign node	The majority of votes provided by u_i to u_j are negative

2.2 Trust Evaluation and Trust Management

Some researchers have focused on developing trust management mechanisms dealing with trust establishment, composition, aggregation, propagation, storage and update processes [11]. However, we focus in this work on the main step which is the trust establishment step. We will focus on the other steps in future works. The trust establishment step consists of developing a trust evaluation model and represents the main component of trust management mechanisms. Indeed, the performance of the trust management system essentially depends on the model introduced to evaluate the degree of trust that can be granted to the various entities involved in the system. We consider that a trust evaluation model is mainly composed of two steps, namely (i) the composition step and (ii) the aggregation step. The other steps such as propagation, updating, and storage will provide other properties such as system response time and scalability.

(i) **The Composition Step** consists of choosing features to be considered in calculating trust values. Several features have been considered in the literature such as honesty, cooperativeness, profile's similarity of profiles, reputation,.... These features can be categorized into various dimensions: (i) global or local; (ii) implicit or explicit; or (iii) related to users, devices or provided services. To measure these different features, the authors use information related to nodes, such as their position, their interaction history, their centrality in the network.

(ii) **The Aggregation Step** consists of choosing a method to aggregate values of different features in order to obtain the final trust value. For this purpose, authors in the literature use static weighted mean, dynamic weighted mean, fuzzy logic, probabilistic models, and so on.

3 Related Works

Various trust-models are proposed in the literature in order to ensure trustworthy services and interactions in SIoT environments. In this section, we try to analyze and compare these different models based on two criteria: (i) the proposed trust evaluation model; and (ii) the resilience face trust-attacks.

Trust evaluation models are composed of two steps, namely (i) **The composition step** and (ii) **The trust aggregation step**. For the trust composition step, authors propose different features such as recommendation, reliability, experience, and cooperativeness. Those features represent abstract concepts aiming to quantify the nodes trust level and are computed by different measures depending on authors goal and background. For example, in [14], the recommendation feature is measured as the number of nodes directly connected to a given node u_i. However, in [17], the recommendation feature is measured as the total mean of rates given to a node u_i. This same measure (mean of rates) is called reputation in some other works. The cooperativeness feature is considered as an indicator to measure a node's knowledge in [17] and is computed as the level of the social interactions between two nodes. However, in [7] the cooperativeness feature is computed as the number of common friends between two nodes.

Given that there is no consensus about trust concept definition, and given the divergence of the proposed features, as well as the divergence of the measure of each feature, this can give birth to thousands of trust evaluation models with different combinations between the features calculated with different measures. We believe that a trust evaluation model must above all fulfill the role of guaranteeing the reliability of the system in which it is involved. This reliability is compromised by the different types of trust-related attacks.

We have chosen in this work to start from the definition of each type of attack. We present an informal description of each attack that we formalized using mathematical measures and equations. We believe that some features and measures proposed in the literature, such as the number of friends in common or the number of relationships in the network, have no relation to the cited trust attacks. Moreover, as it is common in the classic social networks, a malicious node could try to increase the number of its relations in general or the number of its common relations with a given node, before proceeding to attacks. Some other measures, such as the mean rates, could give an idea about the history of a node's interactions and could, therefore, permit to detect some types of attacks. The features proposed in the literature remain insufficient to detect the different types of attacks. Indeed, none of the proposed features can detect, for example, the SPA attack in which a node is hidden under a false identity.

To conclude, the performance of a trust evaluation model mainly depends on the features and measures chosen in the composition phase. Nevertheless, it also depends on the method chosen in the aggregation phase. The weighted mean is most used aggregation method. However, the performed behaviors for each type of trust-related attack are not similar. A weighted mean cannot detect all types of attacks since the features considered and the weights assigned to each feature may differ from one type of attack to another. The problem of detecting malicious nodes being considered as a complex problem and requiring an in-depth analysis of nodes behaviors, and thus, we propose the use of machine learning techniques.

The second criterion of comparison concerns the resilience to trust-related attacks. Some of the cited works focus on trust-attack detection. However, they do not prove the ability of the proposed model to detect trust-attack through evaluations or experimentation. The majority of related works propose model permitting to assign a trust degree to each node in the network. Their goal is to rank nodes according to their trust-values. However, this kind of model does not allow to detect malicious attacks and malicious nodes. This gives the malicious nodes free access to establish different types of attacks in the network. The purpose of our work is to detect malicious nodes in order to block them and obtain a trustworthy system (Table 2).

Table 2. Comparison of related-works

		[18]	[13]	[17]	[7]	[15]	[8]
Trust evaluation model¯	Trust composition	Knowledge reputation experience	Consistency intention ability	Recommend reputation experience	Honesty coopertiveness community-interest	Reliability reputation	Reputation, social relationship, energy-level
	Trust agregation	Fuzzy logic	Weighted mean	Fuzzy logic	Combinatorial logic	Weighted mean	Weighted mean
Goal	Node ranking	✓	✓	✓		✓	
	Attack-detection				✓		✓

4   System Modeling

4.1   Notations

Let $G_u^t = (U, S)$ be a directed graph representing users social network at time t. U is the node set $U = \{u_i | 0 < i \leq n\}$ where n is the number of users. S is the edges set and reflects the friendship relation between users. Each user $u_i \in U$, can be modeled by the 5-tuple $\langle id, age, city, country, devices \rangle$ where $devices$ represents the list of devices that belong to the user u_i.

Let $G_d^t = (D, R)$ be a directed graph representing devices network at time t. D is the node set $D = \{d_j | 0 < j \leq m\}$ where m is the number of devices. R is the edges set where $R \in \{or; sr, wr, lr, pr\}$ represents the different kinds of relations which can occur between devices. *or* represents the owner relationship which occurs between two devices having the same owner. *sr* represents the social relationship which occurs between two devices when their owners have a social relationship. *lr* represents the relation between two devices which are in proximity. *wr* represents the relation between two devices which interact to perform a common task. *pr* represents the relation between two devices which belong to the same category.

Each device $d_j \in D$, can be modeled by the 5-tuple $<id, category, longitude, latitude, services>$ where *services* represent the list of services provided by the device d_j. Each service s_k is modeled by the 4-tuple $<id, endpoint, domain, qos>$ where qos (Quality of Service) represents the service's non-functional characteristics such as its availability, response time, latency, and reliability.

4.2 Problem Definition and Formalization

With the presented notations and definitions, our main problem is to detect malicious users. In a formal way, given a training set of N instances of users associated with a class label $l_i \in \{malicious, bening\}$, the problem is turned first to design an advanced set of M features extracted from the training set. Then, the features designed are used to learn or build a binary classification model y using a given training set such that it takes features X as an input and predicts the class label of a user as an output, defined as $y : u_i \rightarrow \{malicious, bening\}$.

5 Features Design

In this section, we present the composition step of our trust evaluation model. We propose new features permitting to describe and quantify the different behaviors operating in SIoT systems. Our features are derived from the informal description of each type of trust-related attack and allow to distinguish malicious behavior from benign ones.

5.1 Reputation

This feature represents the global reputation of a user u_i in the overall network and is denoted as $Rep(u_i)$. It is computed as the quotient between the number of positive interactions and the total number of interactions (Eq. 1). Positive interactions are interactions with a high rate value. Nodes with a high reputation value are more likely to be attacked by other nodes. Nodes with a low reputation value are more likely to perform trust attacks. The reputation feature, combined with other features, can help in revealing BMA, BSA, SPA and DA attacks.

$$Rep(u_i) = \frac{\sum_{s_k \in S(u_i), (rt(u_j, s_k) >= 3)} m}{|I(u_i, u_j)|} \tag{1}$$

where $rt(u_j, s_k)$ is the rate given by the user u_i to the service s_k and $I(u_i, u_j)$ the set of interactions occurred between u_i and u_j.

5.2 Honesty

Honesty represents whether a user is honest and is denoted as $Hon(u_i)$. A user is considered honest if his rates reflect his real opinion, which means that he doesn't try to give wrong rating values to enhance or decrease other users reputation. Indeed, in BMA, BSA and SPA attacks, the malicious node presents a dishonest behavior. In the BMA attack, the malicious node gives bad votes to a node that provides good quality services, in order to ruin its reputation. In the BSA attack, the malicious node gives good votes to another malicious node that provides poor quality services, with the aim of helping it to promote its reputation. In the SPA attack, the malicious node tries to promote its own reputation by giving itself good votes while its services have poor quality.

The Honesty feature is, therefore, a key feature, which associated with other features, may reveal different types of attacks. To measure and quantify this feature, we compare the user rating vector $Rvec(u_i)$ with the rating matrix using Cosine Similarity Measure (Eq. 2).

$$Hon(u_i) = \sum_{x_j \in Rvec(u_i), x'_j \in Mvec} \sqrt{(x_j - x'_j)^2} \qquad (2)$$

Where x_j is the rate of ith user on j^{th} item, x'_j the average of rates given by all network nodes on item j, $Rvec(u_i)$ is the rating vector of the ith node and Mvec is the mean rating vector representing the average of the rating matrix

5.3 Quality of Provider

Quality of provider represents whether services provided by the user u_i present a good or bad QoS. It is denoted as $QoP(u_i)$. Indeed, malicious node aims at propagating services with bad quality. Services with good quality naturally reach a good reputation in the network. The malicious node must resort to malicious behavior to propagate bad services and will, therefore, perform BMA, BSA, SPA and DA attacks to achieve this goal. QoP feature is therefore essential to distinguish the nodes that likely perform malicious behaviors from other nodes that provide good quality services and do not need to carry out attacks to propagate them.

$$QoP(u_i) = \frac{\sum_{d_j \in D(u_i), s_k \in S(d_j)} QoD(d_j) * QoS(s_k)}{\sum_{d_j \in D(u_i)} QoD(d_j)} \qquad (3)$$

where S_{u_i} is the set of services provided by the ith node, qos(s_k) is the QoS value of the service s_k, and α is a threshold.

5.4 Similarity

Similarity refers to the similarity between user u_i and user u_j and it is denoted as $sU(u_i, u_j)$. This feature is computed based on different features such as profiles, interests, provided services, used devices and the frequency of proximity between a couple of users. It aims to detect affinity between users but can also reveal Self-Promoting Attack (SPA) in which the same user tries to promote his own reputation under a false identity.

5.5 Rating-Frequency

Rating-Frequency refers to the frequency of rating attributed by a user u_i to a user u_j, denoted as $RateF(u_i, u_j)$. It is computed as the number of rates given by a user u_i to a user u_j divided by the total number of rates given by the user u_i. Indeed, if a user u_i performs an attack against a user u_j, we will probably find a high number of rates given by user u_i to user u_j. According to whether these rates are positives or negatives and according to some other features such as the reputation and the QoP of the target user u_j, we can detect a Ballot-Stuffing Attack or a Bad-Mouthing Attack.

5.6 Direct-Experience

Direct-Experience refers to the opinion of a node i about its past interactions with a node j, denoted as $dExp(u_i, u_j)$. It is computed as the quotient of successful interactions between node u_i and node u_j, divided by the total number of interactions between them. The direct experience feature can not therefore directly reveal an attack. But, combined with other features, it helps to distinguish what kind of attack it is. Indeed, taking the example of two nodes u_i and u_j where u_i is a node that provides bad services and therefore has a low QoP value. The Rating frequency value $RateF(u_i, u_j)$ shows that the node u_i is striving to give rates to the u_j node. Indeed, u_i gives a total of 10 votes, of which 6 are attributed to u_j. In this case, it is probably an attack. Other features, such as u_j's reputation and QoP, as well as u_i's honesty, may confirm this hypothesis. The direct experience feature can finally decide whether it is a BMA or BSA attack. Indeed, in the BMA attack, node u_i aims to ruin the reputation of u_j and will, therefore, provide negative rates which result a low value of $dExp(u_i, u_j)$. Whereas, in the BSA attack, the node u_i aims to promote the reputation of u_j, which result a high value of $dExp(u_i, u_j)$.

5.7 Rating Trend

The rating trend feature is measured by the number of positive votes divided by the total number of votes provided by a user. It aims to reveal if a user is rather optimistic or pessimistic. It permit to detect the discriminatory attack (DA) in which the user provides negative votes randomly.

6 Classification Function Design

Once we have chosen the features that describe the behavior of different nodes in the network, the next step consists in choosing a method to aggregate the values of the different features, in order to obtain the final trust value. In the literature, the most common method is the weighted mean. However, we estimate that the performance of the system depends in this case mainly on weights assigned to each feature. Furthermore, the performed behaviors for each type of trust-related attack are different. A weighted mean cannot detect all types of attacks since the features considered and the weights assigned to each feature may differ from one type of attack to another.

The problem of the detection of malicious nodes being considered as a complex problem and requiring an in-depth analysis of nodes behaviors, we propose to use machine learning techniques. To our knowledge, this technique has never been used to measure trust. We consider our system as a classification problem. Indeed, our objective is to detect if a user is malicious or benign. A user is considered malicious if he tries to perform BMA, BSA, SPA or DA attack. If the user didn't perform any of the cited attacks, he is considered as benign. So, for each users u_i, we have two possible classes, namely (i) malicious user class, (ii) benign user class.

Machine learning techniques allowed us to avoid the problem of fixing weights and thresholds. Indeed, the machine learning algorithm will take as input the proposed features, will automatically assign the weights based on the learning data-base and will return as output one of the mentioned classes. The model as proposed in this work does not allow to determine the type of performed attack, but only to detect whether there was an attack or not. We plan in our future work to improve the proposed model, since some attacks may be more dangerous than others depending on the context and the domain. It would be interesting, in this case, to be able to know the type of attack.

7   Results and Evaluations

7.1   Experimental Setup

Data-Set Description. Due to the unavailability of real data, the majority of related works offer experiments based on simulations. In our work, we evaluated the performance of our model based on experiments applied to an enriched real dataset. Sigcomm[1] data-set contains users, their profiles, their list of interests. It contains also social relations between users, interactions occurred between them and frequency of proximity of each couple of users. We generate for each user one or more devices and we divide interactions of a user by his devices. Figure 1 shows statistics and description of the resulting data-set.

Performance Metrics. To assess the effectiveness and robustness of our proposed features using machine learning algorithms, we adopt the accuracy and the standard existing information retrieval metrics of precision, recall, and f-measure.

---

[1] http://crawdad.org/thlab/sigcomm2009/20120715/.

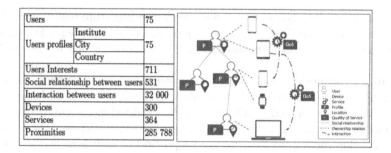

Users		75
Users profiles	Institute	75
	City	
	Country	
Users Interests		711
Social relationship between users		531
Interaction between users		32 000
Devices		300
Services		364
Proximities		285 788

Fig. 1. Data-set description

Learning Methods. We used the different learning algorithms implemented in WEKA [12] tool, to build the binary classification function y. We report here the results of Naive Bayes, Multi-Layer Perceptron and Random Tree learning algorithms (see Fig. 2). We finally opt for the Multi-Layer Perceptron because it has shown the best results in terms of the evaluation metrics. We used 10-fold cross-validation algorithm to evaluate the performance of our features.

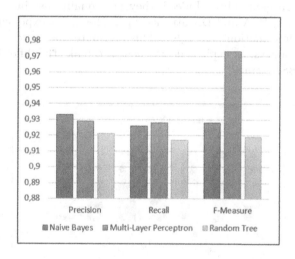

Fig. 2. Comparison of machine learning algorithms

Experiments Procedure. In this work, we propose a trust evaluation model. For this, we proposed, first, new features and measures to describe the behavior of different users. Secondly, we propose to use a new method of aggregation based on machine learning, able to differentiate malicious users from legitimate users.

To prove the performance of each proposed feature, we first measure the information gain for each feature separately. Then, we compare the features that we propose with the most used features in the literature based on common evaluation measures such as recall, precision, and F-measurement. For this, we use the most used aggregation method in the literature which is the weighted mean.

To prove the performance of the proposed aggregation method (Machine Learning), we compare (i) the results obtained by the other works with the weighted mean, (ii) our characteristics with the weighted mean and (iii) our characteristics with Machine Learning. Finally, to prove the resilience of the proposed trust evaluation model, we measure the proportion of malicious nodes detected on different networks with different percentages of malicious nodes ranging from 10 to 50%.

7.2 Experimental Results

Single Features Performance. The Fig. 3 shows the information gain when using one single feature in the learning process. The *similarity* feature has the largest value of information gain. This can be explained by the fact that this is the only feature able to detect Self Promoting Attacks (SPA). *Rating frequency, quality of provider, rating trend, honesty* and *reputation* features present almost equal information gain values. Indeed, they are equally discriminative for the detection of BMA, BSA and DA attacks type. The direct experience attribute has the lowest information gain value. This attribute does not actually detect attacks. But, it allows, as explained previously, to make the difference between a BMA and a BSA attack.

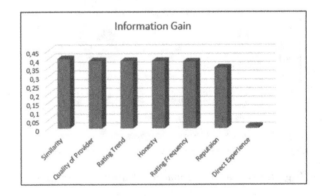

Fig. 3. Evaluation of single features performance

Group Features Performance. We compare our 7 features with 10 features existing in the literature. We implemented the 10 features with experimenting them on our data-set to have fare comparison. Since related-works that propose these features use the weighted mean for the aggregation step, we had to try different weights for each feature used in each related-work. We selected the weights that gave the best results for each work (see Table 3).

In addition, many of the proposed trust evaluation models have objectives of classifying nodes according to their trust degrees, without detecting malicious nodes. So, we had to set the thresholds below which a node is considered as malicious. We have similarly tried different threshold values for each of the related-works and we have chosen the thresholds that give the best results for each model. Table 3 shows the weight and threshold values we have finally selected for each related-work.

Table 3. Parameters for group feature performance evaluation

Related works	Features	Weights	Thresholds
Jayasinghe, U., et al. 2016 [14]	Recommendation	0,62	0,30
	Reputation	0,38	
Truong, N.B., et al. 2018 [19]	Reputation,	0,84	0,22
	Experience	0,16	
Chen, R., et al. 2016 [7]	Honesty	0,74	0,22
	Coopertiveness	0,12	
	Community-Interest	0,14	
Militano, L., et al. 2016 [15]	Reliability	0,37	0,35
	Reputation	0,63	
Our features with weighted mean	Honesty	0,18	0,58
	Reputation	0,19	
	Similarity	0,1	
	Direct Experience	0,06	
	Rating frequency	0,19	
	Quality of Provider	0,18	
	Rating trend	0,1	

We then used the weighted mean for the features we propose in this work. This allowed us to compare and validate the relevance of the features we propose compared to those of the state of the art. Finally, we applied the machine learning on the features that we propose in this work. This allowed us to prove the relevance of the aggregation method that we propose (the machine learning) compared to the most used method in the literature (the weighted mean). Figure 4 shows the results obtained. The features we propose give better results in terms of recall, precision, and f-measurement compared to other works even in the case of aggregation with a weighted mean. The results are even better when we applied the machine learning technique for the aggregation step.

System Resilience. Figure 5 presents the proportions of malicious nodes being detected obtained for an increasing number of malicious nodes performing randomly all kinds of trust-related attack. The proportion remains high (89%) even

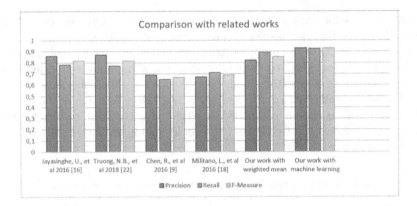

Fig. 4. Comparison with related works

for a system when 50% of the nodes are malicious. Those evaluations prove that our system can ensure resiliency toward each kind of trust-related attack, even facing a high percentage of malicious nodes. We have not continued the assessments for higher percentages, for the simple reason that, if a system has more than 50% malicious nodes, then it is a defective system.

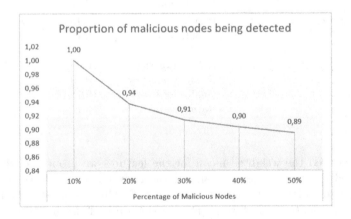

Fig. 5. Proportion of malicious nodes being detected

8   Conclusion and Future Directions

Social Internet of Things (SIoT) is a paradigm where the Internet of Things (IoT) is fused with Social Networks, offering a variety of attractive services and applications. However, facing this emerging paradigm, people feel wary and cautious. They worry divulgence of their data and violation of their privacy.

In this work, we propose a new trust-evaluation model, able to detect malicious nodes, in order to obtain a reliable and resilient system. Our future prospects are to develop a trust-management mechanism based on the proposed trust-evaluation model. This mechanism must ensure not only trust establishment but also the propagation, storage, and updating of trust. This will raise new issues related to the specific characteristics of SIoT environments, such as the scalability, dynamism and constrained capabilities of IoT devices.

References

1. Abdelghani, W., Zayani, C.A., Amous, I., Sèdes, F.: Trust management in social internet of things: a survey. In: Social Media: The Good, the Bad, and the Ugly, pp. 430–441. Swanwea (2016)
2. Ali, D.H.: A social Internet of Things application architecture: applying semantic web technologies for achieving interoperability and automation between the cyber, physical and social worlds. Ph.D. thesis, Institut National des Télécommunications (2015)
3. Atzori, L., Iera, A., Morabito, G.: From "smart objects" to "social objects": the next evolutionary step of the internet of things. IEEE Commun. Mag. 52(1), 97–105 (2014)
4. Atzori, L., Iera, A., Morabito, G., Nitti, M.: The social internet of things (SIoT)-when social networks meet the internet of things: concept, architecture and network characterization. Comput. Netw. 56(16), 3594–3608 (2012)
5. Bao, F., Chen, I., Guo, J.: Scalable, adaptive and survivable trust management for community of interest based internet of things systems. In: 11th International Symposium on Autonomous Decentralized Systems, Mexico City, pp. 1–7 (2013)
6. Calvary, G., Delot, T., Sedes, F., Tigli, J.Y.: Computer Science and Ambient Intelligence. Wiley, Hoboken (2013)
7. Chen, R., Bao, F., Guo, J.: Trust-based service management for social internet of things systems. IEEE Trans. Dependable Secur. Comput. 13(6), 684–696 (2016)
8. Chen, Z., Ling, R., Huang, C., Zhu, X.: A scheme of access service recommendation for the social internet of things. Int. J. Commun. Syst. 29(4), 694–706 (2016)
9. Cho, J.H., Chen, R., Feng, P.G.: Effect of intrusion detection on reliability of mission-oriented mobile group systems in mobile ad hoc networks. IEEE Trans. Reliab. 59(1), 231–241 (2010)
10. Geetha, S.: Social internet of things. World Sci. News 41, 76 (2016)
11. Guo, J., Chen, R., Tsai, J.J.: A survey of trust computation models for service management in internet of things systems. Comput. Commun. 97, 1–14 (2017)
12. Hall, M., Frank, E., Holmes, G., Pfahringer, B., Reutemann, P., Witten, I.H.: The WEKA data mining software: an update. ACM SIGKDD Explor. Newsl. 11(1), 10–18 (2009)
13. Huang, J., Seck, M.D., Gheorghe, A.: Towards trustworthy smart cyber-physical-social systems in the era of internet of things. In: 2016 11th System of Systems Engineering Conference (SoSE), pp. 1–6. IEEE (2016)
14. Jayasinghe, U., Truong, N.B., Lee, G.M., Um, T.W.: RpR: a trust computation model for social internet of things. In: Ubiquitous Intelligence & Computing, Advanced and Trusted Computing, Scalable Computing and Communications, Cloud and Big Data Computing, Internet of People, and Smart World Congress, pp. 930–937. IEEE (2016)

15. Militano, L., Orsino, A., Araniti, G., Nitti, M., Atzori, L., Iera, A.: Trusted D2D-based data uploading in in-band narrowband-IoT with social awareness. In: 2016 IEEE 27th Annual International Symposium on Personal, Indoor, and Mobile Radio Communications (PIMRC), pp. 1–6. IEEE (2016)
16. Mitchell, R., Chen, I.R.: A survey of intrusion detection techniques for cyber-physical systems. ACM Comput. Surv. (CSUR) **46**(4), 55 (2014)
17. Truong, N.B., Um, T.W., Lee, G.M.: A reputation and knowledge based trust service platform for trustworthy social internet of things. Innovations in Clouds, Internet and Networks (ICIN), Paris, France (2016)
18. Truong, N.B., Um, T.W., Zhou, B., Lee, G.M.: From personal experience to global reputation for trust evaluation in the social internet of things. In: GLOBECOM 2017–2017 IEEE Global Communications Conference, pp. 1–7. IEEE (2017)
19. Truong, N.B., Um, T.W., Zhou, B., Lee, G.M.: Strengthening the blockchain-based internet of value with trust. In: International Conference on Communications (2018)
20. Yan, Z., Zhang, P., Vasilakos, A.V.: A survey on trust management for internet of things. J. Netw. Comput. Appl. **42**, 120–134 (2014)

A Certificate-Less Key Exchange
Protocol for IoT

Ivan Marco Lobe Kome[1,2]([✉]), Nora Cuppens-Boulahia[1]([✉]),
Frédéric Cuppens[1]([✉]), and Vincent Frey[2]([✉])

[1] IMT Atlantique, 2 Rue de la Châtaigneraie, 35576 Cesson Sévigné, France
{ivan.lobekome,nora.cuppens,frederic.cuppens}@imt-atlantique.fr
[2] Orange Labs, 4 rue du Clos Courtel, 35510 Cesson Sévigné, France
{ivan.lobekome,vincent.frey}@orange.com

Abstract. Diffie-Hellman key exchange is a popular cryptographic algorithm that allows Internet protocols to agree on a shared key and negotiate a secure connection. It is used in many protocols including SSH, IPsec, SMTPS, and protocols that rely on TLS. In the Internet of Things (IoT), we cannot rely on the PKI architecture to secure communications due to the growing number of connected things. We are proposing to decentralize the encryption keys management while maintaining the property of authentication and secrecy. We use the ability of each node to build a private channel to create a shared key, safe from the eye of an attacker. Our solution provides a solution to build a certificate-less trusted ecosystem for IoT.

Keywords: IoT · Diffie-Hellman · Private channel ·
Ad hoc networks · WPS · Encryption · Wireless security

1 Introduction

Diffie-Hellman (DH) [1] key exchange aims at allowing two parties that have no prior knowledge of each other to jointly establish a shared secret key over an insecure channel. Its security is based on the presumed difficulty of solving the discrete logarithm problem (DLP) [2,3]. To keep this promise, it is strongly recommended to use keys greater than 2048-bits [4] to avoid man-in-the-middle attacks. In the context of Internet of Things, increasing the size of the key is not always a viable solution given the reduced amount of memory, computation power and energy of devices. In fact, when referring to IoT, we are stressing more on class 0 and 1 devices [5]. That describes fewer computation power devices, meaning less than 10KB of RAM and 100kB of Flash. These devices are meant for basic communication to transmit sensor data to servers, most of the time using a gateway. To avoid using longer keys, many are implementing 512-bits Elliptic Curve Cryptography (ECC) which offers the same level of security for smaller key size [6].

© Springer Nature Switzerland AG 2019
A. Zemmari et al. (Eds.): CRiSIS 2018, LNCS 11391, pp. 65–79, 2019.
https://doi.org/10.1007/978-3-030-12143-3_6

Public Key Infrastructure (PKI) is vastly used to establish a link between user's identity and its public key. But issuing and using the certificate are costly and in the context of IoT where billions of connected things are expected to join the Internet, this architecture is not maintainable and will be more and more costly.

The need for more space and computation power for the Diffie-Hellman problem to remain difficult to solve and the cost of a PKI architecture in the context of IoT, lead us to address the following problem: How to secure IoT communications with Diffie-Hellman algorithm in a certificate-less architecture? In this paper we propose an original method, that allows two connected things to mutually create an encryption shared key, with the Diffie-Helman algorithm on a private channel. The proposed solution lightens encrypted communications in IoT as it makes certificates useless. The performance analysis of this solution shows promising results.

The rest of this paper is organized as following: Sect. 2 discusses the Diffie-Hellman challenge in IoT context and why a PKI architecture is not maintainable. It is also dealing with OpenID Connect which is part of our solution. Section 3 presents our solution. We give a security and performance evaluation of our approach in Sect. 4. We present related work about certificate-less protocols in Sect. 5. Finally, Sect. 6 concludes with an outline of future work.

2   Background

2.1   The Diffie-Hellman Problem (DHP)

Encrypting communications relie on functions that are fast to compute but hard to reverse called one-way functions. It requires the use of mathematical problems in cryptographic protocols. The function must be hard to reverse for attackers. The Diffie-Hellman problem is a mathematical problem for the attacker which consists in finding the value of g^{xy} given g^x and g^y. Where g is the generator of some group (elliptic curve or multiplicative group for example) [7–9] and assumed to be public. x and y are randomly chosen integers kept secret. In the most considered of the many variants to the DH problem, the Decisional Diffie-Helman Problem (DDHP) [10], Alice and Bob choose x and y and compute g^x and g^y, respectively. Those values are sent to each other so that each party can compute the shared key $g^{xy} = g^{yx}$.

Table 1 depicts who knows what during the protocol exchange. Eve plays the role of the attacker. The protocol can be easily expandable with other actors using bilinear applications [11]. For instance, if Carol is the third actor, the shared key would be g^{xyz}. With z randomly chosen by Carol.

The problem the attacker must solve is finding x giving g^x or y giving g^y. But it is not easy to compute discrete logs. Otherwise, it would be easier to find g^{xy} after having computed $\log_g g^x = \frac{\ln g^x}{\ln g}$ for the value of x and $\log_g g^y = \frac{\ln g^y}{\ln g}$ for the value of y.

The security of many DHP cryptosystems is then based on what is called the Computational Diffie-Helman (CDH) assumption. But with computation

Table 1. Decisional Diffie-Helman protocol execution: actors knowledge.

Alice	Bob	Eve
g	g	g
g, x	g, y	g
g, x, g^y	g, y, g^x	g, g^x, g^y
$(g^y)^x$	$(g^x)^y$	?

progresses, we can observe man-in-the-middle attacks on DH when keys sizes are ranging from 512-bits to 1024-bits. A famous one is the **Logjam**.

Logjam Attack [12]. It is the most popular form of man-in-the-middle attack on DH. It is a vulnerability against DH from 512-bits to 1024-bit keys. It consists in first downgrading vulnerable TLS connections to 512-bit export-grade cryptography, then computing discrete logs algorithm on that 512-bit group. IETF then made the recommendation to use keys greater than 2048-bits to guarantee security in protocols using DH. The logjam exploits the method based on the number field sieve algorithm [13] to find discrete logarithms.

The attack was performed by David Adrian and associates on TLS and is fully documented on https://weakdh.org/. TLS consists in three phases:

1. **Hello messages:** The client sends a random nonce cr and a list of supported cipher suites with the **ClientHello** message. The server selects the appropriate cipher suite from the list and responds with its nonce sr with the **ServerHello** message.
   An example of cipher suite: *ECDHE-RSA-AES128-GCM-SHA256*.
2. **Key exchange messages:** The server chooses a group *(p,g)*, where p is the prime and g the base. He computes g^b and sends the tuple *(cr, sr, p, g, g^b)* signed using the key sk_S from its certificate $cert_S$. This message is called the **ServerKeyExchange** message. The client responds with g^a in the **ClientKeyExchange** message.
3. **Finished messages** to ensure agreement on the negotiation. Both party compute the secret key g^{ab} and calculate a MAC which exchange in a pair on messages.

The Logjam attack in TLS depicted in Fig. 1 mostly relies on the fact that DHE_EXPORT cipher suites is identical to DHE but were restricted to primes no longer than 512 bits. The discrete log algorithm performed on the most used 512-bit prime produced a database. With a sufficient precomputation, the attacker quickly finds $b = d\log(g^b \mod p_{512})$.

Establishing a cipher key requires each party to be authenticated. The IETF adopted certificates and Public Key Infrastructures to solve this problem.

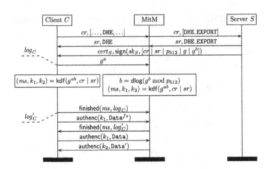

Fig. 1. The Logjam attack on TLS [12]

2.2 Public Key Infrastructure (PKI)

A Public Key Infrastructure guarantees the confidentiality of data, the non-repudiability and the strong authentication of a numeric identity through certification authorities (CA). These organisms are supposed to be trustworthy and publish their public keys. In this architecture, a numerical identity is represented as a certificate [14]. It is a proof of identity made by the certification authority public key and the service identity, all together signed with the certification authority private key. When a user is requesting a service resource, the request is sent with the user certificate. If the certificate is authenticated, the service can then use the public key of the corresponding certificate authority to verify the integrity of received data.

There are no problem in theory with a PKI but vulnerabilities come from CAs and key management. These vulnerabilities are possible because of the lack of control of CAs, which is not always an easy task given that a certificate can certify other certificates: this is called the chain of trust, depicted in Fig. 2. An attacker can certify its public key or certificate authorities private keys can be stolen. For instance, the Stuxnet attack against the Iranian nuclear program was performed thanks to certificates stolen from integrated circuit manufacturers, Realtek Semiconductors and JMicron [15,16].

In the context of IoT, the number of service providers is increasing along with the need to certify them. In fact, there are use cases where connected devices can be considered as service providers.

However, a certificate based architecture has some flaws which can prove to be huge source of attack. Bruce Schneier and Carl Ellison listed ten risks of PKI in [17] and two of them are particularly dangerous for IoT if not corrected. The flaws are the following:

- Untrusted authorities can be part of the chain trust. It is then not obvious to know who is using the key. The secrecy property cannot always be guaranteed either. Moreover each time there is a new untrusted party in the chain brings more complexity and latency into the authentication process.
- Two different actors can have different keys but identical names. And Certificate verification does not use a secret key, only public keys. The risk is

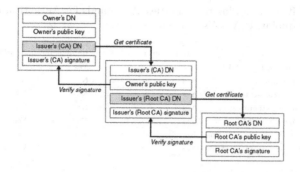

Fig. 2. A certification path from the certificate owner to the Root CA

that an attacker public key is added to the list of verifying public keys. The property of authentication is not always guaranteed.

For the reasons listed above, a PKI is not adapted to IoT. A more distributed and lightweight architecture is more appropriate. We chose another solution to couple authentication with DH.

2.3 OpenID Connect

OpenID Connect 1.0 (OIDC) [18] is a simple identity layer on top of the OAuth 2.0 protocol [19,20]. It allows Clients to verify the identity of the End-User based on the authentication performed by an Authorization Server, as well as to obtain basic profile information about the End-User in an interoperable and REST-like manner. It is implemented by the most used identity providers (Facebook, Twitter, Google). OIDC uses the same architecture defined by OAuth:

- A **Resource Owner (R.O)**.
- A **Client (C)** as the application requesting information about the resource owner.
- An **Authorization Server (AS)** which delivers authorization grants representing the resource owner's authorization.
- A **Resource Server (RS)** hosting owner's resources.

We want in our solution to establish a shared key between two authenticated connected devices. Depending on the properties expected, OIDC has three authentication flows: *authorization code flow, implicit flow, hybrid flow.* The Table 2 depicts OIDC flows according to properties.

Because they are supposed to run the authentication phase without human intervention, we consider a connected device as servers in OIDC paradigm. We then chose the **hybrid flow** to verify connected things identity and to prove their trustworthiness.

Our use of the hybrid flow follows the following steps:

Table 2. OIDC flows according to properties. A.E stands for Authorization Endpoint. T.E is Token Endpoint. U.A is User Agent

Property	Authorization code flow	Implicit flow	Hybrid flow
Tokens returned from A.E	No	Yes	No
Tokens returned from T.E	Yes	No	No
Tokens not revealed to U.A	Yes	No	No
Client can be authenticated	Yes	No	Yes
Refresh Token possible	Yes	No	Yes
One round trip communication	No	Yes	No
server-to-server communication	Yes	No	Varies

– Alice (considered as a C) sends the request to the A.S. Alice needs a *client_id* to make that request. Only a registered C can successfully make that request.
– A.S authenticates Bob (considered as a $R.O$). Bob can only authenticate with a *client_id* and a *client_secret*.
– Alice obtains an authorization code, proof of Bob authentication.

Among all the authorization flows, the hybrid flow is the lighter one. There are less data transmitted and there is no need for the device to handle tokens with this flow.

3   Our Solution: Ad Hoc Private Channel

The concept of our solution is to use the ability of the connected things to build an ad hoc access point and use it as a private channel. The private channel is a Wi-Fi access point protected with a Wi-Fi Protected Access (WPA) passphrase and configured to receive only one device connected at a time. The ssid and passphrase should be at least 128-bit long so that brute force attacks are long enough for the protocol to be entirely executed hidden from the attacker.

This new and ephemeral channel is used to run another DH so that Eve, the attacker, can not be aware neither of the new base nor any other element computed by Alice and Bob, preventing a man-in-the-middle attack. Table Fig. 3 gives an overview of the architecture of the solution. There are four phases in our solution:

The Authentication. It is the first step of the protocol and it performed on the public channel. It consists in making sure that Alice is not initiating a key exchange dialog with Eve, the attacker, but with Bob. Alice, who initiates the dialog, must send a list of the Authentication Servers (AS) where Bob's identity can be verified. Bob responds with one element of the given list. Then follows the OIDC hybrid flow as described in Sect. 2.3. We consider Alice and Bob honest, that means that each of them is supposed to have its OIDC credentials: (*client_id* and *client_secret*). After Bob was authenticated with his credentials, Alice receives an authorization code from the AS, which proves Bob's identity. This authorization must be a nonce. Furthermore, Bob is sure that Alice is trustworthy because he received a request for authentication from the right AS, right after having communicated its AS name to Alice.

The First run. It consists in the running of the DH for the first time, on the public channel, after each actor has authenticated themselves. The first message of this phase, from Alice to Bob, contains the chosen generator g in clear, since it is supposed to be public. At the end of this run, Alice and Bob will have computed the shared key g^{xy}.

Before initiating the second run, Alice will communicate to Bob the access point to connect to and a secret encrypted with the freshly computed shared key. Alice and Bob should be at a Wi-Fi range from each other. The range should be inferior to 46 meters for the traditional 2.4 GHz band and up to 92 m for the 5 GHz band.

The Second run. It consists in switching the generator from g to a new one h. The final shared key is then h^{xy}. This step is always performed on the private channel.

The key_id negotiation. Each actor is in charge of the secure storage of the shared key. After the establishment of the shared key, Alice and Bob must set a common *key_id* so that neither Alice nor Bob have in their respective database, two keys with the same id. A simple way of achieving this task is that Alice proposes first a number and Bob responds with a different number if the one proposed by Alice corresponds to an id in the database. Alice must be able to make an *echo* with a number to end the negotiation. We propose the formalism **key_id:key**.

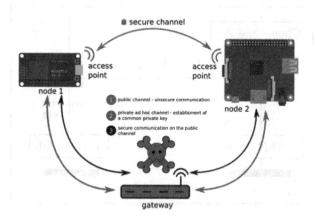

Fig. 3. Solution overview

Once the shared key is established, there is no need for a certificate when initiating the communication. In fact, the communicants only need to know the *key_id* corresponding to the key used to cypher the communication (Figs. 4 and 5).

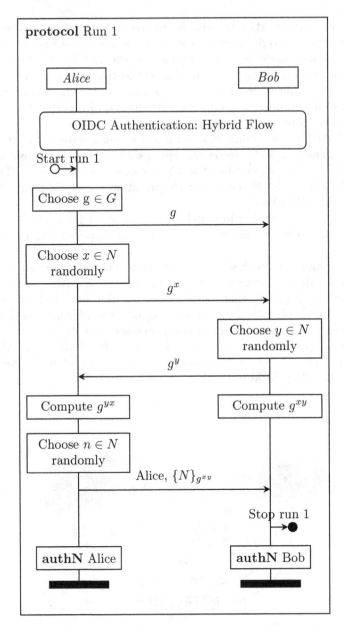

Fig. 4. Sequence diagram of the protocol: Run 1. *Alice* in the message represents the name of the access point where Bob must connect to execute the rest of the protocol.

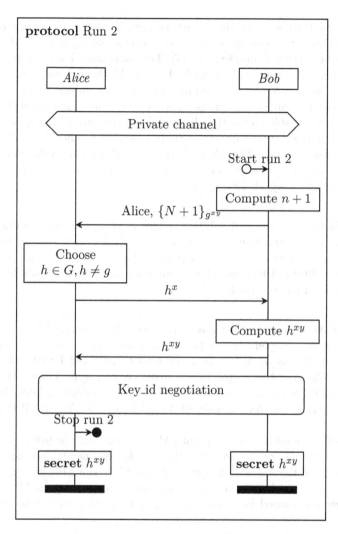

Fig. 5. Sequence diagram of the protocol: Run 2. Bob must send to Alice the value *N+1* via the AP, so that Alice can finish to authenticate Bob with the key established on the first run.

4 Security and Performance Analysis

4.1 Security Analysis

The protocol guarantees a strong authentication of each participants and the secrecy of communications.

Authentication. It is necessary to authenticate each party to avoid man-in-the-middle attacks. With the use of OIDC we can identify each actor taking part in the protocol: the client and the resource server. Unlike a PKI, with OIDC, Carl Ellison and Bruce Schneier questions like *who is using my key ?* and *who John Robinson is he ?* are not unanswered [17]. The authentication property is always satisfied. Each actor is uniquely identified by the AS through the tuple (client_id, client_secret) and each key_id is unique. There is no ambiguity compared to a certificate based architecture. Furthermore, every time an authorization code is released, the AS is able to list the client and the resource owner bounded. This has a better impact on the database than a certificate and their life cycle. In fact, there is no need for the AS to keep track of revoked certificates as each connected device has a ledger of valid keys. Revoking a device is reduced to erasing the couple (key_id, key) from the ledger.

Secrecy. With the proposed solution, there is always at most 3 entities and the encryption is symmetric. So there is no room for an untrusted party. The life expectancy of the ad hoc access point is long enough to build the shared key (less than 30 s) but too short for an intruder to succeed a brute force attack before the end of the protocol.

Attacks on the Private Channel. We use WiFi Protected Setup with PIN protection mode to implement the private channel. There are two famous implementations of attacks on WPA: **Reaver-wps** [21,22] and **Pyrit** [23,24]. Both attacks are following the methodology depicted in Fig. 6. These attacks were perfomed on WPS-Certified routers with 128-bit encryption keys. It takes a minimum of 4 h to recover the correct Wi-Fi Protected Access (WPA/WPA2) passphrase.

Establishing an ad hoc access point (AP) and running the protocol takes less than **10 s**. At the end of the protocol, the attacker has no element he can use to guess the key and the AP is no longer available. Since the AP's life expectancy is shorter than 10 s, it is impossible, in our context, to eavesdrop an AP passphrase and then get the shared key. Our protocol is then invulnerable to brute force attacks.

Attack on DH. As explained in Sect. 2.1, the DH key exchange depends on the presumed difficulty of solving the DHP and on the CDH assumption. The Logjam attack consists of a *precomputation stage* that depends only on the prime p, and a *descent stage* that computes individual logs. The first stage can take days to compute when the second stage only takes seconds. With sufficient precomputation, an attacker can find within seconds the discrete $\log x$ from $y = g^x \mod p$ and break any Diffie-Hellman instances that use a particular p. If the logjam attack takes about a week to break the key (less than 1024-bit keys), in our context, this problem is unsolvable.

Let g be the base in a cyclic group, x and y randomly computed, respectively by Alice and Bob. x and y are the private keys. If Eve, the attacker, is unaware of g, g^y and g^x, computing a sufficient log database can take months or years.

The problem now consists in solving the following system of equations:

$$\begin{cases} y = \frac{\ln h^y}{\ln h} & \text{with } h^y \text{ and } h^x \text{ unknown to the attacker} \\ x = \frac{\ln h^x}{\ln h} & \text{and } h \text{ the base in a cyclic group, also unknown to the attacker} \end{cases}$$

The proposed protocol is raising the level of difficulty of the DHP. It then remains difficult and we can therefore still use a DH modulus size less than 2048-bits and be Logjam-proof.

Another advantage of this architecture is that key management becomes easier. In fact, it is easy to build new keys and revoke old ones.

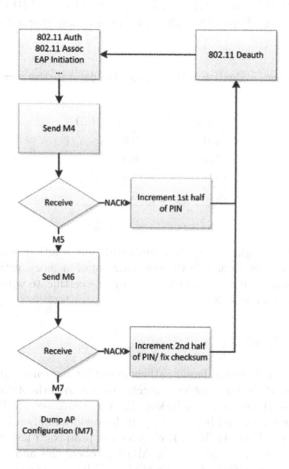

Fig. 6. Brute force methodology. M4, .., M7 are messages exchanged during the WPA authentication with PIN.

4.2 Performance Analysis

We focus on the impact on the memory for this analysis. An objective analysis in term of execution time would require to consider a large variety of processors. This experiment is a work in progress and will be presented in future papers.

Let us consider a node A with 100 keys in the keys database, corresponding to 100 different nodes sharing secrets with A. The Table 3 gives an evolution of the database size in terms of keys bit size. The node A is one of the ESP8266 series, the *ESP-12*. It is a system-on-chip (SoC) produced by Espressif Systems [25] and used on lot of IoT projects. It integrates a 32-bit processor (@80 MHz) as a CPU, 64KB of ROM, 80KB of RAM and 802.11b/g/n WIFI built-in. The hardware is running Micropython [26], a lightweight implementation of Python as an OS.

Table 3. Performance evaluation of key storage. The database size corresponds to 100 keys.

Key size (-bit)	DB size (Ko)
256	3.7
512	6.9
1024	13.3
2048	26.1

Storing and managing encryption keys with our solution have a very low impact on the memory. In fact, in the same amount of memory, with our solution we can store about 7 2048-bit keys where only one certificate with 2048-bit key (about 1.9Ko) can be stored.

5 Related Works

There are any Diffie-Hellman based authenticated key agreement protocols. One of the challenges of the DH protected architecture is to authenticate the parties involved. We can therefore cite solutions like the well-known MTI protocol by Matsumoto, Takashima and Imai [27,28] which provides implicit key authentication in the classical Diffie-Hellman key agreement protocol. Flaws were detected on MTI and led to the creation of the MQV protocol [29] and a whole family of solutions based on MQV [30]. Both MTI and MQV solutions are certificate-based, thus not adapted for IoT for the reasons listed in Sect. 2.2. Another family of solutions are ID-based key agreement protocols based on pairing which consist in associating a Personal Identification Number (PIN) to token [31–34] em with these protocols is that the ID escrow is the new certificate which, compared to our solution, requires a heavier infrastructure. Other certificate-less protocols like Identity Based Cryptography (IBC) have been proposed and are similar to our proposal. In an IBC system, user's ID is considered as her/his public key and the user's private key is generated by a trust authority, called Key Generation Center (KGC) or Private Key Generation (PKG). The disadvantage of that solution is that the trust authority knows the private key and with the example of the attack against the Iranian nuclear program [16], the IBC solution proves to be probably more dangerous.

6 Conclusion

Our solution shows promising results. In fact, we have demonstrated that it is easier to maintain and cheaper to build a shared encryption key using an ad hoc private channel. With our solution, the DHP remains difficult and neither the brute force attack reawer-wps nor the logjam attack are effective to eavesdrop the key. A performance evaluation of the memory consumption reveals that our solution is 7 times more efficient that certificate architecture. In other words, where we can store only one certificate, there is room for 7 keys in our paradigm.

Another advantage of this method is that the shared keys can be refreshed without a third-party involved. Certificates are replaced by key_ids and there is no need to keep track of revoked certificates.

There is however, one limitation in our solution which is the range. In fact, there cannot be a private channel if the nodes are out range from of each other. The range should be within 46 m for the traditional 2.4 GHz band and up to 92 m for the 5 GHz band. The specificity of this method can also be seen as its limitation depending on the use case.

This solution can be very useful to easily build and maintain a trusted ecosystem of connected things. We suggest as a future work, on one hand to implement the four steps of this protocol (authentication, run 1, run 2 and key negotiation) and compare the performances with DTLS in the Constrained Application Protocol (CoAP) [35,36], in terms of packets transmitted and computation time. This is actually a work in progress. On a second hand, we suggest to measure the impact of this solution in a smart home or smart grid architecture.

References

1. Diffie, W., Hellman, M.: New directions in cryptography. IEEE Trans. Inf. Theory **22**(6), 644–654 (1976)
2. Smart, N.P.: The discrete logarithm problem on elliptic curves of trace one. J. Cryptol. **12**(3), 193–196 (1999)
3. Nyberg, K., Rueppel, R.A.: Message recovery for signature schemes based on the discrete logarithm problem. In: De Santis, A. (ed.) Workshop on the Theory and Application of of Cryptographic Techniques. LNCS, pp. 182–193. Springer, Heidelberg (1994). https://doi.org/10.1007/BFb005343
4. Velvindron, L., Baushke, M.: Increase the secure shell minimum recommended Diffie-Hellman modulus size to 2048 bits (2017)
5. Bormann, C., Ersue, M., Keranen, A.: Terminology for constrained-node networks. Technical report (2014)

6. Gura, N., Patel, A., Wander, A., Eberle, H., Shantz, S.C.: Comparing elliptic curve cryptography and RSA on 8-bit CPUs. In: Joye, M., Quisquater, J.-J. (eds.) CHES 2004. LNCS, vol. 3156, pp. 119–132. Springer, Heidelberg (2004). https://doi.org/10.1007/978-3-540-28632-5_9

7. Miller, V.S.: Use of elliptic curves in cryptography. In: Williams, H.C. (ed.) CRYPTO 1985. LNCS, vol. 218, pp. 417–426. Springer, Heidelberg (1986). https://doi.org/10.1007/3-540-39799-X_31

8. Gupta, R., Murty, M.R.: Primitive points on elliptic curves. Compos. Math. **58**(1), 13–44 (1986)

9. Koblitz, N.I.: Introduction to Elliptic Curves and Modular Forms, vol. 97. Springer, Heidelberg (2012). https://doi.org/10.1007/978-1-4612-0909-6

10. Boneh, D.: The decision Diffie-Hellman problem. In: Buhler, J.P. (ed.) ANTS 1998. LNCS, vol. 1423, pp. 48–63. Springer, Heidelberg (1998). https://doi.org/10.1007/BFb0054851

11. Delsarte, P.: Bilinear forms over a finite field, with applications to coding theory. J. Comb. Theory Ser. A **25**(3), 226–241 (1978)

12. Adrian, D., et al.: Imperfect forward secrecy: how Diffie-Hellman fails in practice. In: Proceedings of the 22nd ACM SIGSAC Conference on Computer and Communications Security, pp. 5–17. ACM (2015)

13. Lenstra, A.K., Lenstra, H.W., Manasse, M.S., Pollard, J.M.: The number field sieve. In: Lenstra, A.K., Lenstra, H.W. (eds.) The development of the number field sieve. LNM, vol. 1554, pp. 11–42. Springer, Heidelberg (1993). https://doi.org/10.1007/BFb0091537

14. Housley, R., Ford, W., Polk, W., Solo, D.: Internet x. 509 public key infrastructure certificate and CRL profile. Technical report (1998)

15. Langner, R.: Stuxnet: dissecting a cyberwarfare weapon. IEEE Secur. & Priv. **9**(3), 49–51 (2011)

16. Kelley, M.B.: The Stuxnet attack on Irans nuclear plant was far more dangerous than previously thought. Bus. Insid. **20** (2013)

17. Ellison, C., Schneier, B.: Ten risks of PKI: What you're not being told about public key infrastructure. Comput. Secur. J. **16**(1), 1–7 (2000)

18. Nat Sakimura, John Bradley, Mike Jones, Breno de Medeiros, and Chuck Mortimore. Openid connect core 1.0 incorporating errata set 1. The OpenID Foundation, specification, 2014

19. Hardt, D.: The OAuth 2.0 Authorization Framework. https://tools.ietf.org/html/rfc6749

20. Bradley, J., Denniss, W.: OAuth 2.0 for native apps (2017). https://tools.ietf.org/html/rfc6749

21. Viehbck, S.: Brute forcing wi-fi protected setup. When poor design meets poor implementation (2011). https://code.google.com/archive/p/reaver-wps/

22. Murphy, B.F.: Network penetration testing and research (2013)

23. Lueg, L.: The twilight of wi-fi protected access (2013). https://pyrit.wordpress.com/about/

24. Lueg, L.: Pyrit code source (2013). https://code.google.com/archive/p/pyrit/

25. Espressif Systems. Espressif systems SoCs. https://www.espressif.com/en/products/hardware/socs

26. Damien George. Micropython. https://micropython.org/

27. Matsumoto, T., Takashima, Y., Imai, H.: On seeking smart public-key-distribution systems (1976–1990). IEICE Trans. **69**(2), 99–106 (1986)

28. Wang, S., Cao, Z., Strangio, M.A., Wang, L.: Cryptanalysis and improvement of an elliptic curve Diffie-Hellman key agreement protocol. IEEE Commun. Lett. **12**(2) (2008)
29. Krawczyk, H.: HMQV: a high-performance secure Diffie-Hellman protocol. In: Shoup, V. (ed.) CRYPTO 2005. LNCS, vol. 3621, pp. 546–566. Springer, Heidelberg (2005). https://doi.org/10.1007/11535218_33
30. Blake-Wilson, S., Menezes, A.: Authenticated Diffe-Hellman key agreement protocols. In: Tavares, S., Meijer, H. (eds.) SAC 1998. LNCS, vol. 1556, pp. 339–361. Springer, Heidelberg (1999). https://doi.org/10.1007/3-540-48892-8_26
31. Scott, M.: Authenticated id-based key exchange and remote log-in with simple token and pin number. IACR Cryptology ePrint Archive 2002/164 (2002)
32. Smart, N.P.: Identity-based authenticated key agreement protocol based on weil pairing. Electron. Lett. **38**(13), 630–632 (2002)
33. Shim, K.: Efficient ID-based authenticated key agreement protocol based on weil pairing. Electron. Lett. **39**(8), 653–654 (2003)
34. Chen, L., Cheng, Z., Smart, N.P.: Identity-based key agreement protocols from pairings. Int. J. Inf. Secur. **6**(4), 213–241 (2007)
35. Shelby, Z., Hartke, K., Bormann, C.: The Constrained Application Protocol (CoAP). https://tools.ietf.org/html/rfc7252
36. Raza, S., Trabalza, D., Voigt, T.: 6LoWPAN compressed DTLS for CoAP. In: 2012 IEEE 8th International Conference on Distributed Computing in Sensor Systems, pp. 287–289. IEEE (2012)

Personalized, Browser-Based Visual Phishing Detection Based on Deep Learning

Alberto Bartoli[✉], Andrea De Lorenzo, Eric Medvet, and Fabiano Tarlao

Department of Engineering and Architecture, University of Trieste, Trieste, Italy
{bartoli.alberto,andrea.delorenzo,emedvet,ftarlao}@units.it

Abstract. Phishing defense mechanisms that are close to browsers and that do not rely on any forms of website reputation may be a powerful tool for combating phishing campaigns that are increasingly more targeted and last for increasingly shorter life spans. Browser-based phishing detectors that are specialized for a *user-selected* set of targeted web sites and that are based *only* on the overall *visual appearance* of a target could be a very effective tool in this respect. Approaches of this kind have not been very successful for several reasons, including the difficulty of coping with the large set of genuine pages encountered in normal browser usage without flooding the user with false positives. In this work we intend to investigate whether the power of modern deep learning methodologies for image classification may enable solutions that are more practical and effective. Our experimental assessment of a convolutional neural network resulted in very high classification accuracy for targeted sets of 15 websites (the largest size that we analyzed) even when immersed in a set of login pages taken from 100 websites.

1 Introduction

Phishing campaigns are increasingly more targeted to specific and small population of users and last for increasingly shorter life spans [1,4]. There is thus an urgent need for defense mechanisms that are close to browsers and that do not rely on any forms of blacklisting/URL-based reputation: there is simply no time for detecting novel phishing campaigns and notify all interested users quickly enough.

In this work we investigate the feasibility of browser-based phishing detectors that: (1) are specialized for a *user-selected* set of websites (i.e., we do not insist on detecting phishing attacks directed at any possible target); (2) are based *only* on the overall *visual appearance* of a website (i.e., without relying on any URL-related feature, blacklisting, peculiar features of a given screenshot); (3) allow incorporating a specific website in the set automatically (i.e., with a *systematic* and *website-independent* procedure based solely on screenshots); (4) are simple and fast enough to warn the user in real time.

© Springer Nature Switzerland AG 2019
A. Zemmari et al. (Eds.): CRiSIS 2018, LNCS 11391, pp. 80–85, 2019.
https://doi.org/10.1007/978-3-030-12143-3_7

There have been a number of proposals for attempting to detect phishing pages based solely on their visual features (e.g., [2,3,5]). The framework is based on an image classifier equipped with prior knowledge of the legitimate ⟨protocol, domainName⟩ pair(s) of each website of interest to the user. When the browser has loaded a web page p, the classifier determines whether the screenshot of p belongs to one of the visual classes corresponding to each website to be protected. In case of a match, the tool compares the actual ⟨protocol, domainName⟩ of p to those expected for that website and warns the user in case of a mismatch.

Key advantage of this framework is that it does not require any form of blacklisting or of URL-based reputation. The required tool could be implemented as a browser extension and could possibly be integrated within a password manager. The resulting defensive mechanism would implement the procedure that any technically-savvy and constantly vigilant user applies in practice, except that in this case the procedure would be automated and thus available to every user and continuously. The resulting scenario would thus raise the bar for attackers considerably.

It is fair to claim that approaches of this kind have not been very successful so far, though, the key reasons include the difficulty of actually implementing the above requirements while providing sufficiently high detection accuracy [6]. For example, we are not aware of any actual implementation of the image classifier devised in [5], the screenshot classifiers analyzed in [2] did not deliver adequate accuracy, the large scale classification experiment in [3] considered 16 targeted websites but without injecting pages from other websites (unlike what happens during normal browser usage). In this work we intend to revisit the framework and investigate whether modern deep learning methodologies for image classification may lead to solutions that are practical and effective.

2 Problem Statement and Proposed Approach

The login page of a website may have several different appearances, depending on the user agent declared by the browser (e.g., desktop vs. mobile) and on the resolution of the page rendered by the browser. We say that a screenshot x *looks similar* to the screenshot $x(p)$ of a login page p, denoted $x \sim x(p)$, if the visual appearance of the two screenshots is sufficiently similar to let the user believe that x is indeed the rendering of a login page p. In this work we consider that two screenshots satisfy this definition only if they are screenshots taken from the same login page, possibly with different resolutions. This assumption corresponds to a scenario in which a phishing page is an exact visual replica of a genuine login page, hosted at a (fraudulent) website different from the genuine one. We will consider more general scenarios in future work.

We consider a statically defined list S of websites $s_1, s_2, \ldots, s_{n_S}$ that have a login page and that must be protected from phishing attempts (this set may be personalized on a user basis). The problem input consists of a screenshot x. The corresponding output y must be one of $n_S + 1$ categorical values (*classes*), as follows: if x looks similar to a login page of website $s_j \in S$, then $y = j$; otherwise, $y = n_S + 1$. In other words, the problem does not consist in discriminating between phishing pages and legitimate pages. The problem consists in associating a screenshot with a predefined set of visual classes, including a special class meaning "none of the websites selected for protection" that is necessary in practice.

We explored a solution based on deep learning, specifically, on a neural network in which: the input layer corresponds to a screenshot with a 640×360 pixel resolution with 3 channels (RGB); the output layer consists of $n_S + 1$ neurons, with one-hot encoding of the corresponding classes. We apply a screenshot x to the input layer after the following preprocessing steps. First, we create an image $x^{16:9}$ with 16:9 aspect ratio by either cropping or extending (by wrapping) the bottom part of x. Then, we resize $x^{16:9}$ to 640×360 resolution with the bilinear interpolation of the Pillow Python module. The chosen resolution is high enough to capture small graphical details such as, e.g., logo and text characters shape. We chose a 16:9 aspect ratio because this is the most common screen-ratio for desktop computers (we intend to explore a single classifier for both desktop and mobile platforms in future work).

We used a *convolutional neural network* (CNN) composed of a sequence of four pairs $\langle CN_i, MP_i \rangle$, i.e., $\langle$convolutional layer, maxpool layer$\rangle$, with $i = 1, \ldots, 4$, as follows. CN_1 applies 32 kernels of size $5 \times 5 \times 3, CN_2$ 64 kernels of size $5 \times 5 \times 32, CN_3$ 96 kernels of size $5 \times 5 \times 64, CN_4$ 128 kernels of size $5 \times 5 \times 64$. MP_1 applies 4×4 kernel and 4×4 stride, while the other maxpool layers apply a 2×2 kernel and 2×2 stride. The output of MP_4 is fed to a fully connected layer FC_1, that is followed by another fully connected layer FC_2, that is followed by the output layer SM. Both FC_1 and FC_2 have 200 neurons. The activation function for all the CN and the FC layers is ReLU, while the output layer implements a softmax. We implemented this network architecture with Keras.

For our experimental assessment we collected 1500 screenshots of login pages from 100 websites, 15 different screenshots from each website. For each website, we identified the login page and captured 15 different screenshots of that page differing on the browser windows size resolution. We captured the resolutions that correspond to the 15 most common screen sizes[1], on the grounds that different resolutions may result in very different webpage layouts. We selected 30 websites of the companies most targeted by phishing attacks, according to reports by specialized IT security firms, and 70 websites from the Alexa ranking of the most visited websites. We skipped duplicate websites, sites with pornographic content, sites without a login page. We also skipped websites whose login page was identical to an already collected login page of another website, due to the usage of single sign on.

We trained the network after a *data augmentation* procedure applied to the collected screenshots. This procedure may be used for obtaining a virtually unlimited amount of artificial screenshots different from the real ones but that should be effective for training the multiclass classifier. The procedure consists of the following steps, executed whenever an artificial screenshot x^a is to

---

[1] http://gs.statcounter.com/screen-resolution-stats.

be obtained from a real screenshot x (all random quantities have uniform distribution in a specified interval): (i) modify x and obtain a 16:9 aspect ratio (as in preprocessing); (ii) circular shift vertically and horizontally of a random quantity; (iii) with 50% chance, apply a centered zoom of a random zoom factor and keep size unchanged by cropping; (iv) with 50% chance, either lighten or darken the image; the 3 RGB channels are all lighted or all darkened, with a random multiplicative factor different in each channel such that the overall change never exceed 30% of the original pixel value.

We executed the actual training of the network as follows. Let S denote the set of websites $s_1, s_2, \ldots, s_{n_S}$ whose login page has to be protected from phishing attacks. Let X_S denote the set of login page screenshots of websites in S. Let T, V denote the learning data to be obtained from X_S, i.e., the training set and the validation set respectively. Both T and V are sets of pairs $\langle x, y \rangle$, where x is a screenshot and $y \in \{1, \ldots, n_S + 1\}$ is the corresponding *class* (encoded as one-hot in the output layer of the network): if x is a login page of website $s_j \in S$, then $y = j$; otherwise, $y = n_S + 1$.

At each training epoch, we randomly select a subset of T such that 50% of the pairs are of class $y = n_S + 1$ while the remaining pairs are equally distributed across the other classes. We loop across this subset for constructing a set of artificial screenshots T_a with the data augmentation procedure described above and use T_a for training in the current epoch (the class of an artificial screenshot will be the same as the corresponding real screenshot). We group pairs of T_a in batches of size $b_s = 32$ and execute each epoch for $n_b = 12(n_S + 1)\frac{c_T}{b_s}$ steps, c_T being the median cardinality of classes in T (we use each element of T_a once, hence $|T_a| = 12(n_S + 1)c_T$). We use Stochastic Gradient Descent (SGD) with the following parameters: momentum set to 0.9; learning rate 0.02; gradient clipping with maximum norm value 1.0; dropout with probability 0.1 after each CN layer and with probability 0.3 after each FC layer.

At the end of each training epoch we evaluate the classification accuracy of the current network on a set of validation pairs V_a (the same set for all epochs). We construct this set by randomly selecting a subset of V so that all classes have the same cardinality. We then loop across this subset for constructing a set of artificial screenshots V_a with the data augmentation procedure described above until $|V_a| = 24(n_S + 1)c_V$, c_V being the median cardinality of classes in V. We trained the network for 400 epochs and used the network with higher classification accuracy on V_a ever seen on all the epochs.

3   Experimental Assessment

We assessed three different values for the number of websites to be protected $n_S = 5, 10, 15$, corresponding to $6, 11, 16$ classes respectively (we remark that the large scale classification experiment in [3] considered 16 targeted websites). We constructed the training set T, validation set V and testing set E so as to ensure that: (a) each of the $n_S + 1$ classes has the same cardinality in T and in V; (b) all the remaining data are used in E.

In detail, let S_D be the set of 100 websites of our dataset and let X_D be the corresponding set of 1500 screenshots. We denote each element of X_D by $\langle x, i \rangle$ where x is a screenshot taken from website $s_i \in S_D$. Let X_i denote the subset of X_D containing screenshots taken from $s_i \in S_D$. Initially, we set $T = V = E = X_o = \emptyset$; then:

1. We randomly selected a subset $S' \subset S_D$ such that $|S'| = n_S$.
2. For each website $s_i \in S'$, we randomly partitioned X_i in three subsets X_i^T, X_i^V, X_i^E with the same cardinality; then, we added X_i^T to T, X_i^V to V and X_i^E to E.
3. For each website $s_j \notin S'$, we added X_j to X_o.
4. We randomly partitioned X_o in three subsets X_o^T, X_o^V and X_o^E such that $|X_o^T| = |X_o^V| = |X_i^T|$ (thus, $|X_o^E| = |X_o \setminus (X_o^T \cup X_o^V)|$); then, we added X_o^T to T, X_o^V to V and X_o^E to E.
5. We adjusted all class labels so that elements from S' were of classes $1, 2, \ldots, n_S$ and elements from $S_D \setminus S'$ were of class $n_S + 1$.

We repeated the above procedure 3 times for each value of n_S, each time selecting a different subset S' of websites at step 1 and ensuring that the three subsets have empty intersection. Furthermore, for each selected subset S', we executed a 3-fold cross validation by rotating the roles of sets T, V, E. Thus, we executed 9 different experiments for each value of n_S. For each trained network we computed the performance indexes described below on the testing set E. The *Categorical Accuracy* (CA) is the ratio of correctly classified screenshots while the *Balanced Categorical Accuracy* (BCA) is the arithmetic mean of the accuracy in each class. The *Missed Alarm Ratio (MAR)* is the ratio of screenshots from websites in S' classified as belonging to class $n_S + 1$ (screenshots from websites that should be protected from phishing attacks, but are not recognized as belonging to those sites). The *False Alarm Ratio* (FAR$_I$) is the ratio of screenshots from websites in S' classified as belonging to a class different from the correct class and different from $n_S + 1$ (screenshots from websites that should be protected and that are recognized as a login page, but are attributed to a website different from the real one). The *False Alarm Ratio on other web sites* (FAR$_U$) is ratio of screenshots from websites not in S' classified as belonging to a class different from $n_S + 1$ (screenshots from websites for which a protection from phishing attacks has not been required, but are attributed to a website that should be protected).

Table 1 shows the indexes values, averaged across the 9 experiments. Column ET reports the average execution time for each experiment (on a machine with 18 cores, 128 GB RAM, Xeon(R) E5-2697 v4 @ 2.30 GHz).

4   Discussion and Concluding Remarks

We believe the results are highly encouraging: the multiclass classifier delivers very good performance in each considered index. While such a performance level may not be enough for a full phishing defense, an effective phishing defense

Table 1. Performance indexes, averaged across 9 experiments, for different values of n_S (number of websites to be protected). All values are in percentage, except for ET that is in hours:minutes format.

n_S	CA	BCA	FAR_I	FAR_U	MAR	ET
5	99.0	99.2	0.0	1.0	0.7	4:49
10	98.0	98.2	0.1	2.1	1.7	9:22
15	98.4	98.6	0.3	1.6	1.1	14:17

cannot rely on a single tool: a defense in depth strategy working at different levels is necessary. In this respect, we believe that our proposed approach may indeed be practically viable and may provide complementary capabilities to existing tools. The ability to warn the user of a phishing site without any assumption on the reputation of the IP address, hosting provider, and website may be extremely useful for combating phishing attack strategies that are increasingly shorter and more targeted. While in principle one would like to be protected everywhere, we believe that even a protection on a user-selected set of 10–15 sites may be very useful [3].

Further investigation is obviously needed from several points of view, including in particular the ability to classify correctly screenshots that are not exact replicas of the original login page but that are similar enough to fool a user. To this end, we intend to explore more sophisticated data augmentation strategies and use suitably crafted artificial screenshots in testing as well. Adversarial attacks, i.e., login pages systematically crafted by an attacker to induce the classifier to output an attacker-chosen wrong class, are certainly to be explored as well.

References

1. The Human Factor: People-centered threats define the landscape. Technical report, Proofpoint (2018)
2. Afroz, S., Greenstadt, R.: PhishZoo: detecting phishing websites by looking at them. In: 2011 IEEE Fifth International Conference on Semantic Computing, pp. 368–375 (2011)
3. Chen, T.C., Dick, S., Miller, J.: Detecting visually similar web pages: application to phishing detection. ACM Trans. Internet Technol. **10**(2), 5:1–5:38 (2010)
4. Lazar, L.: Our analysis of 1,019 phishing kits - blog—Imperva, January 2018. https://www.imperva.com/blog/2018/01/our-analysis-of-1019-phishing-kits/. 4 July 2018
5. Maurer, M.E., Herzner, D.: Using visual website similarity for phishing detection and reporting. In: CHI 2012 Extended Abstracts on Human Factors in Computing Systems, CHI EA 2012, pp. 1625–1630. ACM, New York (2012)
6. Varshney, G., Misra, M., Atrey, P.K.: A survey and classification of web phishing detection schemes. Secur. Commun. Netw. **9**(18), 6266–6284 (2016)

Privacy Preserving Data Offloading Based on Transformation

Shweta Saharan[1(✉)], Vijay Laxmi[1], Manoj Singh Gaur[2], and Akka Zemmari[3]

[1] Malaviya National Institute of Technology Jaipur, Jaipur, India
shweta.17oct@gmail.com, vlaxmi@mnit.ac.in
[2] Indian Institute of Technology Jammu, Jammu, India
director@iitjammu.ac.in
[3] University of Bordeaux, Bordeaux, France
zemmari@labri.fr

Abstract. Mobile Cloud Computing (MCC) provides a scalable solution for both storage and computation of data over the Cloud. Though offloading benefits the execution performance, it raises new challenges regarding security. Privacy leakage risks prevent users from sharing their private data with third-party services. State-of-the-art approaches used for secure data storage are cryptography based, having an overhead of key management as well as do not support computation on encrypted data on the cloud server. However, homomorphic techniques support computation on encrypted data and generate an encrypted result, are compute intensive and not advisable due to resource constraint nature of mobile devices. This paper proposes a light-weight technique for privacy-preserving data offloading to the mobile cloud servers supporting computation. Our technique offloads the data to multiple servers instead of a single server. We have performed the security analysis for correctness, secrecy and unknown shares using various similarity measures.

Keywords: Mobile cloud · Privacy · Data · Offloading · Computation

1 Introduction and Background

MCC brings together the fastest growing cloud technology with the ubiquitous smartphone. Cloud application will account for 90% of mobile data traffic by 2019. Mobile Cloud, comes with benefits as well as challenges of mobile computing. With the use of MCC, private data of the mobile user is processed at the cloud side. It leads to exposure of both data and computation to the cloud servers. When a computation is carried on data stored on the cloud, initially it is decrypted for computation, which makes it vulnerable to privacy leakage. Homomorphic Encryption emerged as a solution, which is capable of performing computation on the encrypted data. Homomorphic encryption is too complex and compute-intensive even for computer or laptops, therefore it is not recommendable for resource-constraint mobile devices. There are state-of-the-art approaches for enhancing the privacy of data stored on the cloud. Bahrami and Singhal [2] worked on designing light-weight privacy-preserving method for data storage for cloud. Their approach makes use of pseudo-random permutation based on chaos

A. Zemmari et al. (Eds.): CRiSIS 2018, LNCS 11391, pp. 86–92, 2019.
https://doi.org/10.1007/978-3-030-12143-3_8

systems. Privacy-preserving optimisation framework of Yan et al. [7] make use of masked bloom filter along with Diffie Hellman protocol. Tong et al. [5] proposed privacy-preserving data storage and access for Mobile Health Care. It combines attribute-based encryption for role-based access control. Homomorphic encryption schemes have been widely investigated as a cryptographic primitive for computation enabled privacy preserving approaches. For preserving the privacy of the data, Sánchez et al. [4] separates the sensitive data from non-sensitive data by splitting the data into chunks which are sent to different cloud servers. POP [9] proposed a privacy-preserving photo sharing technique for mobile devices. It detects a Region of Privacy (ROP), as public and secret part. Only the secret region is encrypted, and authorised user can access it and recover original ROP. It makes use of homomorphic encryption. Sedic [8] model makes use of BGV homomorphic encryption for data privacy and high-order back propagation algorithms are executed on cloud for deep learning training. Qin et al. [3] worked on privacy-preserving image feature extraction. It distributes the computation task to different servers. EPCBIR [6] works on encrypted image, in which initially feature vectors are extracted, to improve the search performance, using locality hashing pre-filter tables are constructed. Our approach performs privacy preserved computation without homomorphic encryption as it is resource intensive for mobile devices. Our work aims to provide privacy-preserving data offloading on mobile cloud for computation. We propose a novel, light-weight approach for offloading data to mobile cloud, preserving the privacy of users' data and computation. Our work provides an experimental security analysis of the proposed approach. The rest of the paper describes threat and system model, followed by proposed approach and experimental analysis.

2   Overview

2.1   Threat Model

In the threat model, we assume that cloud servers are malicious and curious, but honest. Cloud servers follow the specified protocol and provide the correct result of the computation, but the servers make efforts to extract information about users' data. The adversary has no access to other cloud nodes and the network, therefore can't cause eaves-dropping.

2.2   System Model

In our model, we consider two entities, data owner/mobile client and mobile Cloud Service Provider (CSP) having multiple cloud servers. We consider that various CSPs that provide similar services are available. The mobile client owns the data to be offloaded for computation. The mobile client splits, transform and offload the data to different servers for computation. The mobile cloud servers perform the required computation on each transformed share and send the computed result to the mobile client. The mobile client merges the result of all servers to get the complete desired result.

3   Proposed Approach

Broadly the proposed approach is divided into 3 stages. Each step of the proposed approach is illustrated in Algorithm 1. Each of the stages is detailed as follow:

1. Share Generation

1. *Split:* Split original image(I) into 'n' parts. 'n' is dependent upon the client and is randomly selected and kept as a secret parameter.
2. *Transformation:* Depending upon operation to be performed, select the filter(F). Pad the split parts and filter to make it of original image size and apply Discrete Fourier Transform (DFT) on each split part and the filter.
3. *Separate Real and Imaginary Part:* For each transformed share and the filter, separate the real and imaginary part. Therefore, the number of shares generated after this stage would be double of 'n' i.e. '2n'.

Algorithm 1. Privacy-Preserving Data Offloading

Input: I: Image, n: Number of Splits, S: Size of Image, T: Transform O: Operation
Output: R: Operation Result

      # Share Generation

1: Divide the Image(I) into 'n' parts
    $\varepsilon \colon \mathfrak{I} \to \mathfrak{I}_1 \times \mathfrak{I}_2 \times \cdots \times \mathfrak{I}_n$
    $I \mapsto I_i = \varepsilon(I)$ where $i = 1$ to n

2: Pad each split (I_i) as well as filter(f) corresponding to the Operation(O) to the original size of I and transform DFT.
    $\tau \colon \mathfrak{I}_1 \times \mathfrak{I}_2 \times \cdots \times \mathfrak{I}_n \to \mathfrak{I}_1 \times \mathfrak{I}_2 \times \cdots \times \mathfrak{I}_n$
    $I_i \mapsto I_i' = \tau(I_i')$ where $i = 1$ to n , $f \mapsto F = \tau(f)$

3: For each transformed part(I_i'), separate the real and imaginary part.
    $\delta \colon \mathfrak{I} \to \mathfrak{I} \times \mathfrak{I}$
    $I_i' \mapsto I_{i.real}, I_{i.img} = \delta(I_i')$, $F \mapsto F_{real}, F_{img} = \delta(F)$

      # Offloading Shares and Processing on Servers

4: Schedule the 'n' parts to different cloud servers for processing as independent requests
    $\varphi \colon \mathfrak{I} \to S_1 \times S_2 \times \cdots \times S_k$
    $I_{i.x} \mapsto S_k = \varphi(I_{i.x}) = (b_1, b_2, \cdots b_k)$ where $i = 1$ to n, $n \leq k$ and $b_i = $ T iff I is affected to server i, $\forall i = 1, 2, \cdots, k, \forall x \in (real, img)$

5: At each server S_i, the image part I_i is multiplied with filter F.
    $O \colon \mathfrak{I} \times \mathfrak{I} \to \mathfrak{I}$
    $I_{i.x} \times F_x \mapsto R_{i.x} = O'(I_{i.x}) \ \forall x \in (real, img)$

      # Result Reconstruction

6: Collecting and assembling the result of all 'i' servers
    $\delta^{-1} \colon \mathfrak{I}_1 \times \mathfrak{I}_2 \times \cdots \times \mathfrak{I}_n \to \mathfrak{I}$
    $R_i \mapsto R_{i.cmp} = \delta^{-1}(R_1, R_2, \cdots, R_n)$

7: Perform the inverse DFT and extract the result from padded data
    $\tau^{-1} \colon \mathfrak{I}_1 \times \mathfrak{I}_2 \times \cdots \times \mathfrak{I}_n \to \mathfrak{I}_1 \times \mathfrak{I}_2 \times \cdots \times \mathfrak{I}_n$
    $R_{i.cmp} \mapsto r_i = \tau^{-1}(R_{i.cmp})$

8: Assemble result of split image
    $\varepsilon^{-1} \colon \mathfrak{I}_1 \times \mathfrak{I}_2 \times \cdots \times \mathfrak{I}_n \to \mathfrak{I}$
    $r_i \mapsto R = \varepsilon^{-1}(r_i)$ where $i = 1$ to n

---

2. Offloading Shares and Processing on Servers. At this stage, each share is offloaded to mobile cloud servers along with the transformed filter corresponding to the operation. The '2n' shares (along with filter) are scheduled over 'k' available servers. These shares are sent as an independent request to each server. At each server, the specified operation is performed over the share using a transformed filter. Each server sends the resultant of their share back to the client.

3. Result Reconstruction. Client assembles all the resultant of all the '2n' shares. Construct a single complex result. The result is extracted from the padded result using the secret placement parameters known to the client only. Inverse Discrete Fourier Transform (IDFT) is applied to each extracted result. All the extracted shares are combined to construct the resultant output of the specified computation on the image data.

4 Experimental Evaluation

To evaluate the proposed algorithm, we conduct various experiments to demonstrate security analysis of our approach on various parameters. Most widely offloaded data on Cloud Servers for computation is in the form of an image, therefore we have tested our approach considering image as data. We evaluated the approach for various operations on different grayscale image taken from CVG-UGR gray level database [1].

As per the threat model, cloud servers are curious to know the data offloaded by the user. Splitting minimises the risk of complete data exposure to a single server. Each server possesses a part of the complete secret only. Real and Imaginary are bifurcated and processed separately, which reduces the risk of detecting the transform which is applied on the data, and makes reconstruction of the original image difficult. The computation performed is modified depending upon the transform performed on the data.

4.1 Correctness

The correctness of the proposed approach is measured using four similarity measures viz. Peak Signal-to-Noise Ratio (PSNR), Structural SIMilarity (SSIM), Mean Squared Error (MSE), and Correlation. We performed four operations on the different types of images. These operations are performed directly over plain data as well as using the proposed approach. The results of both methods are same as shown in Fig. 1. The result of both methods are compared based on four similarity measures and are shown in Table 1. It shows that operations performed by the proposed approach are completely accurate.

4.2 Secrecy

This experiment evaluates the secrecy of the offloaded shares. The offloaded shares should have minimum or no similarity from the original image. Similarity

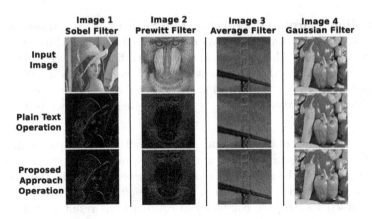

Fig. 1. Result of various operation on different images

Table 1. Correctness of proposed approach

S.No.	Operations	PSNR	SSIM	MSE	Correlation
1.	Sobel filter	∞	1	0	1
2.	Prewitt filter	∞	1	0	1
3.	Average filtering	∞	1	0	1
4.	Smoothing	∞	1	0	1

comparison of the original image with each share based on two similarity measures is shown in Table 2. It depicts that PSNR and SSIM value in all case is very low, which shows that the shares are different from the original image.

Table 2. Similarity comparison between original image to shares

Image	$S1$		$S2$		$S3$		$S4$	
	PSNR	SSIM	PSNR	SSIM	PSNR	SSIM	PSNR	SSIM
Image 1	5.4008	0.0036	5.4089	0.0033	5.4176	0.0035	5.4115	0.0035
Image 2	5.6022	0.0046	5.6122	0.0053	5.6275	0.0045	5.6178	0.0036
Image 3	5.2079	0.0031	5.1920	0.0036	5.1708	0.0033	5.1896	0.0033
Image 4	5.3448	0.0033	5.3309	0.0029	5.3389	0.0024	5.3085	0.0017

4.3   Unknown Shares

To preserve privacy, the cloud server should not be able to detect the similarity among the shares. In case of server collusion, it becomes difficult for the servers to detect whether the share belongs to the same image or not. To test it, we performed the similarity check among all possible combination of shares. The

Table 3. Similarity comparison between the shares

S.No.	Image	SSIM					
		S_1S_2	S_1S_3	S_1S_4	S_2S_3	S_2S_4	S_3S_4
1.	Image 1	0.0256	0.0241	0.0176	0.0176	0.0192	0.0164
2.	Image 2	0.0103	0.0117	0.0037	0.0084	0.0084	0.0137
3.	Image 3	0.0312	0.0147	0.0188	0.0111	0.0225	0.0080
4.	Image 4	0.0199	0.0162	0.0182	0.0186	0.0023	0.0186

similarity between shares is shown in Table 3. All shares S1, S2, S3, S4 are matched with each other i.e. S_1S_2 means comparison between share S_1 and share S_2. The result shows that the resemblance among the shares is very low, which make it difficult for the outsider to detect shares of an original image.

5   Conclusion

In this paper, we propose a novel and light-weight data offloading technique which preserves the privacy of the offloaded data and supports computation. We have evaluated our approach taking image as data. Proposed approach makes use of light-weight transformation for privacy preservation. Operations like edge detection, smoothening etc, which are used for image editing can be performed on the cloud without any disclosure of the image. Our work provides security analysis for correctness, secrecy and unknown shares of the offloaded data and does not disclose the operation being performed. As future work, we would evaluate the resource consumption performance with existing state-of-the-art approaches.

References

1. CVG-UGR image database. http://decsai.ugr.es/cvg/dbimagenes/. Accessed 17 April 2018
2. Bahrami, M., Li, D., Singhal, M., Kundu, A.: An efficient parallel implementation of a light-weight data privacy method for mobile cloud users. In: Proceedings of the 7th International Workshop on Data-Intensive Computing in the Cloud, pp. 51–58 (2016)
3. Qin, Z., Yan, J., Ren, K., Chen, C.W., Wang, C.: Towards efficient privacy-preserving image feature extraction in cloud computing. In: Proceedings of the ACM International Conference on Multimedia - MM 2014, pp. 497–506 (2014)
4. Sánchez, D., Batet, M.: Privacy-preserving data outsourcing in the cloud via semantic data splitting. Comput. Commun. 110, 187–201 (2017)
5. Tong, Y., Sun, J., Chow, S.S.M., Li, P.: Cloud-assisted mobile-access of health data with privacy and auditability. IEEE J. Biomed. Health Inf. 18(2), 419–429 (2014)
6. Xia, Z., Xiong, N.N., Vasilakos, A.V., Sun, X.: EPCBIR: an efficient and privacy-preserving content-based image retrieval scheme in cloud computing. Inf. Sci. 387, 195–204 (2017)

7. Yan, Y., Han, D., Shu, T.: Privacy preserving optimization of participatory sensing in mobile cloud computing. In: 2017 IEEE 37th International Conference on Distributed Computing Systems (ICDCS), pp. 1084–1093 (2017)
8. Zhang, K., Zhou, X., Chen, Y., Wang, X., Ruan, Y.: Sedic: privacy-aware data intensive computing on hybrid clouds. In: 18th ACM Conference on Computer and Communications security - CCS 2011, pp. 515–526 (2011)
9. Zhang, L., Jung, T., Liu, C., Ding, X., Li, X.Y., Liu, Y.: POP: privacy-preserving outsourced photo sharing and searching for mobile devices. In: Proceedings - International Conference on Distributed Computing Systems, July 2015, pp. 308–317 (2015)

DSTC: DNS-Based Strict TLS Configurations

Eman Salem Alashwali[1,2(✉)] and Pawel Szalachowski[3]

[1] University of Oxford, Oxford, UK
[2] King Abdulaziz University (KAU), Jeddah, Saudi Arabia
eman.alashwali@cs.ox.ac.uk
[3] Singapore University of Technology and Design (SUTD), Singapore, Singapore
pawel@sutd.edu.sg

Abstract. Most TLS clients such as modern web browsers enforce coarse-grained TLS security configurations. They support legacy versions of the protocol that have known design weaknesses, and weak ciphersuites that provide fewer security guarantees (e.g. non Forward-Secrecy), mainly to provide backward compatibility. This opens doors to downgrade attacks, as is the case of the POODLE attack [18], which exploits the client's silent fallback to downgrade the protocol version to exploit the legacy version's flaws. To achieve a better balance between security and backward compatibility, we propose a DNS-based mechanism that enables TLS servers to advertise their support for the latest version of the protocol and strong ciphersuites (that provide Forward-Secrecy and Authenticated-Encryption simultaneously). This enables clients to consider prior knowledge about the servers' TLS configurations to enforce a fine-grained TLS configurations policy. That is, the client enforces *strict* TLS configurations for connections going to the advertising servers, while enforcing *default* configurations for the rest of the connections. We implement and evaluate the proposed mechanism and show that it is feasible, and incurs minimal overhead. Furthermore, we conduct a TLS scan for the top 10,000 most visited websites globally, and show that most of the websites can benefit from our mechanism.

1 Introduction

Websites[1] vary in the sensitivity of the content they serve and in the level of communication security they require. For example, a connection to an e-banking website to make a financial transaction carries more sensitive data than a connection to an ordinary website to view public news. A close look at how mainstream TLS clients (e.g. web browsers) treat these differences reveals that they enforce coarse-grained TLS security configurations, i.e. a "one-size-fits-all"

---

[1] Throughout the paper we use the terms website, server, and domain, interchangeably to refer to an entity that offers a service or content on the Internet.

© Springer Nature Switzerland AG 2019
A. Zemmari et al. (Eds.): CRiSIS 2018, LNCS 11391, pp. 93–109, 2019.
https://doi.org/10.1007/978-3-030-12143-3_9

policy. They[2] support legacy versions of the protocol that have known design weaknesses and weak ciphersuites that provide fewer security guarantees, e.g. non Forward-Secrecy (non-FS), and non Authenticated-Encryption (non-AE), mainly for backward compatibility.

Supporting legacy versions or weak ciphersuites provides backward compatibility, but opens doors to downgrade attacks. In downgrade attacks, an active Man-in-the-Middle (MitM) attacker forces the communicating parties to operate in a mode weaker than they both support and prefer. Several studies illustrate the practicality of downgrade attacks in TLS [1,8–12,18]. Despite numerous efforts to mitigate them, they continue to appear up until 2016 in a draft for the latest version of TLS, TLS 1.3 [11]. Previous attacks have exploited not only design vulnerabilities, but also implementation and trust model vulnerabilities that bypass design-level mitigations such as the handshake messages (transcript) authentication. For example, the POODLE [18], DROWN [8], and `ClientHello` fragmentation [10] downgrade attacks.

Clearly, disabling legacy TLS versions and weak ciphersuites at both ends prevents downgrade attacks: There is no choice but the latest version and strong ciphersuites. However, the global and heterogeneous nature of the Internet have led both parties (TLS client vendors and server administrators) to compromise some level of security for backward compatibility. Furthermore, from a website perspective, supporting legacy TLS versions and weak ciphersuites may not only be a technical decision, but also a business decision not to lose customers for another website.

However, we observe that if the client has prior knowledge about the servers' TLS configurations, a better balance between security and backward compatibility can be achieved, which reduces the downgrade attack's surface. Given prior knowledge about the servers' ability to meet the latest version of the protocol and strong ciphersuites, the client can change its behaviour and enforce a *strict* TLS configurations policy when connecting to these advertising servers.

In this paper, we try to answer the following question: ***How to enable domain owners to advertise their support for the latest version of the TLS protocol and strong ciphersuites to clients in a usable and authenticated manner? This is in order to enable clients to make an informed decision on whether to enforce a strict or default TLS configurations policy before connecting to a server.***

Our contributions are as follows: First, we propose a mechanism that enables domain owners to advertise their support for the latest version of the TLS protocol and strong ciphersuites. This enables clients to enforce *strict* TLS configurations when connecting to the advertising domains while enforcing *default* configurations for the rest of the domains. We show how our mechanism augments clients' security to detect certain types of downgrade attacks and server misconfiguration. Second, we implement and evaluate a proof-of-concept for the

---

[2] We tested the following browsers: `Google Chrome` version 67.0.3396.87, `Mozilla Firefox` version 60.0.2, `Microsoft Internet Explorer` version 11.112.17134.0, `Microsoft Edge` version 42.17134.1.0, and `Opera` version 53.0.2907.99.

proposed mechanism. Finally, we examine the applicability of our mechanism in real-world deployment by conducting a TLS scan for the top 10,000 most visited websites globally on the Internet.

2   Background

2.1   Domain Name System (DNS)

Domain Name System (DNS) [17] is a decentralized and hierarchical naming system that stores and manages information about domains. DNS introduces different types of information which are stored in dedicated resource records. For example, the A resource records are used to point a domain name to an IPv4 address, while TXT records are introduced for storing arbitrary human-readable textual information. DNS is primarily used for resolving domain names to IP addresses, and usually this process precedes the communication between hosts. Whenever a client wants to find an IP address of a domain, for example "www.example.com", it contacts the DNS infrastructure that resolves this name recursively. Namely, first, a DNS root server is contacted to localize an authoritative server for "com", then this server helps to localize "example.com"'s authoritative server, which at the end returns the address of the target domain. To make this process more efficient, the DNS infrastructure employs different caching strategies.

2.2   Domain Name System Security Extension (DNSSEC)

DNS itself does not provide (and was never designed to provide) any protection of the resource records returned to clients. DNS responses can be freely manipulated by MitM attackers. DNS Security Extensions (DNSSEC) [7] is an extension of DNS which aims to improve this state. DNSSEC protects DNS records by adding cryptographic signatures to assert their origin authentication. In DNSSEC, each DNS zone has its Zone Signing Key (ZSK) pair. The ZSK's private-key is used to sign the DNS records. Signatures are published in DNS via dedicated RRSIG resource records. The ZSK public-key is also published in DNS in the special DNSKEY record. The DNSKEY record is also signed with the private-key of a Key Signing Key (KSK) pair, which is signed by an upper-level ZSK (forming a trust chain). To validate authentication of the DNS received responses, clients have to follow the trust chain till the root.

2.3   Transport Layer Security (TLS)

Transport Layer Security (TLS) is one of the most important and widely-deployed client-server protocols that provides confidentiality and data integrity on the Internet. It was formerly known as the Secure Socket Layer (SSL). TLS consists of multiple sub-protocols including the TLS handshake protocol that is used for establishing TLS connections. A particularly important and security-sensitive aspect of the handshake is the selection of the protocol version and the cryptographic algorithms with their parameters (i.e. ciphersuites). Every new version of TLS prevents security attacks in previous versions. Some ciphersuites provide more security guarantees than others. For example, Forward Secrecy (FS) is a property that guarantees that a compromised long-term private key does not compromise past session keys [16]. Both finite-field Ephemeral Diffie-Hellman (DHE) and Elliptic-Curve Diffie-Hellman (ECDHE) key-exchange algorithms provide the FS property. On the other hand, RSA does not provide this property. Similarly, Authenticated Encryption (AE) provides confidentiality, integrity, and authenticity simultaneously such that they are resilient against padding oracle attacks [27,29]. GCM, CCM, and ChaCha-Poly1305 ciphers provide the AE property while the CBC MAC-then-Encrypt ciphers do not provide authentication and encryption simultaneously, and hence do not provide the AE property.

2.4 TLS Version and Ciphersuite Negotiation

We base our description on TLS 1.2 [24]. The coming version TLS 1.3 is still a draft [25]. At the beginning of a new TLS handshake, the client sends a ClientHello (CH) message to the server. The ClientHello contains several parameters including the supported versions and ciphersuites. In TLS 1.2 the client sends its supported versions as a single value which is the maximum supported version by the client $vmax_C$, while in TLS 1.3, they are sent as a list of supported versions $[v_1, \ldots, v_n]$ in the supported_versions extension. The $vmax_C$ is still included in TLS 1.3 ClientHello for backward compatibility and its value is set to TLS 1.2. The supported_versions extension is not for pre TLS 1.3 versions [25]. The client's supported ciphersuites are sent as a list $[a_1, \ldots, a_n]$. Upon receiving a ClientHello, the server selects the version and ciphersuite that will be used in that session, and responds with a ServerHello (SH) containing the selected version v_S and the selected ciphersuite a_S. Ideally, these two values are influenced by the client's offered versions and ciphersuites. If the server selected a version lower than the client's maximum version, most TLS clients fall back silently to the lower versions (up to TLS 1.0 in all mainstream browsers today). The silent fallback mechanism can be abused by attackers to perform downgrade attacks as shown in the POODLE [18], a variant of DROWN [8], and ClientHello fragmentation [10] downgrade attacks.

2.5 TLS Downgrade Attacks

In a typical downgrade attack, an active MitM attacker interferes with the protocol messages leading the communicating parties to operate in a mode weaker than they both support and prefer. Downgrade attacks have existed since the very early versions of TLS, SSL v2 [30]. They can exploit various types of vulnerabilities (design, implementation, or trust-model), and target various elements of the protocol (algorithm, version, or layer) [3]. In the absence of handshake transcript authentication, downgrade attacks can be trivially performed. Starting from SSL v3, the handshake transcript is authenticated at the end of the handshake to prevent downgrade attacks. However, experience has shown a series of downgrade attacks that circumvent the handshake transcript authentication. For example, [1, 9, 10, 18]. Figure 1 shows version downgrade as in the POODLE [18] attack.

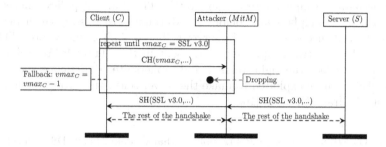

Fig. 1. Version downgrade in the POODLE attack [18].

3   Preliminaries

3.1   Strict Versus Default TLS Policy

Our mechanism affects the client's fine-grained TLS configurations. Namely, the protocol version and ciphersuites. In addition, it affects the client's fallback mechanism. In our proposed mechanism, there are two pre-defined policies (or contexts) for the TLS client configurations: *strict* and *default*. The *strict* policy enforces strong TLS configurations and disables the fallback. We define strong TLS configurations as those that support only the latest version of the protocol and only strong ciphersuites. We define strong ciphersuites as those that support both FS and AE properties simultaneously. The fallback is a mechanism that instructs the client to retry the handshake with weak configurations if the handshake with strong configurations has failed. On the other hand, the *default* policy enforces both strong and weak TLS configurations, and enables the fallback. Weak configurations are defined as those that support both the latest and the legacy versions of the protocol, and both strong and weak ciphersuites. Weak ciphersuites are defined as those that support non-FS or non-AE. Table 1 summarises the *strict* versus *default* policies that we define in our mechanism. Our prototypical TLS client implementation supports TLS versions: 1.0, 1.1, and 1.2, and 14 ciphersuites (similar to those supported in `Firefox` browser version 60.0.2 except that our client does not support the DES ciphersuite). Although TLS 1.3 is present, in our implementation and evaluation (Sect. 6) we consider TLS 1.2 as the latest TLS version. The reason is that TLS is currently in a transition state from version TLS 1.2 to TLS 1.3. TLS 1.3 has not been officially approved as a standard (is still a draft [25]), and is still in its beta version in most mainstream implementations such as `OpenSSL`. However, this does not affect our concept in general as it is applicable to the current deployment where TLS 1.2 is the latest version. Finally we note that in TLS 1.3, FS and AE ciphersuites are enforced by design [25], i.e. strong ciphersuites are implied by TLS 1.3 as a version. Therefore, in TLS 1.3, the *strict* configurations policy boils down to the protocol version and the fallback mechanism. However, there is still a value in our mechanism's ciphersuites policy even in TLS 1.3. Our policy enforces the client to refine its ciphersuites before the `ClientHello` is sent which provides downgrade resilience even when the server is flawed. This is unlike most TLS 1.3 clients, weak and strong ciphersuites are sent in the `ClientHello`, relying on the server to select the right version and ciphersuite. Experience shows that servers' flaws can be exploited to make the server select the wrong version as in `ClientHello` fragmentation [10].

Table 1. The *strict* versus *default* TLS policies that we define in our DSTC mechanism (✓ denotes enabled and ✗ denotes disabled).

Policy	TLS version	TLS ciphersuites	Fallback
Strict	TLS 1.3	FS and AE	✗
Default	TLS 1.3; TLS 1.2; TLS 1.1; TLS 1.0	FS; AE; non-FS; non-AE	✓

3.2 Problem Statement

Achieving both security and backward compatibility is challenging. A *strict* TLS client configurations policy provides stronger downgrade resilience than the *default* one. However, the *strict* policy may render many ordinary legacy servers unnecessarily unreachable, which results in a difficult user experience. On the other hand, the *default* policy (such as mainstream web browsers today), provide backward compatibility but this is achieved at the cost of security. Experience shows that the *default* policy can be abused by attackers to perform downgrade attacks as shown in the POODLE attack [18]. *Can we achieve a better balance between the two extremes? Can we enable clients to enforce fine-grained TLS configurations based on prior knowledge about the servers' TLS configurations? Can we design a usable and authenticated mechanism that allows servers to advertise their support for strong TLS configurations so that clients can enforce a strict TLS configurations policy for connections going to these servers while enforcing a default configurations policy for the rest of the connections?*

3.3 System and Threat Models

Our system model considers the following parties: a TLS client, a TLS server, and a DNS server. A TLS server is identified by its domain name, and the domain owner controls its DNS zone. These parties are standard for TLS connections and are assumed to be honest. As is the case of most real-world systems, the client and server support multiple protocol versions and ciphersuites that vary in the security guarantees they provide. Some of the versions and ciphersuites that the client and server support are weak, and are supported by both parties to be used *if and only if* their peer is indeed a legacy one that does not support the strong configurations. The client and server aim to establish a TLS session using strong configurations. For example, if both parties support the latest version of the protocol (as of this writing, TLS 1.3), then both parties aim to use TLS 1.3. The DNS supports DNSSEC and uses strong signature algorithms and strong keys to sign the zone file which contains all the DNS records. The DNS keys are authenticated keys through a chain of trust in the DNS hierarchy.

In terms of threat model, we consider a MitM attacker who can passively eavesdrop on the transmitted messages, as well as actively modify, inject, drop, and replay messages during transmission. The attacker cannot break sufficiently strong cryptographic primitives (e.g. RSA signatures with 2048 bit ore more) that are properly deployed. The attacker does not have access to the DNS private-key that is used to sign the DNS zone file. We also assume the absence of MitM attackers in the first connection from the client to the DNS server for each domain. However, the MitM can exist in subsequent connections from the client to the DNS server.

3.4   System Goals

Our system goals can be summarised as follows:

- Authentication: TLS clients should be able to verify that the statement advertising the domain's support for the strong TLS configurations in the DNS is genuinely produced by the domain owner.
- Usability: The mechanism should be usable to the clients' end users. It should not incur additional manual configurations on the users.
- Compatibility: The mechanism should be compatible with existing Internet infrastructure. It should not require additional infrastructure or trusted third parties above those in a typical TLS connection.
- Performance: The mechanism should be lightweight. It should incur minimal overhead on the clients' performance.

4   The DSTC Mechanism

4.1   Overview

Our mechanism aims to provide a usable and authenticated method that allows domain owners to advertise their support for strong TLS configurations to TLS clients. This provides the clients with prior knowledge that enables them to take an informed decision on whether to enforce a *strict* or *default* TLS configurations policy, before connecting to a domain. Throughout the paper, we refer to the DSTC record in the DNS as the DSTC policy record.

4.2 DSTC Policy Syntax

In what follows, we describe each directive used in the DSTC policy syntax. Figure 2 shows an example of an ideal DSTC record in a DNS zone file.

- name: Specifies an identifier for the DSTC records. Our mechanism uses a general purpose DNS record (TXT). Therefore, the record must be identified as a DSTC to be interpreted by clients as a DSTC policy record. This directive value must be set to DSTC.
- validFrom: Specifies the DSTC policy issuance date. It indicates the recency of the policy. It acts as a version number for the policy when there are multiple issued policies. The most recent must be the effective one. This directive value takes a date in a dd-mm-yyy format.
- validTo: Specifies the DSTC policy expiry date. It indicates the validity of the policy. This directive value takes a date in a dd-mm-yyy format.
- tlsLevel: Specifies the TLS level that the server advertises. This directive value must be set to strict-config for the *strict* TLS configurations policy to be enforced by the client.
- includeSubDomain: Specifies whether the policy should be enforced to subdomains or not. It takes either 0 to disable the option or 1 to enable it.
- revoke: Specifies whether the domain wants to opt-out from the DSTC policy or not. It takes either 0 to disable the option or 1 to enable it. If enabled, it acts as a poisoning flag. When a server wants to opt-out from the DSTC, it should keep advertising a revoke with value 1 until the expiry date of any previously published DSTC policy. This instructs clients to delete the revoked DSTC from their storage if exists.
- report: Specifies the email address of the domain owner. It takes a string in an email address format. The email can be used by TLS clients to allow the user to report a domain's failure of complying with the advertised policy to the domain owner.

```
tls12   IN TXT
"name:DSTC;validFrom:01-06-2018;validTo:01-06-2019;tlsLevel:strict-config;
includeSubDomain:0;revoke:0;report:config-errors@tls12.com"
```

Fig. 2. An example of a DSTC record in the DNS for the domain "tls12".

4.3 Details

The mechanism can be summarised in three main phases as follows:

1. **Policy Registration:**
   (a) The policy must be defined by the domain owner according to the policy syntax in section Sect. 4.2.

(b) The policy needs to be published as a TXT record in the DNS by the domain owner.

(c) The policy needs to be signed by the domain owner using the private-key of the ZSK. By the end of this step, the signed DSTC policy is publicized in the DNS in the domain's TXT record.

2. **Policy Query and Verification:**

(a) When a client wants to connect to a website, the client queries the DNS to retrieve the domain's DNS records. The DSTC is returned in a signed TXT record.

(b) The client verifies the signature using an authenticated public-key of the ZSK. If the signature is valid, the client verifies the rest of the DSTC policy directives. Based on the verification result, this step returns a value that signals the TLS configuration policy to be enforced: either *strict* or *default* along with a message to clarify the status (e.g. invalid signature) and the reporting email. The *strict* policy is returned only when all the verifications pass. Otherwise, the policy remains *default*.

3. **Policy Enforcement:**

(a) The client receives the TLS configuration policy from the previous step (Query and Verification).

(b) The client enforces the policy according to the policy received: either *strict* or *default*.

After the TLS configurations policy is enforced, which affects the TLS ClientHello offered versions and ciphersuites parameters, the client connects to the server. Figure 3 illustrates the DSTC system and the actors involved. The TLS connection is not part of our mechanism phases, but we include it in Fig. 3 to provide a complete view of the system.

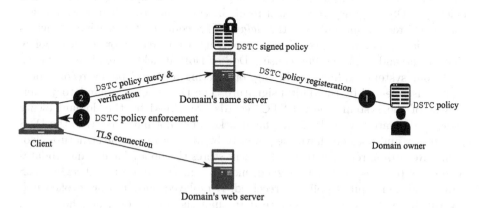

Fig. 3. A high-level overview of the DSTC mechanism.

5 Security Analysis

In our system, the attacker wins under two conditions: First, if he can forge a DSTC policy and present it to a DSTC-supported TLS client as a valid policy. Second, if he can perform an undetectable TLS version or ciphersuite downgrade attack that makes a DSTC-supported TLS client accept weak TLS configurations despite the downgrade-resilience that the DSTC policy provides.

5.1 DSTC Forgery

An active MitM attacker can achieve DSTC forgery if he can add, modify, delete, drop, or replay a DSTC policy record for a particular domain. The attacker's gain from each method can be summarised as follows: First, adding a policy for a domain that did not register a DSTC policy can cause a Denial of Service (DoS) attack for that domain. When DSTC-supported clients enforce a *strict* configurations policy for a domain that actually did not register a DSTC record and does not comply with the policy's requirements (e.g. uses a legacy protocol version), this will result in aborted handshake by the client. Second, modifying a DSTC policy record's directives can cause either DoS or Denial of Policy (DoP) for the concerned domain, depending on the modified directive. DoP prevents a policy from being enforced despite the domain's registration, which results in *default* client configurations which in turn provides weaker downgrade-resilience than desired. For example, modifying the `validTo` directive to an earlier date than it actually is, results in DoP since the policy will be marked as expired by the client at some point of time, and will not be enforced, while it is expected to be enforced by the domain. On the other hand, modifying the `validTo` directive to a later date results in DoS since the policy will be enforced for a domain that is not advertising the policy and may no longer complying with it. Third, deleting a DSTC policy record will result in DoP since the client does not get the DSTC record and enforces the *default* TLS configurations, which provides weaker downgrade-resilience. Fourth, replaying a non recent or revoked policy that has a valid signature can cause a DoS or DoP attacks as explained above.

In our system, adding, modifying, or deleting a DSTC policy record for a domain is defeated by the digital signature. The DNSSEC is a mandatory component of the system where DSTC records are signed by the domain owner using the private-key of the ZSK. The attacker does not have access to the DNS private-key and does not have the power to break it or break the signature algorithm. Regarding replay attacks, the client stores the policy locally and updates or revokes (deletes) it when a signed, more recent (i.e. more recent `validFrom` date), and non-expired policy is received. A replayed outdated or revoked policy will have a less recent issuance date than the stored one, and hence will be detected even if it has a valid signature. Finally, dropping attacks are also defeated by the stored policy from the first connection which is received under the assumption of the absence of MitM in the first connection from client to DNS. If the client has a non-expired stored policy, and the client has not received any new `revoke`-enabled policy to instruct the client to delete it, the absence of the

DSTC record in subsequent DNS queries signals a DSTC dropping attack. Note that connections after the stored DSTC policy expires are considered a first connection and assumed to be in a MitM-free connection.

5.2 TLS Downgrade Attacks

We now show how the DSTC mechanism prevents a class of downgrade attacks that abuse the client's support for legacy configurations and silent fallback. We demonstrate it on real-world downgrade attack scenarios (Fig. 4).

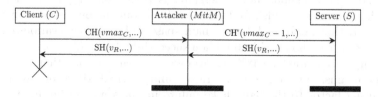

Fig. 4. Illustration of a version downgrade attack with a DSTC-supported client.

The first scenario is inspired by the ClientHello fragmentation version downgrade attack [10]. In this attack, due to a flawed TLS server implementation, if an attacker fragments the ClientHello, the server falls back to TLS 1.0. A *default* client will silently fall back to TLS 1.0 under the assumption that it is connecting to a legacy server. However, with a DSTC-supported client and registered server, this attack is defeated as the client enforces a *strict* TLS policy and does not fallback, hence the attack will be detected and the handshake will be aborted.

The second scenario is inspired by the POODLE version downgrade attack [18]. In this attack, the attacker drops the ClientHello message one or more times. Some TLS clients interpret this as a server compatibility issue and retry to send the ClientHello using a lower version. With a DSTC-supported client, the client does not fallback since it has prior knowledge about the server's support for strong configurations, hence the attack will be detected and the handshake will be aborted.

6 Implementation and Evaluation

6.1 Applicability

To get an insight into the applicability of our proposed mechanism, we conduct a TLS scan (IPv4 space) for the top 10,000 most visited Internet domains globally. The scan provides quantitative data about the supported and preferred TLS versions and ciphersuites in real-world servers. We retrieve the top 10,000 domains list[3] from Alexa Internet [5] on the 5th of May 2018. To run the scan, we use `sslscan 1.11.11` [23], a state-of-the-art open source TLS scanning tool that can perform TLS versions and ciphersuites enumeration through multiple TLS handshakes. The tool supports SSLv2 up to TLS 1.2, and 175 ciphersuites. We run the scan from the SUTD university's campus wired network between the 6th and 12th of May 2018. In terms of ethical considerations, our scan does not collect any private or personal data. The TLS versions and ciphersuites are public data which can be viewed by TLS clients through TLS handshakes. The number of handshakes the tool performs does not represent a danger of DoS.

The total number of servers that completed a successful TLS handshake with one or more TLS versions and ciphersuites is 7080 (70.80%). We do not investigate the reasons of handshake failure as this is outside our scope. However, a recent study that performed domain name-based TLS scans for various domains [4], reports 55.7 million and 58.0 million successful TLS handshakes out of 192.9 million input domains (29.48% on average). Given the fact that our scan is for top domains, our TLS response rate sounds normal. However, one possible contributing factor to the handshake failure in our scan can be due to SUTD university's Internet censorship system that blocks some website categories such as porn and gambling.

In terms of TLS versions, of the responding servers in our results, there are 6888 (97.29%) servers that support TLS 1.2. TLS 1.2 is the preferred version in all the servers that support it. However, there are only 373 (5.27%) servers that support TLS 1.2 exclusively (without any other versions). On the other hand, the number of servers that support at least two version, both TLS 1.2 and TLS 1.1, either exclusively or with other lower versions, is 6462 (91.27%). And the number of servers that support at least three versions, TLS 1.2, TLS 1.1 and TLS 1.0, either exclusively or with other lower versions, is 6202 (87.60%).

In terms of ciphersuites, we examine the servers' ciphersuites in version TLS 1.2 only. The most frequent number of supported ciphersuites (the norm) is 20 ciphersuite, which appeared in 938 servers (13.62%). To count the servers that support FS and/or AE, in each domain in our results, we labeled each supported ciphersuite by one of the following labels: FS+AE, FS+nonAE, nonFS+AE, or nonFS+nonAE. The four labels are based on the two properties: FS and AE. FS is identified by checking if the ciphersuite starts with `ECDHE` or `DHE`, while AE is identified by checking if the ciphersuite contains `GCM`, `CCM`, `CCM8`, or `ChaCha20` strings. There are 6500 (94.37%) TLS 1.2 servers containing at least one FS+AE ciphersuite, either exclusively or with other labels. We find 6483 (94.12%) TLS 1.2 servers that support non-FS or non-AE (i.e. labeled with nonFS+AE, FS+nonAE, or nonFS+nonAE) in addition to one or more FS+AE ciphersuite.

The results show that top domain servers support the strong TLS configurations. At the same time, they maintain support for weak configurations that have known weaknesses and provide fewer security guarantees. Ideally, the clients'

---

[3] The list gets updated daily, according to Alexa's support (in a private communication).

configurations influence the servers' selected configurations. Asserting servers' strong configurations to clients adds a value by providing clients with the confidence to enforce a *strict* TLS configurations policy for connections to these servers, which reduces the downgrade attack surface as we showed in Sect. 5.2.

6.2 Feasibility

To test the feasibility of our concept, we implement a Proof-of-Concept (PoC) for the mechanism. On a machine equipped with 16 GB Random Access Memory (RAM) and Intel Core i7 2.6 GHz processor, and runs Windows 10 (64-bit) OS, we build a virtual private network with a virtual host-only Ethernet adapter using VirtualBox [19]. It includes four virtual machines: Three TLS web servers, a DNS server, and a TLS client. The web servers are equipped with 2 GB of RAM, Intel Core i7 CPU 2.60 GHz processor, and 1000 Mbps wired network card. They run Apache 2.4.18 [6] on Ubuntu 16.04 (64-bit) Operating System (OS). The DNS server is similar to the web servers in specifications except that it has 4 GB RAM and runs BIND 9.10.3 [15]. The DNS server supports DNSSEC and the zone file is signed with a 2048 RSA ZSK. The ZSK is signed with a 2048 RSA KSK. We assume the KSK is validated through a chain of trust. To evaluate a DSTC-supported client, we implement a TLS client using Python 3.6.5 [20] and python's TLS/SSL library [21] on a Linux Ubuntu 18.04 (64-bit) OS on a device equipped with 4 GB of RAM, Intel Core i7 CPU 2.60 GHz processor, and 1000 Mbps wired network card. The client uses OpenSSL 1.1.0g that is shipped with Ubuntu 18.04. In our PoC we assume the highest version of TLS is TLS 1.2. Therefore a DSTC-compliant server should comply to TLS 1.2 and strong ciphersuites. Our client initiates a handshake with the three TLS web servers. The servers are configured as follows: First, to represent a DSTC compliant server that has registered a DSTC record, we configure a TLS 1.2 server with strong ciphersuites, and register a DSTC policy record for it in the DNS. Second, to represent a downgrade attack or misconfigured server, we use a straight-forward method to make the server's version lower than the DSTC requirements, we configure a TLS 1.0 server and add a DSTC policy record for it. Third, to represent a server that has not registered a DSTC record which should not be affected, we configure a TLS 1.1 which does not comply with the DSTC requirements and we do not register a DSTC policy record for it.

As depicted in Table 2, the handshake with the first server succeeds as the server complies with the DSTC requirements. The handshake with the second server fails as the server fails to comply with the DSTC requirements. The handshake succeeds with the third server as the server did not register a DSTC policy record. Our experiment confirms that the concept is technically feasible.

6.3 Performance

To get an insight into the computational cost that our mechanism adds over an ordinary TLS connection, based on scenario 1 in Table 2 (assuming no cached policy in the client) we measure the execution time for the following functions:

Table 2. Test-case scenarios carried from our `python` DSTC-supported client to TLS servers and the effect of DSTC (✓ denotes DSTC registered domain and ✗ denotes unregistered) on the TLS handshake (✓ denotes successful and ✗ denotes failed).

No.	TLS server configurations			Successful handshake
	Version	Ciphersuites feature	DSTC	
1	TLS 1.2	FS and AE	✓	✓
2	TLS 1.0	non-AE	✓	✗
3	TLS 1.1	non-AE	✗	✓

`SigVerify` for the DNS `TXTRRset` records signature verification, `QueryVerify` for the DNS records query and verification (which includes `SigVerify`), `Enforce` for the TLS policy enforcement based on the `QueryVerify` output, and finally, the time for the three functions together. Table 3 presents the measurements using the processor timer in `python`'s `3.6 time` module [22], which is processor-wide timer. Each measurement is repeated 500 times. A TLS socket connection establishment in our client takes 8.16 ms on average (without certificate validation). The mechanism's overall average overhead costs 3.58 ms. We conclude that the computational overhead is affordable which is about 43.87% additional overhead on the TLS socket connection. Our mechanism's overhead can be considered an upper-bound as there is a room for improvements through code optimisation.

Table 3. The mechanism's computational overhead in milliseconds.

No.	Function	Max.	Min.	Avg.
1	`SigVerify`	1.40	0.63	0.72
2	`QueryVerify`	4.99	2.74	3.09
3	`Enforce`	0.86	0.38	0.41
4	`All 3 functions`	6.10	3.23	3.58

7 Related Work

Schechter [26] proposes the HTTP Security Requirements in the Domain Name System (HTTPSSR DNS). It allows domain owners to assert their support for the TLS protocol to prevent TLS layer downgrade (a.k.a. stripping) attacks. However, experience shows that asserting TLS (as a layer only) is not sufficient. Several downgrade attacks that target TLS configurations such as the protocol version or ciphersuite as in the POODLE version downgrade [18] have been shown successful. Dukhovni and Hardaker [13] propose the DNS-based Authentication of Named Entities (DANE). It allows domain owners to bind their own

CA public keys or certificates to detect faked TLS certificates to prevent domain impersonation attacks. Hallam-Baker [14] proposes the Certificate Authority Authorisation (CAA). It allows domain owners to whitelist specific Certificate Authorities (CAs) for their domains to prevent mis-issued certificates. Alashwali and Rasmusssen [2] propose client *strict* TLS configurations against whitelisted domains as a downgrade attacks defense. The domains are added either by the client's users or through servers' HTTP headers. While adding domains through the servers' headers is usable, the *strict* policy can only be enforced starting from the second connections (the first connection is configured before the headers are fetched and hence uses *default* configurations). Our scheme extends this work by leveraging DNS which allows the *strict* policy enforcement before the first connection in a usable and authenticated manner without extra effort from clients' users. Finally, Varshney and Szalachowski [28] propose a general DNS-based meta-policy framework. Overall, none of the previous work have looked at using DNS to enable domain owners to assert strong TLS configurations.

8 Conclusion

We propose a mechanism that allows domain owners to advertise their support for strong TLS configurations through a signed DNS record. The client interprets this record and changes its behaviour to the *strict* policy which affects the TLS version, ciphersuite, and the fallback mechanism. Our prototype implementation and its evaluation show the feasibility of our mechanism. Furthermore, our Internet scan results depict that the majority of servers are ready to benefit from the proposed mechanism.

Acknowledgement. We thank Prof. Andrew Martin for feedback and Monica Kaminska for proofreading. Pawel's work was supported by the SUTD SRG ISTD 2017 128 grant.

References

1. Adrian, D., et al.: Imperfect forward secrecy: how Diffie-Hellman fails in practice. In: Computer and Communications Security (CCS), pp. 5–17 (2015)
2. Alashwali, E., Rasmussen, K.: On the feasibility of fine-grained TLS security configurations in web browsers based on the requested domain name. In: Security and Privacy in Communication Networks (SecureComm) (2018)
3. Alashwali, E., Rasmussen, K.: What's in a downgrade? A taxonomy of downgrade attacks in the TLS protocol and application protocols using TLS. In: Applications and Techniques in Cyber Security (ATCS) (2018)
4. Amann, J., Gasser, O., Scheitle, Q., Brent, L., Carle, G., Holz, R.: Mission accomplished? HTTPS security after diginotar. In: Internet Measurement Conference (IMC), pp. 325–340 (2017)
5. AmazonWS: Alexa Top 1M Global Sites (2018). http://s3.amazonaws.com/alexa-static/top-1m.csv.zip. Accessed 5 May 2018

6. Apache: Apache HTTP Server Project (2018). https://httpd.apache.org. Accessed 6 July 2018
7. Arends, R., Austein, R., Larson, M., Massey, D., Rose, S.: DNS Security Introduction and Requirements (2005). https://tools.ietf.org/html/rfc4033. Accessed 6 July 2018
8. Aviram, N., et al.: DROWN: breaking TLS using SSLv2. In: USENIX Security Symposium, pp. 689–706 (2016)
9. Beurdouche, B., et al.: A messy state of the union: taming the composite state machines of TLS. In: Security and Privacy (SP), pp. 535–552 (2015)
10. Beurdouche, B., Delignat-Lavaud, A., Kobeissi, N., Pironti, A., Bhargavan, K.: FLEXTLS a tool for testing TLS implementations. In: USENIX Workshop on Offensive Technologies (WOOT) (2014)
11. Bhargavan, K., Brzuska, C., Fournet, C., Green, M., Kohlweiss, M., Zanella-Béguelin, S.: Downgrade resilience in key-exchange protocols. In: Security and Privacy (SP), pp. 506–525 (2016)
12. Bhargavan, K., Leurent, G.: Transcript collision attacks: breaking authentication in TLS, IKE, and SSH. In: Network and Distributed System Security Symposium (NDSS) (2016)
13. Dukhovni, V., Hardaker, W.: The DNS-Based Authentication of Named Entities (DANE) Protocol: Updates and Operational Guidance (2015). https://tools.ietf.org/html/rfc7671. Accessed 6 July 2018
14. Hallam-Baker, P.: DNS Certification Authority Authorization (CAA) Resource Record (2013). https://tools.ietf.org/html/rfc6844. Accessed 6 July 2018
15. Internet Systems Consortium: Bind Open Source DNS Server (2018). https://www.isc.org/downloads/bind. Accessed 6 July 2018
16. Menezes, A.J., Van Oorschot, P.C., Vanstone, S.A.: Handbook of Applied Cryptography. CRC Press, Boca Raton (1996)
17. Mockapetris, P.: Domain Names - Implementation and Specification (1987). https://tools.ietf.org/html/rfc1035. Accessed 6 July 2018
18. Möller, B., Duong, T., Kotowicz, K.: This POODLE Bites: Exploiting the SSL 3.0 Fallback (2014). https://www.openssl.org/~bodo/ssl-poodle.pdf. Accessed 6 July 2018
19. Oracle: Virtualbox (2018). https://www.virtualbox.org/wiki/VirtualBox. Accessed 6 July 2018
20. Python: Python (2018). https://www.python.org. Accessed 6 July 2018
21. Python: ssl - TLS/SSL Wrapper for Socket Objects (2018). https://docs.python.org/3.6/library/ssl.html. Accessed 6 July 2018
22. Python: time-Time Access and Conversions (2018). https://docs.python.org/3/library/time.html. Accessed 6 July 2018
23. rbsec: sslscan Tests SSL/TLS Enabled Services to Discover Supported Cipher Suites (2018). https://github.com/rbsec/sslscan. Accessed 6 July 2018
24. Rescorla, E.: The Transport Layer Security (TLS) Protocol Version 1.2 (2008). https://www.ietf.org/rfc/rfc5246.txt. Accessed 6 July 2018
25. Rescorla, E.: The Transport Layer Security (TLS) Protocol Version 1.3 draft-ietf-tls-tls13-28 (2018). https://tools.ietf.org/html/draft-ietf-tls-tls13-28. Accessed 6 July 2018
26. Schechter, S.: Storing HTTP Security Requirements in the Domain Name System (2007). https://lists.w3.org/Archives/Public/public-wsc-wg/2007Apr/att-0332/http-ssr.html. Accessed 6 July 2018

27. Sullivan, N.: Padding Oracles and the Decline of CBC-mode Cipher Suites (2016). https://blog.cloudflare.com/padding-oracles-and-the-decline-of-cbc-mode-ciphersuites/. Accessed 6 July 2018
28. Varshney, G., Szalachowski, P.: A Metapolicy Framework for Enhancing Domain Expressiveness on the Internet. In: Security and Privacy in Communication Networks (SecureComm) (2018)
29. Vaudenay, S.: Security Flaws Induced by CBC Padding-Applications to SSL, IPSEC, WTLS.... In: Theory and Applications of Cryptographic Techniques (2002)
30. Wagner, D., Schneier, B.: Analysis of the SSL 3.0 Protocol. In: USENIX Workshop on Electronic Commerce (EC), pp. 29–40 (1996)

Authenticated Quality of Service Aware Routing in Software Defined Networks

Samet Aytaç[1], Orhan Ermiş[1]($\boxtimes$), Mehmet Ufuk Çağlayan[2], and Fatih Alagöz[1]

[1] Department of Computer Engineering, Bogazici University Istanbul,
34342 Istanbul, Turkey
{samet.aytac,orhan.ermis,fatih.alagoz}@boun.edu.tr
[2] Department of Computer Engineering, Yaşar University, 35100 İzmir, Turkey
ufuk.caglayan@yasar.edu.tr

Abstract. Quality of Service (QoS) aware routing is an ongoing and major problem for traditional networks since they are not able to manage network traffic for immense variety of users due to their inflexible and static architectures. Software Defined Networking (SDN) has emerged to remove these limitations by separating the control plane and the data plane to provide centralized control with the help of programmable controllers. Such improvements also make SDN more flexible than traditional networks in terms of achieving QoS-aware routing for large and medium sized networks. However, providing QoS-aware routing in SDN without using any security mechanism may become a challenging issue. For instance, malicious users in the network may escalate their privileges to monopolize resource utilization. The provision of an authentication mechanism that jointly works with QoS-aware routing is expected to solve the issue. In this paper, we propose an Authenticated QoS-Aware Routing (AQoSAR) for Software Defined Networks to determine routing paths of a single user and a group of users in an authenticated manner. AQoSAR consists of the authentication application and the routing application. In the authentication application, we employ Ciphertext Policy Attribute Based Encryption since it easily operates with huge variety of users by defining attributes such as QoS-aware routing metrics. In the routing application, we propose a routing approach based on a metric list rather than a single metric for determining the QoS level of users. To show the applicability of AQoSAR, the security analysis and the performance analysis are presented.

Keywords: Software Defined Networking ·
QoS Aware Routing in SDN · Attribute Based Authentication ·
Public Key Encryption · Multi-constrained Shortest Path Problem

1 Introduction

Software Defined Networking (SDN) has emerged to remove limitations of traditional networks such as inflexible and static architectures by separating the

© Springer Nature Switzerland AG 2019
A. Zemmari et al. (Eds.): CRiSIS 2018, LNCS 11391, pp. 110–127, 2019.
https://doi.org/10.1007/978-3-030-12143-3_10

control plane and the data plane with the help of programmable devices, namely controllers and switches. Since SDN is able to serve huge variety of users with different expectations, it provides better performance in terms of achieving Quality of Service (QoS) aware routing rather than traditional networks. However, QoS-aware is still open issue for SDN. There have been many studies to solve QoS-aware routing issues in literature such as [6,12,16,21]. OpenQoS in [16] provides QoS-aware routing for multimedia streaming. In [12], OpenQoS is extended for the distributed SDN environment. Dijkstra's shortest path algorithm with switch utilization was proposed [21]. Another study on QoS-aware routing is [6], in which users are isolated by network virtualization mechanism and routing is performed by considering such users.

One of the important characteristics of QoS-aware routing systems is the ability to classify users by considering their privileges. These classifications are necessary to share resources such as bandwidth capacity, latency in the communication, reliability of communications, etc. For instance, high privileged users may request high bandwidth capacity and low latency in communications if they transfer mission critical information for an organization. On the other hand, low or medium privileged users may request high reliability for communications. However, the existence of malicious users may degrade the QoS level by using security vulnerabilities of controllers. Such users may impersonate themselves as high privileged users to monopolize resources of network even if they are low privileged users. Then, controllers become impotent of determining the correct QoS level for users. Therefore, an extra layer should be added for the routing application of controllers to provide a verification mechanism for identities and corresponding privileges of users and groups. This verification mechanism can be accomplished by using an authenticated QoS-aware routing, which is our main motivation for the study. In order to address authenticated QoS-aware routing problem in SDN, variants of Attribute Based Encryption (ABE) schemes [17] can be used since they easily operate with huge variety of users by defining different attributes for QoS aware routing metrics.

ABE is a variant of public-key encryption that employ public-private key pairs together with user attributes in a form of well-defined access policy to encrypt/decrypt plaintexts/ciphertexts. Since user attributes are used rather than user identities in ABE schemes, it can provide fine-grained access control on the encrypted data. ABE schemes are classified as Key Policy Attribute Based Encryption (KP-ABE) [8] and Ciphertext Policy Attribute Based Encryption (CP-ABE) [2]. In KP-ABE, ciphertext is labeled with a set of attributes and secret keys of entities are associated with access structures. In CP-ABE, ciphertext is associated with an access structure and secret keys of entities. In this study, we prefer to use CP-ABE rather than KP-ABE to avoid the key distribution problem among entities in the network.

Our contributions for the study are as follows:

- We propose an Authenticated Quality of Service Aware Routing (AQoSAR) to securely determine routing paths of a single user and a group of users in the network.

- To provide authentication for huge variety users with different expectations, we employ CP-ABE as an authentication mechanism.
- We propose to use metric list rather than using a single metric for the QoS-aware routing to meet different expectations of users.
- Moreover, we provide detailed analysis for the security of the proposed approach against impersonation, collusion, eavesdropping and replay attacks.
- Furthermore, we analyzed the performance of authentication and routing applications of AQoSAR by using numerical evaluations, simulations and asymptotic analysis to show the applicability of proposed approach.

The rest of the paper is organized as follows. We present related works in Sect. 2. In Sects. 3.1 and 3.2, we introduce the authentication and routing applications of AQoSAR, respectively. In Sects. 4 and 5, we present security analysis and numerical evaluations for the proposed approach. Finally, the paper is concluded in Sect. 6.

2 Related Works

In this section, we overview the literature in terms of QoS-aware routing in SDN, authentication mechanisms for SDN and Attribute Based Authentication.

2.1 QoS Aware Routing in SDN

SDN applications can perform different routing approaches with the abstract view of a network and by using real time switch statistics. In [16], a network virtualization algorithm to isolate tenants and perform a QoS-aware routing algorithm on those tenants was proposed. In [4], users specify their bandwidth capacity expectations for each service. While system provides the bandwidth capacity to user, it also optimizes utilization of a switch.

Statistics of switches are also important for routing in SDN. In [12], an extended version of Dijkstra's shortest path algorithm was proposed. The proposed approach uses switch utilization as a weight of a node in order to compute the shortest path. In [21], NSV-Guard was proposed to construct paths in a secure manner. NSV-Guard computes trust values of switches by using switch statistics such as number of successfully delivered packets and the probability of successfully relaying packets. Then, NSV-Guard utilizes the path with the highest trust score. A QoS aware routing mechanism, namely OpenQoS, was proposed in [5] for achieving QoS in multimedia streaming. OpenQoS provides QoS by only considering multimedia flows. Then, paths of multimedia flows are computed by minimizing the delay for a constant jitter. An extended version of OpenQoS was proposed in [6] to operate on the distributed SDN environment for providing QoS-aware routing in multimedia streaming.

2.2 Authentication Mechanisms for SDN

Authentication is an open problem for SDN as far as the QoS-aware routing is concerned. The existence of programmable devices may cause security vulnerabilities such as malicious users may take the control of these entities to monopolize resource utilization in the network. Use of authentication mechanism is a pervasive approach in SDN in order to prevent network from such malicious attempts. For instance, in [22], a lightweight authentication mechanism that operates between controller and switches was proposed. Another example usage of authentication mechanisms in SDN is the authentication between switches and users in the network. Mechanisms in [14,15] are example for such usage of authentication in SDN. In both mechanisms, user authentication is performed by using a trusted third party to regulate authentication in the network. Once the user is authenticated, its access to resources are controlled with respect to the user policy definitions in the authentication server.

The provision of authentication mechanism is also provided solutions for existing attack models for traditional networks such as the DNS flood attack. Such attacks are a type of Distributed Denial of Service (DDoS) attacks that endanger the availability of DNS servers. In [18], a countermeasure was proposed by using IP spoofing to distinguish authenticated SDN queries in DNS requests while discarding unauthenticated ones. In [24], the model provides automated initialization for IPSec configurations in order to authenticate OpenFlow switches.

2.3 Attribute Based Authentication

ABE schemes are mostly used for providing the fine-grained access control on the encrypted content. One use of ABE variants is to verify users with respect to the attributes assigned them. Such usage is called as Attribute Based Authentication (ABA) [9,10,13,23]. Scheme in [13] is one of the example usage for ABA schemes. The proposed scheme uses group signature in order to provide group authentication. In [23], a hierarchical ABA scheme for cloud systems was proposed. The approach provides user based and attribute based hierarchical ABA for two scenarios. In [9,10], privacy preserving ABA systems were proposed for health systems. In both frameworks, different privacy levels are used for entities in the network. Then, these levels are used in order to authenticate users.

Another usage of ABA framework is the use for resource constrained devices as proposed in [1]. In the proposed framework, verification of identities is realized in a proxy server rather than the device itself due to the excessive computational cost of verification. Another examples for the use of ABA schemes together with proxy server are given in [3] and [11] to provide proxy signature for the privacy of secret keys of sender entities.

QoS-aware routing protocols, which are presented throughout this section, rely on QoS expectations of users in SDN. However, all of the protocols use a single metric for each assigning the QoS level of a user. Therefore, it is hard to achieve optimal QoS for each user when the diversity of users increases. To address the problem, in AQoSAR, we use a metric list for QoS-aware routing instead of a single metric. Moreover, to the best of our knowledge, there is no use of security mechanism that jointly works with QoS-aware routing in SDN. Without using any security mechanism, providing QoS-aware routing may become open to security vulnerabilities. Therefore, malicious users in the network may take the control of the controllers in order to utilize the most of resources. To address the security issues, we employ CP-ABE as an authentication mechanism.

3   AQoSAR: Authenticated QoS Aware Routing

In this section, we introduce Authenticated QoS Aware Routing (AQoSAR) for SDN. AQoSAR is a novel approach to achieve both QoS and authentication while determining routing paths of a user and a group of users in the network. As shown in Fig. 1, AQoSAR consists of two applications, namely the authentication application and the routing application. The authentication application is responsible for verifying identities of users and groups by considering their privileges defined as QoS metric list. The authentication process can be realized by using the certificate authority and the authentication application in the controller. The certificate authority is responsible for the distribution of certificates to users with respect to their privileges. The authentication application is a computer program that runs on the controller to verify certificates of users. When the certificates of users are verified, the list of authenticated users is transmitted to the routing application ((1) in Fig. 1). Later, routing application determines paths for authenticated users by considering the metric list of each user. As part of a routing application, statistics of switches and links are collected by controller ((2) in Fig. 1). Controller transmits network statistics to the routing application ((3) in Fig. 1). With the metric lists of users and the network statistics, routing application constructs an appropriate path for each user or group.

3.1   Authentication Application

Authentication application of AQoSAR is used for increasing the security of QoS-aware routing. The application prevents malicious users from accessing routing benefits of privileged users. Authentication operation is performed by considering user privileges with respect to their QoS metric list. Authentication application consists of two protocols, namely single user authentication protocol and group authentication protocol. The application uses ElGamal encryption algorithm [7], Schnorr signature [19] and CP-ABE algorithm [2] for confidentiality, authentication among entities and authentication for QoS-aware routing, respectively. Notations for the authentication application are as given in Table 1.

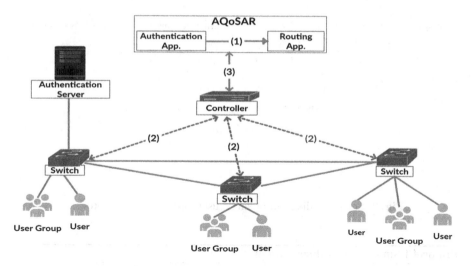

Fig. 1. Overview of AQoSAR

Single User Authentication. Sequence diagram of the single user authentication protocol is as shown in Fig. 2. Authentication of a user is realized in two steps. In the first step, a certificate that is produced by certificate authority is used. In the second step, a nonce which is encrypted with CP-ABE is used.

Table 1. Notations for the authentication application.

Symbol	Definition	Symbol	Definition
CA	Certificate authority	ME_n	n^{th} Member of group
C	Controller	MA	Group Manager
e	Entity	MS_n	n^{th} Message
$E_{ABE,\gamma}$	Attribute based encryption for metric list γ	n	Randomly Generated Nonce
E_k	Encryption with key k	PK_e	Public key of entity e
G	Group	SK_e	Secret key of entity e
$h()$	Hash function	$SK_{ABE,e}$	Secret ABE Key of entity e
ID_e	ID of entity e	t	Timestamp
U	User	γ_e	Metric list of entity e

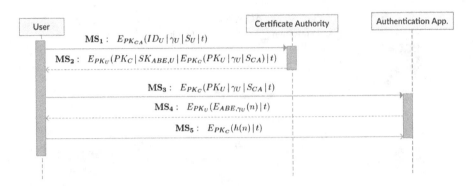

Fig. 2. Sequence diagram of single user authentication protocol

---

Protocol 1 Single User Authentication

1.1 : U signs γ_U, ID_U and t with SK_U, encrypts them with PK_{CA} and sends it to CA.

$\quad$ **MS$_1$** : $\quad E_{PK_{CA}}(ID_U \,|\, \gamma_U \,|\, S_U \,|\, t)$

2.1 : CA decrypts MS_1 with SK_{CA}, then verifies S_U with PK_U.

2.2 : CA generates $SK_{ABE,U}$ based on γ_U.

2.3 : CA signs PK_U and γ_U with SK_{CA}, then encrypts them with PK_C.

2.4 : CA encrypts $(PK_C \,|\, SK_{ABE,U} \,|\, E_{PK_C}(ID_U \,|\, \gamma_U \,|\, S_{CA})$ and t with PK_U, then sends it to U.

$\quad$ **MS$_2$** :

$E_{PK_U}(PK_C \,|\, SK_{ABE,U} \,|\, E_{PK_C}(PK_U \,|\, \gamma_U \,|\, S_{CA}) \,|\, t)$

3.1 : U decrypts MS_2 with SK_U and redirects $E_{PK_C}(E_{SK_{CA}}(PK_U \,|\, \gamma_U) \,|\, t)$ to C.

$\quad$ **MS$_3$** : $\quad E_{PK_C}(PK_U \,|\, \gamma_U \,|\, S_{CA} \,|\, t)$

4.1 : C decrypts MS_3 with SK_C, then verifies S_{CA} with PK_{CA}.

4.2 : C generates a nonce and encypts it with E_{ABE,γ_U}

4.3 : C encrypts $E_{ABE,\gamma_U}(n)$ and t with E_{PK_U} and sends it to U.

$\quad$ **MS$_4$** : $\quad E_{PK_U}(E_{ABE,\gamma_U}(n) \,|\, t)$

5.1 : U first decrypts MS_4 with SK_U, then decrypts $E_{ABE,\gamma_U}(n)$ with $SK_{ABE,U}$.

5.2 : U take hash of n with $h()$, encrypts $h(n)$ and t with PK_C and sends it to C.

$\quad$ **MS$_5$** : $\quad E_{PK_C}(h(n) \,|\, t)$

6.1 : C decrypts MS_5 with SK_C.

6.2 : **if** $h(n)$ is correct **then**

6.2.1 : $\quad$ Authentication of U is completed.

6.3 : **else**

6.3.1 : $\quad$ Authentication of U is failed.

6.3.1 : **end if**

Let U be the user, SK_U is secret key of user U, PK_U is public key of user U, γ_U is metric list of user U, $\S_U$ is signature of user U and $SK_{ABE,U}$ is CP-ABE key of user U. In addition, CA denotes Certificate Authority and C denotes controller. Single user authentication protocol for a user U operates as given in Protocol 1 (Fig.3).

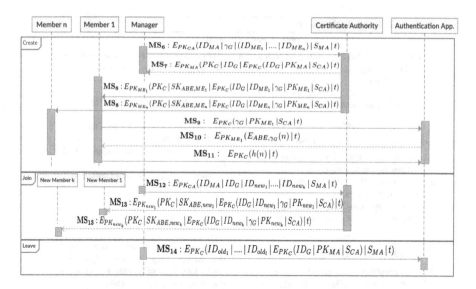

Fig. 3. Sequence diagram of group authentication protocol

Group Authentication. In group authentication, we use the extended version of the single user authentication protocol. First, users, who form the group, are delegated as group managers. Group managers are responsible for determining the metric list for the QoS-aware routing. After the metric list of the group is determined, certificate authority distributes certificates to group members. Then, users can connect to the Internet or other resources of the network via using these metrics.

Let G be the privileged group, MA be manager of the group G and ME_n denotes n^{th} member of group. SK_{MA} is secret key of manager MA, PK_{MA} is public key of manager MA, S_{MA} is signature of manager MA. SK_{ME_n} is secret key of member ME_n, PK_{ME_n} is public key of member ME_n, SK_{ABE,ME_n} is CP-ABE key of member ME_n. γ_G is metric list of group G. In addition, CA denotes certificate authority and C denotes controller. Group user authentication protocol for group G operates as shown in Protocol 2.

Protocol 2 Group Authentication

Create Group Operation:

1.1 : MA signs ID_{MA}, γ_G, $ID_{ME_1}|....|ID_{ME_n}$ and t with SK_{MA}.

1.2 : MA encrypts
$(ID_{MA}|\gamma_G|(ID_{ME_1}|....|ID_{ME_n})|S_{MA}|t)$
with PK_{CA} and send it to CA.

$$MS_6:$$
$$E_{PK_{CA}}(ID_{MA}|\gamma_G|(ID_{ME_1}|....|ID_{ME_n})|S_{MA}|t)$$

2.1 : CA decrypts MS_6 with PK_{CA}, then verifies S_{MA} with PK_{MA}.

2.2 : CA signs $(ID_G|PK_{MA})$ with SK_{CA} and encrypts it with PK_C.

2.3 : CA encrypts $E_{PK_C}(ID_G|PK_{MA}|S_{CA})$, PK_C, ID_G and t with PK_{MA} and sends it to MA.

$$MS_7:$$
$$E_{PK_{MA}}(PK_C|ID_G|E_{PK_C}(ID_G|PK_{MA}|S_{CA})|t)$$

3.1 : CA generates $SK_{ABE,ME}$ based on γ_G.

3.2 : **for each** ME in $(ID_{ME_1}|....|ID_{ME_n})$ **do**

3.2.1 : CA signs PK_{ME} and γ_G with SK_{CA}.

3.2.2 : CA encrypts $(\gamma_G|PK_{ME}|S_{CA})$ with K_C.

3.2.3 : CA encrypts $E_{PK_C}(\gamma_G|PK_{ME}|S_{CA})$, PK_C, $SK_{ABE,ME}$ and t with PK_{ME} and sends it to ME.

3.2.4 : **end for**

$$MS_8:$$
$$E_{PK_{ME_1}}(PK_C|SK_{ABE,ME_1}|E_{PK_C}(\gamma_G|PK_{ME_1}|S_{CA})|t)$$

4.1 : ME_1 decrypts MS_8 with SK_{ME_1} and redirects $E_{PK_C}(\gamma_G|PK_{ME_1}|S_{CA}|t)$ to C.

$$MS_9 : E_{PK_C}(\gamma_G|PK_{ME_1}|S_{CA}|t)$$

5.1 : C first decrypts MS_9 with SK_C, then verifies S_{CA} with PK_{CA}.

5.2 : C generates a nonce and encypts it with E_{ABE,γ_G}.

5.3 : C encrypts $E_{ABE,\gamma_G}(n)$ and t with $E_{PK_{ME_1}}$ and sends it to ME_1.

$$MS_{10} : E_{PK_{ME_1}}(E_{ABE,\gamma_G}(n)|t)$$

6.1 : ME_1 first decrypts MS_{10} with SK_{ME_1}, then decrypts $E_{ABE,\gamma_G}(n)$ with SK_{ABE,ME_1}.

6.2 : ME_1 take hash of n with $h()$, encrypts $h(n)$ and t with PK_C and sends it to C.

$$MS_{11} : E_{PK_C}(h(n)|t)$$

7.1 : C decrypts MS_{11} with SK_C.

7.2 : **if** $h(n)$ is correct **then**

7.2.1 :   Authentication of ME_1 is completed.

7.3 : **else**

7.3.1 :   Authentication of ME_1 is failed.

7.3.1 : **end if**

Join Operation:

1.1 : MA signs $ID_{MA}|ID_G|(ID_{new_1}|....|ID_{new_k})$ with SK_{MA}.

1.2 : MA encrypts

1.2 : $(ID_{MA}|ID_G|ID_{new_1}|....|ID_{new_k}|S_{MA}|t)$ with $E_{PK_{CA}}$ and sends it to CA.

$$MS_{12}:$$
$$E_{PK_{CA}}(ID_{MA}|ID_G|ID_{new_1}|....|ID_{new_k}|S_{MA}|t)$$

2.1 : CA decrypts MS_{12} with PK_{CA}, then verifies S_{MA} with PK_{MA}.

2.2 : CA generates $SK_{ABE,new}$ based on γ_G.

2.3 : **for each** ME in $(ID_{new_1}|....|ID_{new_n})$ **do**

2.3.1 : CA signs PK_{new} and γ_G with SK_{CA}.

2.3.2 : CA encrypts $(\gamma_G|PK_{new}|S_{CA})$ with K_C.

2.3.3 : CA encrypts $E_{PK_C}(\gamma_G|PK_{new}|S_{CA})$, PK_C, $SK_{ABE,new}$ and t with PK_{new} and sends it to new.

2.3.4 :   **end for**

$$MS_{13}:$$
$$E_{PK_{new_1}}(PK_C|$$
$$SK_{ABE,new_1}|E_{PK_C}(ID_G|ID_{new_1}|\gamma_G|PK_{new_1}|S_{CA})|t)$$

Leave Operation:

1.1 : MA signs $(ID_{old_1}|....|ID_{old_t})$ and $E_{PK_C}(ID_G|PK_{MA}|S_{CA})$ with SK_{MA}, encrypts it with PK_C and sends it to C.

$$MS_{14}:$$
$$E_{PK_C}(ID_{old_1}|....|ID_{old_t}|$$
$$E_{PK_C}(ID_G|PK_{MA}|S_{CA})|S_{MA}|t)$$

2.1 : C decrypts MS_9 with SK_C, then verifies S_{MA} with PK_{MA}.

2.2 : C decrypts $E_{PK_C}(ID_G|PK_{MA}|S_{CA})$ with SK_C, then verifies S_{CA} with PK_{CA}.

2.3 : C adds $(ID_{old_1}|....|ID_{old_t})$ to the blacklist of group G.

In addition to the separate uses of the single user authentication and the group authentication protocols, they can be combined in order to determine the multi-level QoS-aware routing for user. For instance, some users may have high privileges when they are communicating as a group member in a specific location and they may have low privileges when communicating as a single user. As a consequence, it is possible to assign different QoS levels for users by considering their memberships for group in the network.

3.2 Routing Application

This application performs routing operations based on QoS metric list of users and groups. The routing application, analyzes incoming packets with respect to privileges of their owners. Then, the application determines the correct path for that packets by considering the network statistics collected from switches. QoS level for each user and group can be determined by using the combination of the following metrics:

- **Availability:** This metric defines availability expectation of a user. Availability of a switch is determined by using the packet drop ratio of a switch.
- **Reliability:** This metric defines reliability expectation of a user. Reliability of a switch is determined by the up-time of a switch.
- **Cost:** This metric defines the node weight for calculating the shortest path. Cost has nominal values, where $\mathcal{C} = \{utilization, delay, min\text{-}hop\}$.
- **Bandwidth Capacity:** This metric defines bandwidth capacity expectation of a user.
- **Criticality:** The metric is used for defining criticality of packets to be transmitted for each user. Criticality can only have $+1$ or -1 values.

As an example use case scenario, to meet the reliability and the availability expectations of users, the routing application defines reliability and availability levels for each switch by considering the packet drop ratio and the up-time of a switch. Then, routing application detects and isolates switches with low reliability and low availability for high privileged users that request more secure communication.

QoS routing problem in SDN is defined as a constraint shortest path problem in [5]. Since we have multiple metrics for QoS-aware routing, we define our routing problem as a multi-constraint shortest path (MCSP) problem. We prefer to use the cost metric of a user as a weight of MCSP problem. For other constraints of MCSP problem, we use availability, reliability and bandwidth capacity metrics of users. In our formulation, (i, j) pair represents link between node i and node j. Let $P(s, t)$ be the set of all paths from source node s to destination node t. For any path $p \in P(s, t)$, we define cost function $f_c(p)$ as:

$$f_c(p) = \sum_{(i,j) \in p} c_{ij} \tag{1}$$

c_{ij} is cost of (i, j) link. If cost metric of user is utilization, c_{ij} denotes utilization of (i, j), if the metric is delay, c_{ij} denotes delay on (i, j) and if the metric is min-hop, c_{ij} is 1. We define our availability constraint for path p as follows:

$$f_a(p) = \begin{cases} 1, & \forall s \in p, a_s \geq a_u \\ 0, & \text{otherwise} \end{cases} \tag{2}$$

s denotes a switch, a_s denotes the availability level of the switch s and a_u denotes availability metric of user u. We define our reliability constraint for path p as follows:

$$f_r(p) = \begin{cases} 1, & \forall s \in p, r_s \geq r_u \\ 0, & \text{otherwise} \end{cases} \tag{3}$$

r_s denotes reliability level of a switch s and r_u denotes reliability metric of user u. We define our bandwidth capacity constraint for path p as follows:

$$f_b(p) = \begin{cases} 1, & \forall (i, j) \in p, b_{(i,j)} \geq b_u \\ 0, & \text{otherwise} \end{cases} \tag{4}$$

$b_{i,j}$ denotes bandwidth capacity of (i, j) link and b_u denotes bandwidth metric of user u. Then, we can formalize our MCSP problem as:

$$p^* = \arg\min_p \{f_c(p) \mid p \in P(s, t),$$
$$f_a(p) = 1, f_r(p) = 1, f_b(p) = 1\} \tag{5}$$

When a new flow arrives to a switch, it forwards the first packet of the flow to the controller. If source node or destination node of the flow is authenticated user, path of the flow is constructed based on the path construction procedure. If both source and destination nodes are unauthenticated users, default routing procedure on the controller is performed.

The path construction procedure of routing application is as shown in Procedure 1. The procedure is a modified version of Dijkstra's shortest path algorithm which calculates the shortest path based on the cost metric of authenticated user. In addition, procedure eliminates nodes and links which do not satisfy availability, reliability and bandwidth capacity constraints of a user. If there is no path which satisfies QoS constraints of an authenticated user, criticality metric of the user is used for determining the next step. If the criticality metric of user is $+1$, packets of user are identified as critical packets. Therefore, all packets that come from the user are dropped. If the metric is -1, QoS constraints of users are discarded and the path which offers lower cost is used.

In AQoSAR, each path has a life-time determined by users or groups. When the life-time of a specific path is exceeded, flows related to the path are automatically removed from flow tables of switches. Therefore, users and groups are able to assign specific metrics based on their QoS expectations for a specific time interval.

Procedure 1. Path Construction

Input:

G: Graph

s: Source Node

d: Destination Node

u: Authenticated User

$\{r_u, a_u, c_u, b_u\}$: reliability, availability, cost and metrics of u

1: **procedure** PATHCONSTRUCTOR
2:     $dist[s] \leftarrow 0$
3:     $prev[s] \leftarrow$ undefined
4:     **for** each node n in graph G **do**
5:         **if** $n \neq s$ **then**
6:             $dist[n] \leftarrow \infty$
7:             $prev[n] \leftarrow$ undefined
8:             add n to Q
9:         **end if**
10:     **end for**
11:     **while** Q is not empty **do**
12:         $p \leftarrow$ node in Q with min $dist[p]$
13:         remove p from Q
14:         **if** p == destination **then**
15:             return $dist[p], prev[p]$
16:         **end if**
17:         **for** each neighbor r of p **do**
18:             **if** ($r_r < r_u \parallel a_r < a_u \parallel b_{(p,r)} < b_u$) **then**
19:                 remove r from Q
20:             **else**
21:                 calculate $c_{(p,r)}$ based on c_u
22:                 **if** $dist[p] + c_{(p,r)} < dist[r]$ **then**
23:                     $dist[r] \leftarrow dist[p] + c_{(p,r)}$
24:                     $prev[r] \leftarrow p$
25:                 **end if**
26:             **end if**
27:         **end for**
28:     **end while**
29:     return $dist[p], prev[p]$
30: **end procedure**

---

4   Security Analysis Of AQoSAR

In this section, we analyze the security of AQoSAR against impersonation, replay, collusion and eavesdropping attacks.

Theorem 1. *Under the difficulty of discrete logarithm problem, single user authentication is secure against impersonation attacks.*

Proof. To access routing privileges of legitimate users in the single user authentication protocol, adversary should impersonate messages MS_1, MS_3, MS_5 of legitimate users.

$$\mathbf{MS_1}: \quad E_{PK_{CA}}(ID_U \mid \gamma_U \mid S_U \mid t)$$

In MS_1, an adversary tries to impersonate itself as a legitimate user. As defined in MS_1, user signs the message by using Schnorr signature. Since Schnorr signature is secure against impersonation attacks as proposed in [19], adversary should have SK_U to impersonate MS_1. Without obtaining SK_U, the adversary cannot impersonate itself as a legitimate user.

$$\mathbf{MS_3}: \quad E_{PK_C}(PK_U \mid \gamma_U \mid S_{CA} \mid t)$$

In MS_3, an adversary can impersonate itself as a legitimate user and tries to generate MS_3 which is signed by CA. Since Schnorr signature is secure against impersonation attacks, the adversary is not able to obtain SK_{CA} from MS_3.

$$\mathbf{MS_5}: \quad E_{PK_C}(h(n)|t)$$

To impersonate MS_5, adversary need to have the nonce in MS_4. MS_4 is encrypted with both PK_U and E_{ABE,γ_U}. Even adversary obtains MS_4, she should have SK_U and $SK_{ABE,U}$ to decrypt the message, which is as hard as the discrete logarithm problem. Therefore, it is not possible for the adversary to impersonate a legitimate user. Thus, by considering the security of messages MS_1, MS_3, MS_5, the single authentication protocol is secure against the impersonation attacks.

Theorem 2. *Under the difficulty of discrete logarithm problem, group authentication provides resistance against impersonation attacks.*

Proof. We can use the assumption in the proof of Theorem 1 in order to show the security against impersonation attack for the group authentication protocol of AQoSAR. An adversary should impersonate a legitimate user in the group by using messages MS_6, MS_9, MS_{11}. Since MS_6 and MS_9 is signed by using Schnorr signature scheme and it is not possible to obtain SK_{CA} and SK_{MA} from messages, an adversary cannot impersonate a legitimate user. To generate MS_{11}, adversary should have SK_{ME} and $SK_{ABE,ME}$, which is as hard as the discrete logarithm problem. To perform impersonation attack to join and leave operation, an adversary should impersonate MS_{12} and MS_{14}, respectively. Since both messages are signed with SK_{MA}, adversary cannot impersonate a legitimate user. Thus, the group authentication protocol is secure against the impersonation attack.

Collusion attacks are one of the most important security threats for ABE variants. In this attack model, a group of adversaries try to use the aggregated set of their attributes to obtain the plaintext from ciphertext that is encrypted by using CP-ABE. Let a_1 and a_2 be adversaries that try to collude their SK_{ABE} to escalate their routing privileges. For instance, let a_1 has $\gamma_1 = \{m_1, m_4\}$ and a_2 has $\gamma_2 = \{m_2, m_3\}$. a_1 and a_2 can perform collusion attack to attain $\gamma_c = \{m_1, m_2, m_3, m_4\}$. A nonce is encrypted with metric list in both protocols (MS_4, MS_{10}) by $E_{ABE,\gamma}(n)$. As defined in [2], secret keys are randomized and cannot be combined in CP-ABE. Therefore, AQoSAR is secure against collusion attacks.

Replay attack is a type of active attacks that messages of entities are repeated maliciously. As a countermeasure to replay attacks, we use a timestamp value in each messages between MS_1 and MS_{14}.

Eavesdropping is a passive attack that adversary capture messages between entities and extract information from captured messages. As a countermeasure to eavesdropping, messages of both authentication protocols ($MS_1 - MS_{14}$) are encrypted with the public key of the receiver entity. Since ElGamal encryption scheme is indistinguishable under the chosen-plaintext attack [20], it is not possible to extract secret key of receiver entity from ciphertext. Therefore, AQoSAR is secure against eavesdropping attack.

5   Performance Analysis of AQoSAR

In this section, we present performance analysis of AQoSAR. First, we give numerical evaluations for the performance of AQoSAR by using simulations. Then, we analyze the performance of AQoSAR by using asymptotic analysis. Finally, we investigate the performance of routing application by using queueing theory. All simulations were carried out by using FloodLight controller, Openv Switch, Mininet environment on Intel i7-6700 HQ processor and 12 GB RAM memory. We run our simulations 100 times for each simulations.

We investigate the time required to execute authentication application with respect to changes in the number of attributes used for CP-ABE for group of five users as shown in Fig. 4. Since CP-ABE execution time depends on the number of attributes used for generating secret key, the time required to establish authentication proportionally increases with the number of attributes.

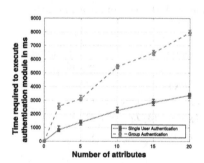

Fig. 4. Time required to execute authentication application with respect to change in the number of attributes

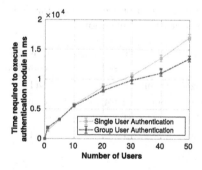

Fig. 5. Time required to execute authentication application with respect to change in the number of users

We also investigate effects of changes in the number of users on the time required to execute authentication application as shown in Fig. 5. In our simulations, we use metrics in the Sect. 3.2 as QoS metrics and attributes for CP-ABE.

Therefore, we assume that the QoS metric list of each user or each group is the subset of these metric set. Simulation results show that the total time required to execute the authentication application for a group of ten users and ten single users take the same amount of time since each user in the group authentication has to communicate with the group manager during the certificate distribution. On the other hand, when the number of users is greater than ten, the effect of certificate distribution decreases as shown in Fig. 5. Moreover, numerical evaluations also show that the total execution time for the group authentication application for 50 users is approximately 13 s, which shows the applicability of AQoSAR for medium-sized groups.

In addition, we present analysis for the authentication application with respect to the computation cost and the communication cost. Let n be the number of participants, k be the number of joining participants, l be the number of leaving participants and T_{EXP} be the time required to compute modular exponentiation operations (since it is the most time consuming operations for executing CP-ABE, Schnorr Signature and El Gamal), the communication cost and computation cost analysis results are as shown in Table 2. Communication cost is used for representing the total number of messages exchanged to perform authentication. Single user authentication is performed with five message per user as given in Table 2. Communication cost of create group and join operations depends on the number of participants in the group. Since leave operation is performed with one message, it is independent from the number of leaving participants. For the computation cost, single user authentication and leave operation are realized in constant time, however, create and join operations depends on the number of participants.

Table 2. Asymptotic analysis for the computation and the communication cost of authentication application.

Operation	Communication cost	Communication complexity	Computation cost	Computation complexity
Single user auth.	5	$O(1)$	$17 \cdot T_{EXP}$	$O(1)$
Create group	$2 + 4 \cdot n$	$O(n)$	$8 \cdot T_{EXP} + 13 \cdot T_{EXP} \cdot n$	$O(n)$
Join	$1 + 4 \cdot k$	$O(k)$	$4 \cdot T_{EXP} + 13 \cdot T_{EXP} \cdot k$	$O(k)$
Leave	1	$O(1)$	$4 \cdot T_{EXP}$	$O(1)$

For the performance analysis of routing application, we assume that the controller is a single server in the network, arrival rate of users determined by a Poisson process and job service times have an exponential distribution. Therefore, $M/M/1$ queue is used. Expected service time ($E[S]$) of routing application can be formalized as follows:

$$E[S] = \frac{n^2 \cdot \overline{b}}{b_{max}} + n^2 \cdot \overline{a} + n^2 \cdot \overline{r} \qquad (6)$$

where n denotes number of switch in the network, b_{max} denotes maximum bandwidth capacity in the network, $\bar{b}$, $\bar{a}$, $\bar{r}$ denotes average bandwidth capacity metric, average availability metric and average reliability metric of users in system, respectively. Then, service rate (μ) is:

$$\mu = \frac{1}{E[S]} = \frac{b_{max}}{n^2 \cdot (\bar{b} + b_{max} \cdot (\bar{a} + \bar{r}))} \tag{7}$$

The average number of users in system, denoted as L_s, is calculated by using the following equation:

$$L_s = \frac{\lambda \cdot n^2 \cdot (\bar{b} + b_{max} \cdot (\bar{a} + \bar{r}))}{b_{max} - \lambda \cdot n^2 \cdot (\bar{b} + b_{max} \cdot (\bar{a} + \bar{r}))} \tag{8}$$

where λ denotes arrival rate of users and ρ denotes utilization ratio of system. We calculate the average time that each user spends in the system by using the equation below:

$$W_s = \frac{n^2 \cdot (\bar{b} + b_{max} \cdot (\bar{a} + \bar{r}))}{b_{max} - \lambda \cdot n^2 \cdot (\bar{b} + b_{max} \cdot (\bar{a} + \bar{r}))} \tag{9}$$

Fig. 6. Average number of users in system with respect to arrival rate of users

Fig. 7. Average time a user spends in the system with respect to arrival rate of users.

We also present simulations for the average number of users in the system with respect to the arrival rate of users and the average time a user spends in the system with respect to the arrival rate of users as shown in Figs. 6 and 7, respectively. For these simulations, we assume that the network consists of 20 switches and $\bar{b}/b_{max}$, $\bar{a}$, $\bar{r}$ values to calculate L_s and W_s are equal to 0.5. As a result, routing application operates efficiently for the arrival rate of uses up to 80/min, which is also higher than the efficient execution time of authentication application for medium-sized groups. Therefore, routing application can easily operate on the group of authenticated users.

6   Conclusion

In this study, we have proposed an Authenticated Quality of Service Aware Routing (AQoSAR) in SDN. AQoSAR consists of two applications, namely the authentication application and the routing application. The authentication application is able to provide authentication for a single user and a group of users. The routing application constructs paths of users based on network statistics and QoS metric list of users. We have showed that AQoSAR is secure against impersonation, collusion, replay and eavesdropping attacks. In addition, we have presented detailed performance analysis for AQoSAR. Numerical evaluations of authentication and routing application show that AQoSAR provides promising results when it is used for medium-sized groups. Implementation of AQoSAR on a real-life scenario is left as a future work.

Acknowledgement. This work was supported in part by the Scientific and Technical Research Council of Turkey (TUBITAK) under Grant 117E165 and in part by the Turkish State Planning Organization (DPT) through the TAM Project under Grant 2007K120610.

References

1. Aghapour, S., Ameri, M., Mohajeri, J.: A multi sender attribute-based broadcast authentication scheme. In: International Symposium on Telecommunications. IEEE (2016)
2. Bethencourt, J., Sahai, A., Waters, B.: Ciphertext-policy attribute-based encryption. In: Symposium on Security and Privacy. IEEE (2007)
3. Bin, W., Yan, R.: An attribute-based anonymous authentication scheme. In: International Conference on Emerging Intelligent Data and Web Technologies. IEEE (2013)
4. Dutra, D., Bagaa, M., Taleb, T., Samdanis, K.: Ensuring end-to-end QoS based on multi-paths routing using SDN technology. In: Global Communications Conference. IEEE (2017)
5. Egilmez, H., Dane, T., Bagci, T., Tekinalp, M.: OpenQoS: an OpenFlow controller design for multimedia delivery with end-to-end quality of service over software-defined networks. In: Signal & Information Processing Association Annual Summit and Conference. IEEE (2012)
6. Egilmez, H., Tekinalp, A.: Distributed QoS architectures for multimedia streaming over software defined networks. In: Transactions on Multimedia. IEEE (2014)
7. ElGamal, T.: A public key cryptosystem and a signature scheme based on discrete logarithms. In: Blakley, G.R., Chaum, D. (eds.) CRYPTO 1984. LNCS, vol. 196, pp. 10–18. Springer, Heidelberg (1985). https://doi.org/10.1007/3-540-39568-7_2
8. Goyal, V., Pandev, O., Sahai, A., Waters, B.: Attribute-based encryption for fine-grained access control of encrypted data. In: Conference on Computer and Communications Security. ACM (2006)
9. Guo, L., Zhang, C., Sun, J., Fang, Y.: PAAS: a privacy-preserving attribute-based authentication system for ehealth networks. In: International Conference on Distributed Computing Systems. IEEE (2012)

10. Guo, L., Zhang, C., Sun, J., Fang, Y.: A privacy-preserving attribute-based authentication system for mobile health networks. In: Transactions on Mobile Computing. IEEE (2014)
11. Hong, H., Sun, Z., Xia, Y.: Achieving secure and fine-grained data authentication in cloud computing using attribute based proxy signature. In: International Conference on Information Science and Control Engineering. IEEE (2017)
12. Jiang, J., Huang, H., Liao, J., Chen, S.: Extending Dijkstra's shortest path algorithm for software defined networking. In: Network Operations and Management Symposium. IEEE (2014)
13. Khader, D.: Attribute-based authentication scheme. In: Ph.D. dissertation. University of Bath (2009)
14. Kuliesius, F., Dangovas, V.: SDN-driven authentication and access control system. In: The International Conference on Digital Information, Networking, and Wireless Communications. SDIWC (2014)
15. Kuliesius, F., Dangovas, V.: SDN enhanced campus network authentication and access control system. In: International Conference on Ubiquitous and Future Networks. IEEE (2016)
16. Porxas, A., Liny, S., Luoz, M.: QoS-aware virtualization-enabled routing in software-defined networks. In: Next Generation Networking Symposium. IEEE (2015)
17. Sahai, A., Waters, B.: Fuzzy identity-based encryption. In: Cramer, R. (ed.) EUROCRYPT 2005. LNCS, vol. 3494, pp. 457–473. Springer, Heidelberg (2005). https://doi.org/10.1007/11426639_27
18. Sahri, N., Mao, J.: Collaborative spoofing detection and mitigation - SDN based looping authentication for DNS services. In: Computer Software and Applications Conference. IEEE (2016)
19. Schnorr, C.P.: Efficient identification and signatures for smart cards. In: Brassard, G. (ed.) CRYPTO 1989. LNCS, vol. 435, pp. 239–252. Springer, New York (1990). https://doi.org/10.1007/0-387-34805-0_22
20. Tsiounis, Y., Yung, M.: On the security of ElGamal based encryption. In: Imai, H., Zheng, Y. (eds.) PKC 1998. LNCS, vol. 1431, pp. 117–134. Springer, Heidelberg (1998). https://doi.org/10.1007/BFb0054019
21. Wang, M., Liu, J., Mao, J., Cheng, H., Chen, J.: NSV-guard: constructing secure routing paths in software defined networking. In: International Conferences on Big Data and Cloud Computing, Social Computing and Networking, Sustainable Computing and Communications. IEEE (2016)
22. Won, K., Park, S., You, J.: Mynah: enabling lightweight data plane authentication for SDN controllers. In: Computer Communication and Networks. IEEE (2015)
23. Yang, H., Oleshchuk, V.: Traceable hierarchical attribute-based authentication for the cloud. In: Workshop on Security and Privacy in the Cloud. IEEE (2015)
24. Li, Y., Mao, J.: SDN based access authentication and automatic configuration for IPSec. In: International Conference on Computer Science and Network Technology. IEEE (2015)

On Consent in Online Social Networks: Privacy Impacts and Research Directions (Short Paper)

Sourya Joyee De$^{(\boxtimes)}$ and Abdessamad Imine$^{(\boxtimes)}$

LORIA-CNRS-INRIA Nancy Grand-Est, Nancy, France
sourya-joyee.de@inria.fr, abdessamad.imine@loria.fr

Abstract. The EU General Data Protection Regulation (GDPR) recognizes data subject's consent as a legitimate ground of data processing. At present, consent mechanisms in OSNs are either non-existent or not GDPR compliant. While the absence of consent means a lack of control of the OSN user (data subject) on his personal data, non-compliant consent mechanisms can give them a false sense of control, encouraging them to reveal more personal data than they would have otherwise. GDPR compliance is thus the only way to obtain meaningful consents, thereby protecting user privacy. In this paper, we discuss the characteristics of valid consent as per the GDPR, analyze the present status of consent in OSNs and propose some research directions to arrive at GDPR compliant consent models acceptable to users and OSN providers (data controller). We observe that evaluating privacy risks of consents to data processing activities can be an effective way to help users in their decision to give or refuse consents and hence is an important research direction.

Keywords: Online Social Networks (OSN) · Privacy · Consent · GDPR · Privacy risk

1 Introduction

The EU General Data Protection Regulation (GDPR) [4], which has come into force across Europe from 25th May 2018, recognizes consent of data subject as a legitimate ground of data processing. The central aim of promoting the notion of consent is to provide data subjects control over their personal data.

Today, users reveal a wide variety of personal data in Online Social Networks (OSNs), not only to the OSN provider (the data controller) but also to third party applications and other users. OSNs involve a wide variety of data processing activities, such as face recognition and friend suggestion. At present, consent mechanisms for these processing activities are either non-existent or not GDPR compliant. This situation, in the absence of other legitimate reasons for data processing, is undesirable. The absence of consent means a lack of choice

This work is supported by ANR project SEQUOIA ANR-14-CE28-0030-01.

© Springer Nature Switzerland AG 2019
A. Zemmari et al. (Eds.): CRiSIS 2018, LNCS 11391, pp. 128–135, 2019.
https://doi.org/10.1007/978-3-030-12143-3_11

and consequently, a lack of control of the data subject on how his data is processed. Non-compliant consent mechanisms can give users a false sense of control, encouraging them to reveal more personal data than they would have otherwise [8]. Data controllers, third parties and/or governments may misuse the huge data repository accumulated by OSNs for surveillance, profiling leading various forms of discrimination and other privacy harms. Other malicious entities can misuse the data for identity theft, stalking, shaming, defamation and bullying, to say the least. On top of this, non-compliant data controllers are subject to hefty fines by the GDPR and may suffer loss of reputation among an increasingly privacy-conscious population when privacy harms come to light.

Quitting OSNs to protect one's privacy is not an effective measure. OSN providers can still possess the data of past members and collect information about non-users. Moreover, users derive various social benefits from OSNs, such as establishing new friendships and reviving and strengthening existing ones [2]. Therefore, the right approach to ensure user privacy is for data controllers to be compliant to privacy regulations and compliance of consent mechanisms constitute a major step in this direction. Achieving consent compliance is not an easy task in OSNs. Often, user privacy depends both on the data subject's consent and other users' actions. Users face many cognitive and structural challenges in their decision to give or refuse consent [8]. Moreover, a compliant consent mechanism must have certain characteristics and to be practical, must be acceptable to both users and OSN providers. These issues open up new research directions to be explored. Privacy risk evaluation of consents for data processing activities can be an effective way to help users to decide whether to give or refuse consents and is an important research direction. The GDPR encourages informing users about the privacy risks of personal data processing.

In this paper, we first discuss what constitutes a "valid consent" according to the GDPR in Sect. 2 and then, in Sect. 3, we analyze the current state of consent in OSNs, with a focus on examples from Facebook, the leading OSN provider. Finally, in Sect. 4, we propose some research directions to arrive at GDPR compliant consent models acceptable to both OSN providers and users.

In this paper, we use the terms "data subject", "data controller", "third party", "personal data" and "data processing" as defined by the GDPR. In the context of OSNs, users are the "data subjects", the OSN service provider is the "data controller" and third party application providers are the "third parties" as defined in the GDPR. We also use the terms "personal data" and "data processing" in the sense of the GDPR.

2   Valid Consent as in the GDPR

A valid consent, as in Articles 4 and 7 of the GDPR, must be (1) freely given, (2) specific, (3) informed and (4) obtained by a clear affirmative action of the data subject. Below, we briefly describe these characteristics.

Freely Given. The WP29 guideline on consent [1] describes how to assess whether a consent is indeed freely given using the following criteria: (1) the relationship between the data controller and the user, (2) the conditionality and (3) the granularity of the consent and (4) if the withdrawal of consent is detrimental for the user. It is unlikely that consent is freely given if there is a *power imbalance* between the data controller, such as an employer, and the data subject who may fear significant negative consequences if he does not give consent. If the performance of a contract is *conditional* on the consent to data processing not necessary for the execution of the contract, then consent is not freely given. If a data controller seeks the consent for several purposes bundled together, then it lacks *granularity* as the data subject does not have the freedom to give or deny consent for each purpose. Refusal or withdrawal of consent must not be *detrimental* to the user. If a user gives consent to Facebook's facial recognition feature meant for tag suggestions, detection of fake accounts etc., it is not "freely given" as the data subject has to accept all purposes even if he finds only one of them acceptable.

Specific. When several data processings have the same purpose, consent may be sought for all of them together. However, if a data processing has multiple purposes, then consent must be sought for each of them. Specificity of consent promotes transparency as the data subject knows about each purpose of data processing, increases his control over these purposes and safeguards against function creep. Facebook's facial recognition feature does not allow users to give "specific" consent as the provider does not ask for consent for each purpose.

Informed. To really enable data subjects to understand what they are consenting to and to exercise their rights, such as the *right to withdraw consent*, the data controller must provide, in plain and clear language, a minimal set of information including its own identity, the purposes of processing and the data that are to be collected and used. Informed consent thus promotes transparency.

Clear Affirmative Action. Data subjects must give consent in an active motion or declaration. Thus, opt-out and pre-ticked opt-in boxes in consent forms are invalid under GDPR. For example, Twitter requires users to uncheck pre-ticked boxes to opt-out of targetted advertising, making the resulting consent invalid. Silence, inactivity or simply proceeding with a service without any action are not consents.

3   Consent in Online Social Networks: Present Status

In OSNs, personal data is transferred from the data subject to the data controller (OSN provider), or third party application providers or other data subjects. These data transfers can be summarized into: (1) data subject-data controller interaction, (2) data subject-third party interaction and (3) data subject-data subject interaction. The last type of interaction is unique to OSNs. Several data processing activities can be related to each interaction and, according to the GDPR, all such activities require user consent to be legitimate. At present, such consent mechanisms in OSNs are either non-existent or if they exist, are mostly not GDPR compliant. In the following sub-sections, for each interaction, we discuss the current state of consent in OSNs. Facebook is a leading OSN provider, which has been questioned over the years by regulators and privacy advocates about its privacy practices [7]. It is yet to be seen how Facebook manages to comply with the GDPR. With this in mind, we focus mainly on Facebook for examples of consent mechanisms.

Data Subject-Data Controller Interaction. Targetted advertising, based on personal data available from user profiles and activities or from external sources, is the primary source of revenue for OSNs today. Advertising platforms can be exploited to cause privacy problems, such as inferring users' full phone numbers just from the knowledge of their e-mail addresses [11]. In response to the GDPR, Facebook has recently started seeking consent on whether to include data from its partners such as other websites to show advertisements, but it gives no options to users to say no to targetted advertisements. In contrast, Snapchat and Twitter have enabled their users to opt-out of targetted advertising [10]. However, opt-out and pre-ticked opt-in boxes in consent forms, under the GDPR, do not indicate "clear, affirmative action" and hence, do not constitute valid consent. Facebook's face recognition feature can be used to scan the profile picture and other photos and videos of a user to compute a template which can then be matched with other photos and videos in Facebook. The current consent mechanism allows the user to give consent for all purposes of face recognition or none at all, thus lacking in specificity and granularity. Users may be interested to enable the facial recognition feature for detecting fake profiles but not for photo tagging. So, refusal of consent leads to losing out on otherwise useful service(s) and hence is detrimental to the user.

Data Subject-Third Party Interaction. When using third party applications on the OSN platform, users often have little comprehension of how much data they are sharing, with whom and that they are also responsible for sharing their friends' information [6]. Recently, an app called "thisisyourdigitallife" was used to gather the personal data of its users and their friends in the disguise of a paid psychological test on Facebook. This data was then shared with Cambridge Analytica which may have used it to influence choices in elections. Such data sharing, without valid user consent, may lead to many harms like loss of jobs and insurance and suppression of free speech [5]. To use third party gaming applications on Facebook, users must agree to disclose personal data such as their public profile, name, e-mail address, date of birth, friend list etc., by clicking on a "Play Now" button. Although Facebook provides an explanation below this button that clicking it implies that the user agrees to disclose a list of personal data, the positioning of this explanation and the bundling of the actions of playing the game and giving consent may be misleading for data subjects. It is questionable whether clicking on the "Play Now" button is indeed a "clear, affirmative action" of the data subject. Moreover, satisfactory information about the purposes of data processing is not always available to the users. Therefore, the consent given in this case appears to be neither fully "informed" nor "specific".

Data Subject-Data Subject Interaction. In Facebook, even if a user does not consent to sharing some personal data, the actions of other users can reveal this data. Wall posts or comments by one user may contain personal data of others. A friend may make public a user's wall posts originally meant only for friends. Another relevant scenario is where user A wants to upload a photo including his friend user B on Facebook, but user B does not. It is also possible to infer personal data, not disclosed by the data subject, from that revealed by his network, i.e., his friends, friends-of-friends and groups [12]. Facebook privacy settings, which is a consent mechanism meant to enable users to control the personal data they share with their network, cannot deal with these scenarios. "People You May Know" is an important Facebook feature that opens up the scope of data subject-data subject interaction by allowing one user to easily access the personal data of another. It suggests a user A's profile to another user B based on their mutual friends, common groups, networks (such as school, university, work) and uploaded contacts. In its current form, Facebook does not seek consent from A before suggesting him as a potential friend to B, increasing the accessibility of A's profile to B without A's consent. Like NewsFeed, this feature does not make more information publicly available, but makes it easier for a potential misuser to get to this information [6].

4 Research Directions Towards Consent Compliance

While the lack of a consent mechanism deprives users of control over their personal data, a non-compliant consent mechanism can give users a false sense of control encouraging them to reveal more data than they would have otherwise. So, the research community must focus on converging towards GDPR compliant consent models that are acceptable to both users and service providers. To this end, we propose some research directions in this section. These research efforts would be multi-disciplinary in nature, involving the contributions of computer scientists, legal experts and psychologists.

Privacy Risk Evaluation for "Well-Informed" Consent. A consent mechanism presents users with a set of choices. To help them make the right decision, the data controller should provide information about the data processing activity, its purpose and the personal data involved. Users often do not read long privacy notices, yet they need deeper understanding and background to make informed choices. Even if they read, they lack the expertise to understand the consequences of their consents and are often ready to give up on privacy for small, immediate benefits [8]. In the Cambridge Analytica scandal, people gave up their own personal data and that of their friends in exchange for small monetary benefits. These data ended up being used to influence election results, a long-term harm for the society. One way to address these problems in OSNs could be to design a tool that can assess on behalf of the user the privacy risks of each consent. Usability surveys can help to construct the right interface for communicating these risks to users. This risk information will be short, simple but concrete enough for the user to get a view of the consequences of their consent and help them arrive at a decision. In other words, it greatly enhances the "informed" characteristic of a valid consent. The GDPR, in its Recital 39, promotes this idea of making users aware of risks of personal data processing. Privacy risk evaluation has been utilized for other services to help users make meaningful choices of privacy settings [3].

Inter-provider and Intra-provider Risk Evaluation. Several pieces of data, aggregated over time, can lead to various privacy harms [8]. An average user may engage with several OSNs (not to mention other services) each of which usually involves several data processing activities. To truly avoid all privacy harms, the decision to consent for a data processing activity must depend on the consents already given to other data processing activities. Thus, researchers should focus on designing intra-provider and eventually inter-provider privacy risk evaluation mechanisms that take into account personal data revealed for all data processing activities for a given OSN and those for all OSNs that a data subject uses, respectively.

Balancing Privacy Risks and Social Benefits. Users have to deal with several cognitive and structural hurdles to arrive at meaningful decisions regarding consents to data processing activities [8]. Apart from privacy risks, they must also consider various social benefits, such as building new friendships and reviving and maintaining existing ones [2], for which they participate in OSNs. Automating the decision-making process of balancing privacy risks and social benefits for all data processing activities can take the burden off users. A similar approach was adopted recently to help users manage the privacy settings of OSN attributes [2].

Collaborative Consent and Risk-Based Friend Selection. While the OSN provider is obligated to obtain valid consent to process data in the absence of another legitimate basis, other users are under no legal obligations to obtain the data subject's consent before sharing his personal data. Friends of a user may publicly share data that were meant to be seen only by friends or post photos of the user without the latter's consent. Potential misusers may also infer personal data of the user from the data revealed by his friends about themselves. The design of collaborative consent mechanisms could be a fruitful research direction in this context. Using such mechanisms, a user and his friends can together decide which personal data they share and to what extent so that it is difficult to infer with high confidence any personal data that has been kept private. These mechanisms could also be used to resolve data disclosure scenarios where the user sharing some data is not the data subject (for example, a photo of A shared by B) or is only one of the data subjects (for example, a photo of A and B shared by B) [9]. Another solution approach could be to design mechanisms that enable users to choose friends based on the privacy risks they pose, both in terms of unintended disclosure and the inference of personal data from those revealed by the friends about themselves.

5   Conclusion

At present, consent mechanisms in OSN are either absent or are not compliant to the newly enforced GDPR. Such a scenario poses severe privacy problems for data subjects as the latter have no true control on their personal data. Consent compliance is an important step towards protecting user privacy. In this paper, we discussed the characteristics of valid consent according to the GDPR, analyzed the present status of consent in OSNs and proposed some research directions to arrive at GDPR compliant consent models that are acceptable to OSN users and OSN providers.

References

1. Article 29 Data Protection Working Party. Guidelines on Consent under Regulation 2016/679 (2018)
2. De, S.J., Imine, A.: To reveal or not to reveal - balancing user-centric social benefit and privacy in online social networks. In: Proceedings of the 33rd Annual ACM Symposium on Applied Computing (ACM SAC 2018). ACM (2018)
3. De, S.J., Métayer, D.L.: Privacy risk analysis to enable informed privacy settings. In: 2018 IEEE European Symposium on Security and Privacy Workshops, Euro S&P Workshops 2018, London, UK, 23–27 April 2018, pp. 95–102 (2018)
4. European Commission: General Data Protection Regulation (2016)
5. Fruchter, N., Specter, M., Yuan, B.: Facebook/Cambridge Analytica: Privacy Lessons and a Way Forward (2018). https://internetpolicy.mit.edu/blog-2018-fb-cambridgeanalytica/
6. Hull, G., Lipford, H.R., Latulipe, C.: Contextual gaps: privacy issues on Facebook. Ethics Inf. Technol. **13**(4), 289–302 (2011)
7. New York Times: Mark Zuckerberg Testimony: Senators Question Facebook's Commitment to Privacy (2018). https://www.nytimes.com/2018/04/10/us/politics/mark-zuckerberg-testimony.html
8. Solove, D.J.: Introduction: privacy self-management and the consent dilemma. Harv. Law Rev. **126**, 1880 (2012)
9. Squicciarini, A.C., Xu, H., Zhang, X.: CoPE: enabling collaborative privacy management in online social networks. J. Am. Soc. Inf. Sci. Technol. **62**(3), 521–534 (2011)

10. Sweeney, J.: GDPR and the Major Social Networks: What You Need to Know (2018). https://blog.makemereach.com/gdpr-facebook-twitter-snapchat-linkedin-what-you-need-to-know
11. Venkatadri, G., et al.: Privacy risks with Facebook's PII-based targeting: auditing a data Broker's advertising interface. In: IEEE Symposium on Security and Privacy (SP), pp. 221–239 (2018)
12. Zheleva, E., Getoor, L.: To join or not to join: the illusion of privacy in social networks with mixed public and private user profiles. In: Proceedings of the 18th International Conference on World Wide Web, pp. 531–540. ACM (2009)

Enhancing Collaboration Between Security Analysts in Security Operations Centers

Damien Crémilleux[1]([✉]), Christophe Bidan[1], Frédéic Majorczyk[1,2], and Nicolas Prigent[3]

[1] CentraleSupélec, Rennes, France
{damien.cremilleux,christophe.bidan}@centralesupelec.fr
[2] DGA-MI, Bruz, France
frederic.majorczyk@intradef.gouv.fr
[3] LSTI, Saint-Malo, France
neeko@neekotech.fr

Abstract. Security Operations Centers (SOCs) collect data related to the information systems they protect and process it to detect suspicious activities. In this paper we explain how a SOC is organized, we highlight the current limitations of SOCs and their consequences regarding the performance of the detection service. We propose a new collaboration process to enhance the cooperation between security analysts in order to quickly process security events and define a better workflow that enables them to efficiently exchange feedback. Finally, we design a prototype corresponding to this new model.

Keywords: Security and privacy · Intrusion detection systems · Network security · Collaboration · Security Operations Center

1 Introduction

Most of the large information systems are monitored by a Security Operations Center (SOC). A typical SOC collects from thousands to millions of security events every day [1] with the objective of finding which of them require priority attention. The high volume of irrelevant security events and the way they are currently handled lead to the fact that real attacks are often missed and ignored. Consequently, there is a delay up to several months between an intrusion and its discovery. Security analysts in SOCs being put under pressure results in poor judgments when looking at security events and in a high burnout rate [2].

In order to improve efficiency of SOCs and solve the problems stated above, this paper proposes the following contributions:

- An analysis of the current limitations of SOCs, in Sect. 2. This paper describes SOCs with insight gained from interviews with security analysts.

A. Zemmari et al. (Eds.): CRiSIS 2018, LNCS 11391, pp. 136–142, 2019.
https://doi.org/10.1007/978-3-030-12143-3_12

- A new process to enhance the cooperation between the different security analysts, in Sect. 3. This process is established with the creation of rules to define security meta-events and the creation of a specific feedback loop between groups of security analysts.
- A design to support our new process, in Sect. 4. The limitations and the feedback from the evaluation we performed help our design of a prototype for a visualization tool dedicated to a better collaboration.

2   Security Operations Centers and Their Limitations

We interviewed twelve security analysts, all male with one to ten years of experience in the field, in one-to-one interviews. During the interviews, experts provided insights regarding the collaboration happening in SOCs between Tier 1 and Tier 2 analysts. Tier 1 analysts, the biggest category in number, are responsible for continuously monitoring the alert queue, and for the quick triage of the security alerts. If there is a procedure in the knowledge base for a given event, they follow it, resulting in a qualified incident or a false positive. Otherwise the suspicious event is sent to Tier 2 analysts. Tier 2 analysts perform two main tasks. First, they analyze unknown events that are suspicious, and following the result of their investigation, create a new qualified incident if needed. Second, they manage the incidents and the creation of an appropriate response.

Based on our findings, we highlight the current limitations inside a SOC and divide them into two aspects: process and technology. The process issues are:

- *Lack of creativity.* Tier 1 analysts follow written procedures that severely limit creativity and they stay with what they know, resulting in failure to react appropriately to novel operational scenarios.
- *Lack of feedback.* Once their decision is made, Tier 1 analysts lose track of their actions. They do not have the result of the analysis of Tier 2 analysts and therefore will not know if they acted correctly.
- *Repetition of the same task.* Tier 1 analysts perform repetitive tasks following known procedures. This aspect is also true for Tier 2 analysts. Because Tier 1 analysts keep sending the same type of events, Tier 2 analysts have to deal with them. The consequence is a loss of time and a diminished appreciation for the work accomplished by Tier 1 analysts.

The technology issues are:

- *Numerous data, and numerous data sources that are not linked.* Even with only IDSes alerts as main data source, Tier 1 analysts face a huge volume of security events and only have seconds or minutes to accomplish their task. This challenge also exists for Tier 2 analysts, the amount of data given to them being prodigious, in the order of millions of security events. Moreover the data sources are various: antivirus, IDSes alerts, system events, network traffic, etc., and are not necessarily linked one with the others. Thus an expertise in each of these data sources is required, and correlation and pivoting between pieces of data is a difficult task.

- *Progression of threat escalation.* It is particularly important to evaluate if an event is isolated or if it is a part of a bigger scenario. The knowledge of the current context, threats and incidents currently happening help the security analysts to take a decision.
- *Rhythm of networks.* Security analysts learn the rhythm of the network. They recognize frequent events and know which will follow them. The understanding of such events and of the typical amounts of errors in the system is currently insufficiently exploited, even if we should mention that it is a part of the collection strategy required in [3].

3   A New Collaboration Process

The limitations exhibited persuade us to propose a new collaboration process which introduces the concept of security meta-event and the creation of a feedback loop between Tier 1 and Tier 2 analysts. The purpose of security meta-events is to avoid, for Tier 1 analysts, to have to continuously deal with the same type of events. Instead of repeating the same procedures, events are regrouped in a security meta-event, an identified sequence of similar security events belonging to the same data source. Security meta-events should be easily created by Tier 1 analysts. Tier 2 analysts should have the possibility to refine it and collaborate around it, so we use rules based on signature to describe security meta-events. Rules are designed so that all analysts can quickly grasp their meaning. When creating a rule for a security meta-event, the key point for a Tier 1 analyst are: a name, a comment (used to explain more precisely the rule), a filter (stating which events should match with pattern matching).

When manipulating rules Tier 2 analysts have the possibility to improve them with: a label (the status of meta-events linked to the rule), a person (the Tier 2 analyst in charge of the remediation), an end date if needed, an interval (the minimum time needed between two matched events to create a new security meta-event). The values of the label field can be a suspicious meta-event, qualified incident, or noise (false positive alerts). Suspicious meta-events are those which are composed of security events currently happening in the system. A Tier 2 analyst has not looked at this meta-event and a response has not yet been found. By contrast, after an examination by a Tier 2 analyst, the meta-event can become a qualified incident. The rule describing this security meta-event can now be used to create future qualified incidents, if the analyst estimates that it is important to know when new events matching this rule arrive.

We now present in Fig. 1 a new workflow we designed that uses the concept of security meta-events and implements a feedback loop to empower Tier 1 analysts. The differences it exhibits with the current workflow used in SOCs are shown in bold and brown. Tier 1 analysts are now sending suspicious meta-events instead of single events, when faced with unknown suspicious security events. By using meta-events defined by rules, significant time can be saved. After the analysis of the meta-event, Tier 2 analysts have the possibility of modifying the rule if they estimate that it can be improved. Whatever the result, feedback is given to

Tier 1 analysts, empowering them. They can now create rules, and improve their knowledge over time with the continuous feedback given by Tier 2 analysts.

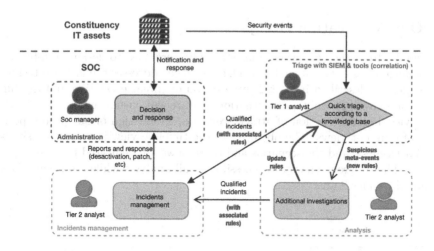

Fig. 1. Proposed workflow for a SOC.

At the beginning, there are no rules inside the system. With the constant creation and modification of rules, Tier 1 analysts see the rate of irrelevant events diminish so they can be more efficient in accomplishing their task. This workflow facilitates the work of Tier 1 analysts while still keeping them under the supervision of Tier 2 analysts. The limitations regarding the lack of creativity and feedback for Tier 1 analysts are also addressed since Tier 1 analysts have to think about the creation of relevant rules and understand the changes made by Tier 2 analysts to their rules. We advocate that this improvement helps Tier 1 analyst stay motivated, to accomplish their task more easily and results in an improved efficiency of the SOC.

An evaluation was performed in order to validate this new process. Eleven experts out of the twelve performed the job of a Tier 1 analyst with [4] on the VAST 2012 challenge, (50000 IDS alerts over three days of capture). We ask them to judge if this new process is improving the efficiency of a SOC. With an average rating of 4.1 out of 5, the experts answer positively. They judged that meta-events were a good way to keep the volume of irrelevant security events low. The fact that security events were sent in groups, in meta-events, was declared very useful for both Tier 1 and Tier 2 analysts. The introduction of rules to enhance the collaboration between analysts was appreciated. Rules and their comments helped the analysts to quickly understand the context of the security events. Three expert pointed out that the skill of Tier 1 analysts was a limiting factor of our solution. However, we advocate that this was already the case before the introduction of meta-events. Similarly, we believe that Tier 1 analysts will improve their knowledge and so the rules they create thanks to the feedback of Tier 2 analysts. Another point of interrogation for two experts was the evolution of the rules and their growing number over time. The interface presented in the next Section tries to answer this point.

4   Our Application Design

The results from the evaluation and our study were used to design an interface to exchange rules between analysts. This interface addresses the last two technical challenges described in Sect. 2, progression of threat escalation and rhythm of networks, by proposing quick situational awareness, visual correlation of incidents, visual reconstruction of attack scenarios. The design of our prototype is made of different views. The objective of the timeline view is to provide situational awareness, and the scenarios and rules views are dedicated to these types of data. The different views are accessible to all analysts while modifying data is limited to Tier 2 analysts.

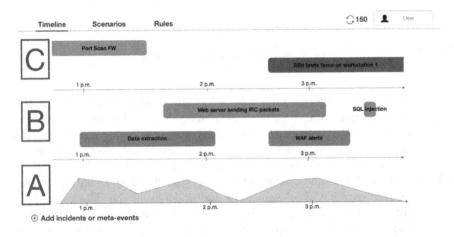

Fig. 2. Timeline view.

The timeline shown in Fig. 2 is the central view, provides high-level awareness of the rhythm of the network and enables visual correlation of incidents. It is divided into three sections, according to a gradient of gravity. The unclassified alerts are represented on a time chart in zone (A), giving an idea of the volume of security events arriving. The suspicious meta-events are then shown in the zone (B) and qualified incidents in zone (C). The color of the meta-events and the incidents on the timeline are indicators of the related scenarios of attacks, if unknown grey is used. The timeline form enables the analyst to understand the time relation between the security events and redraw the story behind them.

Analysts can access scenarios in the scenarios view. Sparklines are used in small multiples[1] to display the current trend for each scenario over time. For

---

[1] A series of similar graphs with same scale and axes to compare them easily.

each scenario, analysts have access to the number of rules and events composing it. They can modify its characteristics or delete it if needed. New scenarios can be added. The rules view is based on the same principle that the scenario view.

5   Related Work

Sundaramurthy et al. [2] performed anthropological studies of SOCs, evaluated the security analyst burnout in SOCs, and tried to find causes. Four factors are cited as the origin for the high burnout rate: lack of skills management, lack of empowerment, insufficient possibility to express creativity and lack of growth. The collaboration inside a security team is also addressed by Rajivan et al. [5] who focus on the team situational awareness. Some observations are relevant to our subject, even if the teams in their study are not working in a SOC. The authors emphasize the need for a better collaboration and cooperation inside security analysts teams. A collaboration tool is proposed with OCEANS [6] with web-based interface, however designed only for Tier 2 analysts.

Timelines are present in [7], a visual system for analyzing, examining and investigating time-series data. In [8] analysts can investigate network flow using timelines with specific glyphes to plot events. NStreamAware [9] leverages timelines with sliding slices and feature selection. Franklin et al. propose a design for an alerts management system resulting in an inbox metaphor prototype [10], with mail displayed on a timeline. In our proposition the design integrates the concept of timeline with the different teams and escalation process of SOCs.

6   Conclusion

In this paper, we have presented a description of the workflow currently in place in SOCs. We have emphasized their limitations deriving in a high turn over and detrimental to the efficiency of the SOC. In order to enhance the collaboration between security analysts working inside a SOC, we have proposed a new collaboration process and a design prototype using security meta-events defined by rules, with a feedback loop between Tier 1 an Tier 2 analysts. The evaluation shows that our contribution makes a positive impact with respect to SOC efficiency and experts of the field acknowledge our approach.

References

1. Zimmerman, C.: Ten Strategies of a World-Class Cybersecurity Operations Center. The MITRE Corporation, McLean (2014)
2. Sundaramurthy, S., et al.: A human capital model for mitigating security analyst burnout. In: SOUPS 2015. USENIX Association, July 2015
3. Prestataires de détection des incidents de sécurité. Référentiel d'exigences. ANSSI (2017)
4. Crémilleux, D., et al.: VEGAS: visualizing, exploring and grouping alerts. In: NOMS, pp. 1097–1100. IEEE (2016)

5. Rajivan, P., Cooke, N.: Impact of team collaboration on cybersecurity situational awareness. In: Liu, P., Jajodia, S., Wang, C. (eds.) Theory and Models for Cyber Situation Awareness. LNCS, vol. 10030, pp. 203–226. Springer, Cham (2017). https://doi.org/10.1007/978-3-319-61152-5_8
6. Chen, S., et al.: OCEANS: online collaborative explorative analysis on network security. In: VizSec 2014 (2014)
7. Stoffel, F., Fischer, F., Keim, D.A.: Finding anomalies in time-series using visual correlation for interactive root cause analysis. In: VizSec 2013 (2013)
8. Phan, D., et al.: visual analysis of network flow data with timelines and event plots. In: Goodall, J.R., Conti, G., Ma, K.L. (eds.) VizSEC 2007. Mathematics and Visualization. Springer, Heidelberg (2008). https://doi.org/10.1007/978-3-540-78243-8_6
9. Fischer, F., Keim, D.A.: NStreamAware: real-time visual analytics for data streams to enhance situational awareness. In: VizSec 2014 (2014)
10. Franklin, L., et al.: Toward a visualization-supported workflow for cyber alert management using threat models and human-centered design. In: VizSec 2017 (2017)

RIICS: Risk Based IICS Segmentation Method

Khaoula Es-Salhi[1(✉)], David Espes[2(✉)], and Nora Cuppens[1(✉)]

[1] IMT Atlantique - LabSTICC, Cesson-Sévigné, France
{khaoula.es-salhi,nora.cuppens}@imt-atlantique.fr
[2] University of Western Brittany - LabSTICC, Brest, France
david.espes@univ-brest.fr

Abstract. Nowadays, one of the major challenges in industrial business world is integrating industrial control systems (ICS) with corporate systems (IT) and keeping the integrated system secured. Connecting this two totally different networks has numerous benefits and advantages, but introduces several security problems. *Defense-in-depth* is one of the most important security measures that should be applied to integrated ICS systems. This security technique consists essentially of *"Segmentation"* and *"Segregation"*. Segmentation of an integrated ICS may be based on various types of characteristics such as technical characteristics, business impact, risk levels or other requirements defined by the organization. This paper presents RIICS (**R**isk based **IICS** **S**egmentation) a new segmentation method that aims to simplify security zones identification by focusing on systems characteristics that are really relevant for segmentation especially technical industrial specificities and risk.

Keywords: Cyber-security · Corporate system · ICS · SCADA ·
Integration · Network segmentation · Risk analysis

1 Introduction

Integrating an Industrial Control System (ICS) with a Corporate System (IT) exposes both of them to several security problems [1,3]. Very important number of industrial entities and infrastructures are so critical that any successful cyber attack on these entities can cause significant damages to business, to environment and more severely to national security and people safety.

Defense-in-depth is a highly recommended security measures for Integrated ICS [2,6]. It protects against security issues [6] by dividing the system into encapsulated security zones to create multiple layers of defense. The Defense-in-depth mainly uses Segmentation and Segregation techniques. Segmentation consists of creating multiple security zones that can be separately controlled, monitored and protected [14]. A security zone is a set of *Components* or sub-systems connected within one sub-network governed by a single authority and one security policy [15].

© Springer Nature Switzerland AG 2019
A. Zemmari et al. (Eds.): CRiSIS 2018, LNCS 11391, pp. 143–157, 2019.
https://doi.org/10.1007/978-3-030-12143-3_13

The system's characteristics that should be considered for segmentation are not obvious. Segmentation of an Integrated ICS may be based on various aspects such as functional characteristics, risk levels, business impacts or other requirements defined by the organization. Engineering expertise and intuition are not enough to perform Integrated ICS segmentation because it may be error-prone and produce inaccurate results. The work may take more time than necessary while some important aspects may be neglected. Using a framework or a working method is always very useful because it guarantees more valuable results more quickly. Although some segmentation solutions have been suggested by some research works [6, 13, 14], they still are not generic enough.

Therefore, we propose RIICS (**R**isk based **IICS S**egmentation), a new segmentation method that aims to simplify security zones identification by focusing on systems characteristics that are really relevant for segmentation such as technical industrial specificities and risk.

This paper is structured as follows. Section 2 presents the state of the art related to IICS segmentation. Section 3 presents the RIICS method. It explains the principle, the concepts and the main steps of the method. The fourth section describes our validation tests, explains the test methodology, and discusses the results. For the rest of this document, we will use the abbreviation IICS to refer to "Integrated ICS".

2   State of the Art

Multiple research works have been conducted on IICS Systems segmentation. They can be classified into three categories in accordance with their approach to addressing the issue and the aspects they take into account.

The first category of studies mainly includes general security guides such as NIST [2], ISA [7–10, 17] and ANSSI [4, 5] guides. They are very valuable resources for getting started on the subject as they provide fairly simple definitions of the concepts. They all agree that the segmentation should be implemented on a case-by-case basis, based on a risk assessment of the system. However, their recommendations remain rather superficial as most of the work has to be done by the organization without having any precision on how to proceed. In fact, many questions remain unanswered, especially regarding the aspects to be taken into account in order to achieve segmentation.

The second category of studies, [6, 11], addresses the subject with a more practical approach since they use a well-defined reference architecture as the basis for their solutions. They suggest implementing multiple layers of defence by creating multiple security zones. They mainly use the Purdue model logic framework for the control hierarchy, developed by the International Society of Automation IEC 62264 (ISA-95) ISA-99-1. This model defines five functional levels that are used in these documents as the main criteria for delineating security zones. The results of such studies are quite accurate. However, their solutions are not generic and can only be adopted for systems similar to the reference system or, at best, for learning.

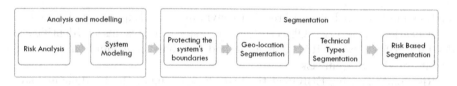

Fig. 1. RIICS principle

The third category of studied documents tries to solve the problem in a more generic way. Their solutions are in the form of generic rules and guidance where security zones are abstractly defined. We believe that this approach can lead to great results if conducted with deep focus on the aspects that are really relevant for IICS segmentation. This is an important ingredient that the studied documents do not unfortunately ensure because only the functional aspect, using the IEC 62264 (ISA95) model, is taken into account. This is definitely not enough to cover most of the IICS Systems.

Therefore, we defined a new generic IICS Segmentation method that try to fill these gaps. This is why we have defined a new generic IICS segmentation method that aims at filling these gaps by taking the best of each approach and focusing on security-oriented aspects such as risk.

3   Risk Based IICS segmentation Method

3.1   The Principle

RIICS is a new IICS segmentation method that aims to ensure efficient zoning to meet actual security needs of IICS. The principle of RIICS is illustrated in Fig. 1. The segmentation is done in two phases. First, the system is analyzed and modeled to create the system's model that represents the main input of the segmentation phase.

The system's modeling is based on the meta-model presented in Sect. 3.2 and on a risk analysis of the whole system. An IICS model primarily focuses on system components and their interconnections. Risk analysis allows the evaluation and attribution of risk levels to the system's components (Sect. 3.2).

At the second phase, the system should first have its boundaries protected before being segmented. The segmentation operation consists, next, of grouping the system's components according to their geolocation, technical type and risk level characteristics in three cycles. Simply stated, components that have the same geolocation, the same technical type and the same level of risk together constitute a single security zone.

3.2   Analysis and Modelling

Risk Analysis

Components modeling requires the evaluation of their associated risk. This should be carried out using a risk analysis. We suggest using the EBIOS [16] risk analysis method. EBIOS is a French acronym meaning Expression of Needs and Identification of Security Objectives (**E**xpression des **B**esoins et **I**dentification des **O**bjectifs de **S**écurité). It is a method for analysis, evaluation and action on Information System risk.

Risk analysis using EBIOS at the first phase of the method is done in 4 steps as illustrated in Fig. 2.

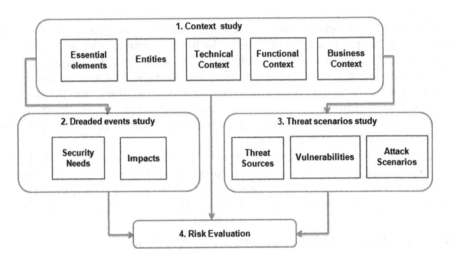

Fig. 2. EBIOS steps

Studying the Organization's Context

The first step of risk analysis is to study in depth the technical, functional and business context of the organization. For the study to be conducted properly, sufficient knowledge of the company's data, business processes, existing security policy and procedures, business model and competitors is required.

The objective of this step is to:

- Model the company's assets
- Model the system architecture (components and connections)
- Acquire sufficient knowledge about technical, functional and business specificities of the company's assets.

Modeling the system relies on the meta-model of Fig. 3. For EBIOS, a company disposes of a set of assets. Assets are any valuable resource necessary to achieve the organization's objectives. There are two types of them: essential elements and entities. Essential elements are deployed, managed and protected by entities. Entities are assets such as sites, personnel, equipment, networks, software or systems. Essential elements potentially involve feared events that can occur as a result of an threat scenario operated by a threat source. Threat scenarios exploit entities vulnerabilities.

– **Essential elements**
Essential elements of a company are its most important assets. They usually have many security requirements that should be analyzed and considered by the risk analysis. Processes and digital data are good examples of essential elements.

  • **Processes**
    A Process is a set of interrelated or interacting activities, which transforms input information into and output. A system is organized into multiple processes. Each process may contain one or more components. Processes identification should be done by the company. In general, an organization standard such as ISO9001 is applied to partition the system into multiple processes. Processes use one or more system components to ensure their operation.
    Order placement processes, billing processes, industrial control process, and secret recipe manufacturing processes are examples of essential elements processes. Special attention should be paid to confidentiality and integrity for IT processes and availability for industrial processes.

  • **Digital Data**
    All data stored, manipulated or exchanged by components such as databases and file systems. They are highly valued by the company and usually are critical assets.
    Clients personal data, invoices, orders and SCADA logs are examples of precious data.

– **Entities**
Entities are assets of the system that perform core functions, process, store and transmit essential elements. These include physical locations, computing and human resources, networks, applications and software... As far as our method is concerned, we pay special attention to Components and Connections because they are the primary focus of the method.

  • **Components**
    A *"Component"* is any device capable of communicating through the system network regardless its functions or the technologies it uses. A Component is characterized by its its technical type, the geographical site it belongs to as well as its risk level.

    * **Geographical Location**
      Components geographical location is also relevant for segmentation [2]. Two physically distant sites systematically constitute two different security zones. "Physically distant" sites are sites that are either connected by wireless *Connection* or non physically protected wired *Connection.*

    * **Technical Types**
      A *Component* can be an Information Technology (IT), Operation Technology (OT) *Component.*
      IT *Components*
        · Are "Enterprise data centric": Cover the spectrum of systems that support corporate functions;

· Focus on higher level processes and transactions that manipulate data;

· Focus on data confidentiality and integrity;

· The main humans role is manipulating (reading, creating and updating) the data.

OT *Components*

· Are "Thing (product) centric": Deal with the physical transformation of products and services;

· Focus on physical industrial processes. They are mission-critical task-specific systems where controlling the physical equipment should be done with great precision;

· Focus on safety and availability;

· The main humans role is supervising and controlling the industrial processes.

A *Component* can, otherwise, be an IT-OT *Component*. We introduced this new type to distinguish *Components* that are designed to use both types of technologies IT and OT such as workstations.

According to these security guides and standards [2,5,7,9,10,12], *Components* of different technical types must be separated into different security segments because they have different security requirements.

* **Risk Level**

Components are also characterized by their risk level. It can have one of the risk levels of Table 1. Components risk evaluation will be explained in Sect. 3.2. Evaluating the risk levels of the Components is the main motivation for using a risk analysis method.

Connections

A "*Connection*" is any channel that can be used by two (or more) *Components* to communicate with each others. It can be physical, where the *Components* are directly linked by a physical (wired or a wireless) connection, or logical, where the *Components* are linked through a succession of physical *Connections*.

Identify the Feared Events and Estimate Their Gravity

Feared events are security violations (in terms of confidentiality, integrity and availability) to one or more essential elements of the system under study. An example of feared events is the access to some essential elements (such as a clients database) by a non authorized external person. Each feared event is associated with a gravity level. Feared events gravity is the extent of its impact on one or more of the company's essential elements. It can have one of the gravity scale values from Table 3. Gravity estimation is done with a qualitative approach that needs good knowledge of the organization's system and business.

Analyze Threat scenarios and estimate the likelihood of the attack

Threat scenarios are operating mechanisms applied by threat sources (competitors, enemies, internal opponents, human error...) to violate security of entities (especially components) in order to achieve a feared event on one or more

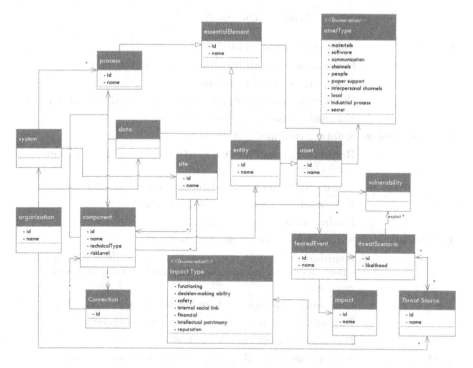

Fig. 3. EBIOS meta-model

Table 1. The risk levels   **Table 2.** The likelihood scale

Negligible risk	1. Low	This is unlikely to happen
Considerable risk	2. Probable	This may happen
Critical risk	3. Significant	There is a significant risk that this will occur
Extreme risk	4. Strong	This should happen one day

essential elements. A threat scenario can be either intended or accidental. Basic threats typically involve exploiting system vulnerabilities at the organizational, functional, operational, or design level. Vulnerabilities are identified based on a security diagnosis. Special attention should be paid to potential threat scenarios and vulnerabilities in relation with components and their connections.

Each threat scenario is associated with a level of likelihood from Table 2. This depends on the attractiveness of the target for the threat source and how easily the attack can be achieved. Threat sources should be identified and qualified in terms of capacity and motivation.

Evaluate the Risk Level

The objective of this step is to assign a risk level value from Table 1 to each component of the system. This requires that the feared events of all the essential elements hold by the components to be identified, their gravity estimated, all

Table 3. The gravity scale

1. Low	**Safety:** No threat to safety
	Regulatory/Legal: Internal sanction at the most
	Company's image: No impact
	Financial: Low potential financial (e.g., few dozens of dollars)
	Business: Loss of some few prospects
2. Considerable	**Safety:** Small material damage
	Regulatory/Legal: Small Contractual penalties with some small clients
	Company's image: Local impact, limited number of actors
	Financial: e.g., some thousands of dollars
	Business: Loss of small clients
3. Critical	**Safety:** Considerable material damage
	Regulatory/Legal: Strong contractual penalties with major clients, civil or criminal cases, non-compliance with law or regulation
	Company's image: Wide perimeter impact
	Financial: Dozens of thousands of dollars annually
	Business: Loss of important clients
4. Major	**Safety:** Big material damage, Danger on Human safety
	Regulatory/Legal: Major non-compliance with the law or regulation, massive invasion of privacy, criminal conviction, contractual penalties with multiple actors
	Company's image: Scandal
	Financial: Hundreds of thousands of dollars annually
	Business: Loss of partnership, Massive loss of clients

threat scenarios related to these feared events listed and their likelihood estimated.

The risk level of a Component is a function of feared events gravity and their likelihood. For one feared event and one threat scenario, the risk level is calculated using the the risk levels grid in Fig. 4.

The risk level of a component should always be calculated assuming the worst case using the following formulas:

- The associated risk to an event and a scenario $Risk(event, scenario)$ is calculated using the risk levels grid.
- The risk associated to a feared event is calculated based on the most probable threat scenario:

$$Risk_{event} = Max_{scenarios}(Risk(event, scenario))$$

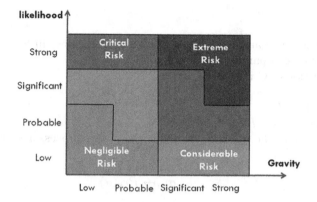

Fig. 4. Risk levels grid

- The risk associated to an essential element equals the most important risk of its feared events:

$$Risk_{essential} = Max_{events}(Risk_{event})$$

- The risk associated to component is the most important risk associated to the essential assets it holds:

$$Risk_{component} = Max_{essentials}(Risk_{essential})$$

3.3   Segmentation

Once the components and connections are completely modeled, components are then straightforwardly grouped by their geolocation, technical types and risk levels. The segmentation can be formalized using mathematical objects as below to summarize the method and provides a useful starting point for implementation.

Preliminary:
Let S an IICS system, S = <C,Ge> where:

- C is the set of components of S,
- Ge is the set of all the geographical sites of S.
- $R = \{NEGLIGIBLE, CONSIDERABLE, CRITICAL, EXTREME\}$ is the set of all possible risks levels.
- $T = \{TI, TO, TIO\}$ is the set of all possible technical types.

Notations:
$\forall c \in C,$

- $tt_c \in T$ is the technical type of c.
- $site_c \in Ge$ is the site to which c belongs.
- $risk_c \in R$ is the risk level of c.

<u>Definitions:</u>

1. Let $\Sigma_{(S)}$ the set of all possible segmentations of the system S,
$\Sigma_{(S)} = \{ \sigma/\sigma$ is a partition of C $\}$
σ is a partition of C if:
   - $\emptyset \notin \sigma$
   - $\bigcup_{A \in \sigma} A = C$
   - $\forall A, B \in \sigma,\ A \neq B \Rightarrow A \cap B = \emptyset$

2. For each cycle of the method, we define the cycle's processor function as:

$$Pr_g : \Sigma_{(S)} \to \Sigma_{(S)}$$
$$\sigma \mapsto Pr_g(\sigma)$$

$$Pr_g(\sigma) = \{A' \subset C/\forall c, d \in A', \exists A \in \sigma \text{ where } c, d \in A \text{ and } g(c) = g(d)\}$$

where g is the cycle's grouping function that depends on the cycle and respects the following definition:

$$g : C \to G$$
$$c \mapsto g(c)$$

G is a set of grouping values such as sites, technical types and risk levels. Thus:

   - The technical grouping function is:

$$tech : C \to T$$
$$c \mapsto tech(c) = tt_c$$

   - The geolocation grouping function is:

$$geo : C \to Ge$$
$$c \mapsto geo(c) = site_c$$

   - The risk level grouping function is:

$$risk : C \to R$$
$$c \mapsto risk(c) = risk_c$$

3. We finally define RIICS as:

$$RIICS_{(S)} : \Sigma_{(S)} \to \Sigma_{(S)}$$
$$\sigma \mapsto Pr_{risk} \circ Pr_{tech} \circ Pr_{geo}$$

Let us assume that $\sigma_{initial}$, is the initial segmentation of the system S, $\sigma_{result} = RIICS_{(S)}(\sigma_{initial})$, is the result of the application of RIICS on the system S.

Application Example

As an application example of the segmentation phase, let us assume that we have the modeled system of Fig. 5. The example IICS system consists of a Corporate sub-system and an industrial system geographically divided into two sites. The corporate system belongs to the first site and only contains one ERP and one CRM. They are connected to the SCADA Server and historian from the ICS system of the first site. For simplicity, we assume that the components risks are already evaluated as depicted by the Figure. The technical types are assigned based on the definitions provided in Sect. 3.2. For example, ERP and CRM are IT components, whereas, SCADA Servers, PLCs, sensors and actuators are OT components. The segmentation is then straightforwardly done in 3 steps as illustrated by the figure.

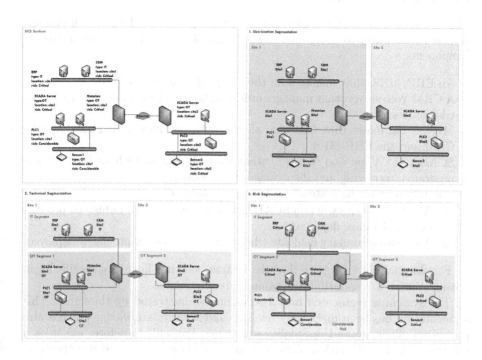

Fig. 5. Application example

1. The first step consists of grouping components by their geo-location. The system is composed of two geographical sites, therefore, we obtain two geographical segments.
2. Next, we group components according to their technical types inside the already identified geographical segments. The first geographical segment is then divided into two technical segments (one for IT components, and another for OT components). Whereas, the second geographical segment remains unchanged because it only contains OT components.
3. Finally, components are grouped based on their risk inside the already identified segments. Only one risk based segment is then added inside the "OT Segment 1". The other risk based segments are identical to the previously identified segments.

4   Tests and Validation

In order to validate our method, we carried out a validation test. The principle is to compare the results obtained by our method to a segmentation made over time (without a method) on a test system. The test system and the validation criteria will be presented later in this paper.

4.1   The Test System

The test system is illustrated by Fig. 6. It is based on a real system in production. It consists of two geographically separate sites and includes the following components:

- An ERP/MES: that manages all the company's resources.
- A CRM Web server: that manages orders, validates them, and launches industrial processes.
- MySQL database: that Contains all the business data. It is shared by the CRM and the ERP-MES.
- SCADA (PCView and WinCC): that controls PLCs, such as loading new programs, retrieving and displaying information. . .
- The ICS part of the system consists of two field sites.
  1. A main field site where a SCADA network and a set of industrial production devices are deployed.
  2. A remote secondary field site where a remote production unit is deployed.

For simplicity, we suppose that the system does not have any specific legal, organizational or responsibilities grouping requirements.

The system is segmented into 3 segments as illustrated by the figure. This segmentation has been made only by skills and security knowledge but has also proven its efficiency and optimality over time. We will, therefore, use it as a reference for our validation tests. For more readability, we will use the term *Ex-Segmentation* to refer to this existing segmentation.

4.2   Test Methodology

The test plan consists of applying our segmentation method on our test system and comparing the results with the *Ex-Segmentation*.

This allows us to validate our method on a real existing system with effective segmentation under real conditions and on a long term basis. However, this approach has the disadvantage of being very expensive and inflexible because creating a good test system is time-consuming and finding existing test systems is not easy.

Validation Criteria

In order to compare the results obtained by RIICS with the *Ex-Segmentation*, we used the concept of **Segmentation efficiency and accuracy**. It is a new comparison metric we defined.

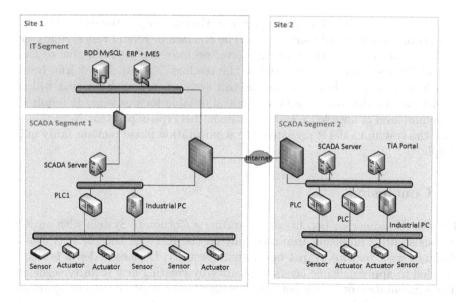

Fig. 6. The IIC test system

The efficiency of a method on a set of test systems is the mean of the accuracy of the results obtained for each system. A result's accuracy depends on how much the result is similar to the expected one. In our case, a segmentation's result's accuracy is a function of the distance between the segmentation obtained using RIICS and the *Ex-Segmentation*. The distance between two segmentations of a same system is the minimum cost to transform a segmentation into the other one by performing a set of only the following actions:

- Move only one component at a time from one segment to another.
- Remove one segment
- Merge two segments

Each action has a cost of 1. For example, the distance between two segmentations, where it is necessary to move two components of their segments, is equal to 2. Accuracy is calculated based on the distance using the following formula:

$$accuracy = \frac{1}{1 + distance}$$

When two segmentations are the same, the distance between them equals 0, the accuracy then equals 1 (the maximum value). On the other hand, when distance increases, the accuracy decreases towards 0.

4.3   Results and Discussion

The application of RIICS to the test system resulted in a segmentation similar to the *Ex-Segmentation* (Fig. 6). The distance between the two segmentations is equal to zero. This result does not guarantee the efficiency of the method because it was obtained with only one system. The creation of several test systems with an Ex-Segmentation being very expensive, we have not yet been able to carry out all the tests necessary to validate the method. Nevertheless, initial results remain encouraging. Furthermore, the test system's risk analysis, that will not be detailed in this paper, is clearly not affordable for everyone. It requires a minimum level of knowledge and expertise in this type of practice. Nevertheless, once the system model is prepared, the segmentation phase remains fairly quite simple.

5   Conclusion

Despite the numerous benefits of integrating a Corporate System with an ICS, serious security problems arise especially on the ICS side because it is usually designed with very low, if not nonexistent, security. Defense-in-depth is recommended to apply multiple layers of security by creating new security segments. The segmentation of IICS is not trivial as they have heterogeneous configurations and much specificity.

This paper presents RIICS, a new IICS segmentation method that aims to ensure efficient zoning to meet actual security needs of IICS. It is based on a risk analysis and a meta-model that helps to model systems. Systems models are used by the method to delineate security zones by grouping components of the same characteristics. We agree that the risk analysis requires some level of expertise to be conducted, however the segmentation phase is very simple.

We carried out a validation test to validate our method results. The first results were rather accurate. However, we still have many more tests to do before we can confirm the effectiveness of the method. It is especially necessary to apply the method to a variety of systems with different configuration and various functional and business specificities. The cost of finding or creating test systems remains, however, significantly high.

Note that RIICS is also applicable to Information Systems (without any industrial system), because it is generic and because IS are subsystems of IICS. Furthermore, RIICS could be improved by including segregation concepts to provide more guidance for inter-zones flows protection.

References

1. Cai, N., Wang, J., Yu, X.: SCADA system security: complexity, history and new developments. In: 6th IEEE International Conference on Industrial Informatics (2008)
2. Stouffer, K., Lightman, S., Pillitteri, V., Abrams, M., Hahn, A.: Guide to industrial control systems (ICS) security. In: NIST Special Publication, vol. 800, no. 82 (2015)
3. Pires, P.S.M., Oliveira, L.A.H.G.: Security aspects of SCADA and corporate network interconnection: an overview. In: IEEE International Conference on Dependability of Computer Systems, pp. 127–134 (2006)

4. ANSSI: Classification Method and Key Measure (2013)
5. ANSSI: Detailed Measures (2013)
6. CSSP, DHS: Recommended practice: improving industrial control systems cybersecurity with defense-in-depth strategies US-CERT Defense In Depth, October 2009
7. Security for Industrial Automation and Control Systems: Terminology, Concepts, and Models.: Howpublished. ISA-99 Standard 62443-1-1 (Draft2, Edit4) (2013)
8. Enterprise - Control System Integration. Part 2: Object Model Attributes. ISA-95 Standard 95.00.02 (Draft 9) (2001)
9. Enterprise - Control System Integration Part 3: Activity Models of Manufacturing Operations Management: Howpublished. ISA-95 Standard 95.00.03 (Draft 16), 2004
10. Enterprise - Control System Integration Part 1: Models and Terminology: Howpublished. ISA-dS95 Standard (Draft 14) (1999)
11. Obregon, L.: Secure Architecture for Industrial Control Systems. SANS Institute, InfoSec Reading Room (2015)
12. Zerbst, J.-T., Hjelmvik, E., Rinta-Jouppi, I.: Zoning Principles in Electricity Distribution and Energy Production Environments. In: 20th International Conference on Electricity Distribution (2009)
13. Khaoula, E., David, E., Nora, C.: A new segmentation method for integrated ICS. In: The Fifteenth International Conference on Privacy, Security and Trust (PST) (2017). IEEE Commun. Surv. Tutor. (2013)
14. Network Segmentation for Industrial Control Environments. Wurldtech, AGE, March 2016
15. Mahan, R.E., et al.: Secure data transfer guidance for industrial control and SCADA systems. Report to US Department of Energy, PNNL-20776 (2011)
16. De la Défense Nationale, Secrétariat Général: EBIOS-Expression des Besoins et Identification des Objectifs de Sécurité, Méthode de Gestion des risques (2010)
17. Unver, H.O.: An ISA-95-based manufacturing intelligence system in support of lean initiatives. Int. J. Adv. Manuf. Technol. **65**(5–8), 853–866 (2013)

Effectiveness and Impact Measurements of a Diversification Based Moving Target Defense

Manel Smine[(✉)], Nora Cuppens, and Frédéric Cuppens

IMT Atlantique, Brest, France
{manel.smine,nora.cuppens,frederic.cuppens}@imt-atlantique.fr

Abstract. Moving Target Defense techniques have been proposed to increase uncertainty and apparent complexity for attackers. In this paper, we first study the related work on quantification effectiveness and the impact of a diversification based MTD techniques. Then, we propose a new model that relies mainly on the knowledge that the adversary has about the target system to compute the effectiveness and the impact and also to figure out the optimal MTD diversification of a target system.

Keywords: Moving Target Defense ·
Effectiveness and impact quantification · Optimal diversification

1 Introduction

At the present time, enterprise networks use technologies which are implemented to satisfy business needs such as data processing, communication and customer support. Administrators of enterprise network are supposed to keep access lists to add or remove users, avoid potential intrusions by scanning the system and limit communications between the Internet and internal hosts by modifying the rules of firewalls. Once the system is deployed, updating the system is complex task which forces the administrators to change the configuration less often, which leaves the configuration unchanged for a long period of time. Therefore, attackers will have an asymmetric advantage due to the static nature of enterprise networks. Attackers will generally have as much time as necessary to perform target network reconnaissance (e.g., networks, services, etc.). Attackers will also have enough time to study and determine the potential vulnerabilities of enterprise networks, launch the attack at the best time and eventually maintaining a backdoor without being discovered for a long period of time.

An approach called Moving Target Defense (MTD) has been proposed in [1,2] as a concept that aims to control the changes in systems or infrastructures in order to: (1) increase the complexity of performing attacks for attackers through increasing their uncertainty about the target system or infrastructure, and (2) reduce the window in which the information the adversary has already collected about the target system are useful to perform attacks against it.

A. Zemmari et al. (Eds.): CRiSIS 2018, LNCS 11391, pp. 158–171, 2019.
https://doi.org/10.1007/978-3-030-12143-3_14

A diversification based MTD approach can be used to change the aspects and the configurations of a system to present a variable attack surface to the attackers. The key aspect in diversification consists of the ability to introduce the same functionality while slightly varying the internal software or using unique variants of a piece of software. The idea is to create space from which we can make a selection to change/diversify a property of the considered system. This is the case for IP addresses, memory space as well as port numbers. A diversification example can be the change of the port number for SSH service from the standard port number 22 to another port number. This will make more difficult for an attacker who targets the SSH service to find it since he/she needs to scan all open ports.

One of the main challenges is how to quantify the effectiveness and the impact of a diversification based MTD technique. In this paper, we propose a model for quantifying the effectiveness and the impact of a diversification based MTD technique which can be used to figure out the optimal MTD diversification of the target system. The rest of this paper is organized as follows: Sect. 2 studies the related work of the MTD quantification. Section 3 proposes a new model for an MTD quantification of the effectiveness and the impact which can figure out an optimal diversification. Finally, Sect. 4 concludes the work.

2 Related Work

Evaluating defense strategies against attacks relies traditionally on game based intrusion evaluation [4,6,10]. These works provided a general framework for evaluating attack and defense strategies, however, they are not useful for quantifying the efficiency and impact of diversification-based moving target defense.

Several research in measurement of the quantification of the effectiveness of a MTDs has been done. In [12], Zhuang et al. proposed a model for quantifying the effectiveness of diversification-based MTDs by measuring attacker success rate for various settings of the target system before and after the diversification. In [3], Collins proposed a means for evaluating the strength of network-based moving target defenses by measuring the attacker success rate over time. Peng et al. [9] model a Cloud-based service with several heterogeneous and dynamic attack surfaces and used a probabilistic service deployment strategy that exploits attack surfaces heterogeneity for making the considered service more resilient against attacks. Peng et al. [9] quantifies the efficiency of their approach by measuring considered service survival rate over time.

Zaffarano et al. [11] proposed a model for defining and measuring MTD effects applied to a network environment. The proposed approach uses several metrics: (1) productivity metric that measures the completion rates of both users tasks and attack tasks, (2) success metric that quantifies the number of succeeded tasks and attacks, (3) confidentiality metric that measures how much tasks information is exposed to eavesdroppers and how much attacks tasks can be detected, and (4) integrity metric which quantifies how much tasks information is transmitted without modification or corruption as well as the accuracy of the information viewed by an adversary. The main limitation of this quantification approach is that, regardless which target system is considered, users tasks and attacks have the same importance in the different proposed quantification metrics. We will show later that both the impacts of attacks and the importance of the hosted services could vary regarding the target system.

Another multi-dimensional metric was introduced by Jafarian et al. in [8] which measures MTDs based on 3 metrics: (1) deterrence metric that measures the cost for the attacker in terms of additional time taken to perform an attack, (2) deception metric which quantifies the ratio of failed attacks due to effects of an MTD, and (3) detectability metric which measures the ratio of the number of probes required with an active MTD to the number of probes required in the static case. The proposed model is particularly useful to quantify the effectiveness of MTDs for disrupting and delaying attackers rather than quantifying their effectiveness in strict prevention of attacks.

In [5], Connell proposed a model for quantifying the efficiency of moving target defense diversification-based mechanisms. The proposed model is composed of 4 layers:

- The service layer that represents the set of services to be protected
- A weakness layer that represents the vulnerabilities that may be exploited
- A knowledge layer that represents the knowledge that an adversary should have to exploit a vulnerability
- An MTD layer that represents the available MTD techniques

By expressing the effects that MTDs have on required knowledge as a probability, they propagate those values to also calculate the chances of a software weakness being exploited and determine an overall value for the effectiveness of the MTD. This model seems to be interesting, however, it is based on a strong hypothesis since it requires the knowledge of all the target system vulnerabilities and possible attacks that can exploit them. We believe that if the set of all target system vulnerabilities are known, it is better to correct them rather than using an MTD based approach, to prevent an attacker from exploiting them. In addition, the proposed model does not take into consideration vulnerabilities that can be possibly discovered (i.e., Zero days vulnerabilities).

More recently, [5] proposes a framework that measures how different MTD techniques can affect the information an attacker needs to exploit a system's vulnerabilities so as to introduce uncertainty and reduce the likelihood of successful attacks. Authors shows that their model can be used to compare two sets of MTDs and to select an optimal set of MTDs that maximize security. The main drawbacks of the proposed model is that: (1) it does not take into consideration the impact that MTD techniques may have on the target system, and (2) the model requires the knowledge of the target system's vulnerabilities to be able to quantify MTDs ensured security levels.

The model we proposed in this paper overcomes most of the limitations of previously mentioned approaches. First, instead of considering that all attacks have the same impact on the target system [11], our model offers the possibility to associate a weight for each attack that will represent the impact that the attack would have in the target system. The efficiency of a diversification-based MTD depends then on the weights of the attacks that are prevented. Second, instead of relying on the knowledge of all the vulnerabilities of the target system to quantify an MTD efficiency [5], our model relies on the set of a well known attacks (e.g., DoS, Men in the middle, SQL injection, etc.) to be specified by the security administrator and that should be prevented on the target system. Third, differently to the approaches [3,5,8,9], our model quantifies the impact (i.e., the bad effects of the application of MTDs) of the application of MTDs on the functioning of the target system.

3 The Quantification Model

In this section, we present our model to compute the effectiveness and the impact of an MTD-diversification based approach.

3.1 MTD Effectiveness

Our model relies mainly on the knowledge that the adversary has about the target system in order to quantify the amount by which adversary knowledge about the target system is reduced after applying the diversification.

The knowledge $\mathcal{K}_{\mathcal{A}}$ that an adversary $\mathcal{A}$ can have about the system is described in the following definition.

Table 1. List of properties of an infrastructure

Server	Network	Router
OS version	Network IP address	Router IP addresses
List of services	Number of routers	Ports
List of open ports	Number of subnets	Security group
Mac address	Routes	
IP address	Number of active servers	

Definition 1 (Adversary Knowledge). *Given an infrastructure $\mathcal{I}$. The knowledge of an adversary $\mathcal{A}$ about the target system $\mathcal{I}$ is*

$$\mathcal{K}_{\mathcal{A}}^{\mathcal{I}} = \{(p_1, v_1), \cdots, (p_n, v_n)\}$$

where:

- *p_i is a property of $\mathcal{I}$,*
- *v_i is the true value of the property p_i in $\mathcal{I}$.*

We denote $\mathcal{P}_{\mathcal{K}_{\mathcal{A}}^{\mathcal{I}}} = \{p_1, \cdots, p_n\}$ the set of properties which the adversary $\mathcal{A}$ knows their values in $\mathcal{I}$.

Depending on the strategy used to activate the MTD diversification-based technique (i.e., proactive or reactive strategy), adversary knowledge about the target system can be differently computed. If a proactive strategy is considered, MTD techniques are launched at will, the worst case is then to be considered, that is, the adversary is supposed to know each single information about the target system. However, if a reactive strategy is used, that is, MTD is launched on environmental information changes, such as the detection of abnormal actions, then the adversary knowledge could be estimated by analyzing the tasks (e.g., scanning, fingerprinting, etc.) that was performed by an adversary to collect information about the target system. To illustrate, let us consider that scanning and fingerprinting operations were detected, we suppose that the adversary knows IP addresses and port numbers of all services running in the target system. Moreover, we consider that the adversary knows the operating system versions of all the machines running in the target network.

Table 1 describes some of the properties that an adversary will try to gather their values in an infrastructure. In fact, the importance of the knowledge of each property may differ according to the goal of the adversary. To capture the importance of the knowledge of each property, we will use the set of attacks against which the administrator wants to protect the set of hosted infrastructures. For that, we will suppose that the set of attack families that the system should be protected against is to be specified by the security administrator of the target system.

Definition 2 (Attack required property). *Given an infrastructure $\mathcal{I}$ having a set of properties $\mathcal{P}_{\mathcal{I}}$ and an attack θ. θ-required properties $\mathcal{P}_\theta$ are a set of properties in $\mathcal{P}_{\mathcal{I}}$ whose knowledge are required to perform θ on $\mathcal{I}$.*

We give the following example to illustrate the previous definition.

Example 1. Consider an Infrastructure $\mathcal{I}$ containing a web server and database services and having the following set of properties:

- IP_w: the IP address of the server hosting the web service
- P_w: the port of the web service in the server hosting it
- IP_n: the gateway IP address of the network containing the servers hosting the services
- IP_d: the IP address of the server hosting the database service
- P_d: the port of the database service in the server hosting it.

Let us suppose that an adversary wants to perform a Denial of service (DoS) over the database service. Since, it is required to know the IP address and the port of the target service to perform a DoS attack, then the required properties $\mathcal{P}_{DoS}$ for performing a DoS over the database service are $\mathcal{P}_{DoS} = \{IP_d, P_d\}$.

It is obvious that the effects of an attack differ from a target system to another. To illustrate, let us take the two following use cases in which we consider two attacks: DoS and SQL injection.

- Let's consider a first use case in which a database is used to store information about users purchases such as purchased items, total amount of paid money and the number of credit card used to purchase the bought items. As we know, DoS does not have much impact since the collected information can be saved later by always keeping them in a register or a memory until the return of the service availability, or by using a backup database server. However, if the attacker succeeds in retrieving information from the database using SQL injection, specifically the credit card numbers, it is disastrous for the client and for the reputation of the company. So, clearly SQL injection attack impacts are much more important than the impacts that can cause a DoS attack.
- In the second use case, we suppose a target system that uses a database to save stock market data used by the system users to buy and sell securities, such as shares of stock and bonds and other financial instruments. By taking into consideration the fact that the data contained in the database are publicly available, so the impact of getting the information stored in the database via SQL injection in this case is not so important. But if the attacker succeeds to make the database server inaccessible by performing a DoS over the server, it might be very harmful for target system users since they will not be able to access the values of their interactions and cannot get the values of their actions which may make them losing a lot of money.

We believe that a good MTD quantification model should allow the administrator of this target system to specify the impact importance of each considered attack regarding the other attacks. To the best of our knowledge, our model is the first that considers the severity of the set of attacks to prevent in the quantification of the MTDs efficiency.

Definition 3 (Attacks weights).   *Given a target system $\mathcal{I}$ and the set of attacks that should be prevented $\Theta = \{\theta_1, \cdots, \theta_n\}$. We will assume that a weight w_{θ_i} is assigned to each attack θ_i such that:*

$$\sum_{i=1}^{n} w_{\theta_i} = 1$$

We expect attacks weights to reflect the severity of the impact of each attack on the target system. The greater the severity of the attack, the greater the weight assigned to the attack.

Definition 4 (Weight property).   *Given a target system $\mathcal{I}$ having a set of properties $\mathcal{P}_\mathcal{I} = \{p_1, \cdots, p_n\}$. Let us suppose that $\Theta = \{\theta_1, \cdots, \theta_m\}$ is the set of attacks to prevent in $\mathcal{I}$ and that each θ_i has a weight w_{θ_i}. The weight of each property $p_i \in \mathcal{P}_\mathcal{I}$ is:*

$$w_{p_i} = \frac{\displaystyle\sum_{p_i \in \mathcal{P}_{\theta_i}} w_{\theta_i}}{\displaystyle\sum_{p_i \in \mathcal{P}} \left(\sum_{\theta_i \in \Theta_{\mathcal{P}_i}} w_{\theta_i} \right)}$$

where $\mathcal{P}_{\theta_i}$ is θ-required properties (Definition 2) and $\Theta_{\mathcal{P}_i}$ is the set of attack that requires $\mathcal{P}_i$.

To illustrate property weight computation, we give the following example.

Example 2. Let us consider the same Infrastructure $\mathcal{I}$ and properties as in Example 1. Let us suppose that the administrator of $\mathcal{I}$ wants to prevent the following attacks:

- θ_{DoS}: DoS over the hosted services in $\mathcal{I}$. We suppose that its weight w_{DoS} is equal to 1/5.
- θ_{MIM}: Man in the middle attack (ARP spoofing) over the server hosting the web service. We suppose that its weight w_{MIM} is equal to 4/5.

Then, the weight of the property representing the IP address of the web server IP_w of $\mathcal{I}$ is the number of attacks that requires IP_w which are MIM and DoS attacks, and we divide that by the number of attacks required for all the properties in the target system. As a result, the weight of the property IP_w is:

$$w_{IP_w} = \frac{w_{DoS} + w_{MIM}}{w_{DoS} + w_{MIM} + 3 \times w_{DoS} + w_{MIM}}$$
$$= 5/12$$

and the weight of the property representing the port of the database service P_d of $\mathcal{I}$ is:

$$w_{P_d} = \frac{w_{DoS}}{w_{DoS} + w_{MIM} + 3 \times w_{DoS} + w_{MIM}}$$
$$= 1/12$$

Definition 5 (MTD efficiency). *Given a set of attacks Θ, an adversary $\mathcal{A}$, and an infrastructure $\mathcal{I}$ that is diversified to $\mathcal{I}'$ using a diversification-based MTD approach $\mathcal{M}$. The efficiency $\mathcal{E}_{\mathcal{M}}^+$ of $\mathcal{M}$ to prevent the adversary $\mathcal{A}$ to perform the set of attacks in Θ is quantified as follows:*

$$\mathcal{E}_{\mathcal{M}}^+ = \sum_{p_i \in \mathcal{P}_{\mathcal{K}_{\mathcal{A}}^{\mathcal{I}}} \setminus \mathcal{P}_{\mathcal{K}_{\mathcal{A}}^{\mathcal{I}'}}} w_{p_i}$$

where $\mathcal{P}_{\mathcal{K}_{\mathcal{A}}^{\mathcal{I}}} \setminus \mathcal{P}_{\mathcal{K}_{\mathcal{A}}^{\mathcal{I}'}}$ represents the set of properties whose values in $\mathcal{I}$ are known to $\mathcal{A}$ and their values in $\mathcal{I}'$ are unknown to $\mathcal{A}$.

Example 3. We will use the same configurations as in Example 1. That is, we consider the same Infrastructure $\mathcal{I}$ and properties as in Example 1 and we suppose that the administrator of $\mathcal{I}$ wants to prevent the following attacks:

- θ_{DoS}: DoS over the hosted services in $\mathcal{I}$
- θ_{MIM}: Man in the middle attack (ARP spoofing) over the server hosting the web service.

Using Definition 4, we get:

$$w_{IP_w} = 5/12, \quad w_{IP_d} = w_{P_w} = w_{P_d} = 1/12 \ \ and \ \ w_{IP_n} = 1/3 \qquad (1)$$

Let us suppose now that we have applied a diversification-based MTD approach $\mathcal{M}$ on $\mathcal{I}$ to create the infrastructure $\mathcal{I}'$. The mechanism $\mathcal{M}$ does the following:

- Randomly choose a new address IP for the server hosting the web service.
- Randomly change the gateway IP of the network that hosted the two servers.

We will suppose that the adversary $\mathcal{A}$ knows all the properties of $\mathcal{I}$ ($\mathcal{P}_{K_{\mathcal{A}}^{\mathcal{I}}} = \{IP_w, IP_d, P_w, P_d, IP_n\}$). Let us now suppose that $\mathcal{I}$ is replaced by $\mathcal{I}'$. Since the value of the two properties IP_w and IP_n was randomly replaced in $\mathcal{I}'$, then the set of property that $\mathcal{A}$ knows about $\mathcal{I}'$ is:

$$\mathcal{P}_{K_{\mathcal{A}}^{\mathcal{I}'}} = \{IP_d, P_w, P_d\} \qquad (2)$$

Then using Definition 5 with (1) and (2) we can quantify the efficiency of $\mathcal{M}$ as:

$$\mathcal{E}_{\mathcal{M}}^+ = 5/12 + 1/3 = 3/4.$$

Our model for quantification of the efficiency of a diversification-based MTD techniques is based mainly on the knowledge the adversary has about the target system before the application of the diversification technique. In reactive strategies, the knowledge of the adversary about the target system could be calculated based on the observed events, such as network scanning, port scanning, OS fingerprinting, and so on. However, this will not be possible when considering a proactive strategy. To overcome this limitation, once we decide that it is time to diversify the system, we will consider that the adversary knows all the properties of the system to be diversified.

Semantically, MTDs efficiency quantification computed by our model could be directly transformed to an attack probability measurement. Under the hypothesis that all the properties required by considered attacks are correctly specified in our model, that is every target system property that could be used to perform an attack θ should be part of the set of required property $\mathcal{P}_\theta$, an efficiency measurement represents theoretically a probability of $1/4$ that the considered attacks (the attacks that the system target administrator wants to prevent) can still be performed by the adversary. In proactive strategies, the computed attacks applicability probability (i.e., efficiency) holds just after the application of the used diversification-based MTD technique. However, it is not possible to guarantee the same attacks applicability probability over the time since, in proactive strategy, we are not expecting to know the set of actions performed by the adversary in the target system. In the other side, if a reactive strategy is considered, it is possible to measure the change of the attacks applicability probability by observing the actions that the adversary is performing in the target system. Once the attacks applicability probability exceeds a specific threshold, the target system should again be diversified.

3.2 MTD Application Impact

The application of MTD technique over a system may have an impact on its correct functioning. As far as we know, no impact quantification model has been proposed in the literature for MTD-based approaches. In this section, we propose a new model for quantifying the impact of the application of an MTD-based approach over a system. We argue that our impact quantification model can measure the impact of any MTD-based technique over any kind of system.

In our proposed model, two kinds of impact are considered: a functional impact and a continuity of service impact. The functional impact quantifies the magnitude by which system services may deviate from their correct functioning. The continuity of service impact computes the period of inaccessibility of the target system services during the application of the MTD-based technique.

Functional Impact

Definition 6 (Service required configuration). *Given a service S that is running in a platform. S-required configurations C_s are a set of configurations that are required for a correct working of the service.*

In fact, the required configuration could be seen as a relationship between a property as introduced in Sect. 3.1 and a constraint. To illustrate the previous definition, we give the following example.

Example 4. Consider an infrastructure $\mathcal{I}$ containing a web service. Suppose that the web service users are always using the port 80 to access to the web service. In order to preserve the accessibility of the web service to its users, a required configuration is then a relationship between the property P_w representing the port number associated with a web service and the constraint saying P_w should be equal to 80.

As soon as several services are running on the target system. Depending on the considered system, some services might be more important than others. To illustrate, let us take the example of a university information system hosting several services such as mailing, inscription, distance and online courses, video-conferencing, etc. Let us suppose that the access to these services requires the authentication to a Single Sign On service. Clearly, the Single Sign On service should have more importance than other services since, if not provided correctly, the university students and employees cannot use any of the other services.

Definition 7 (Services weights). *Given an infrastructure $\mathcal{I}$ and the set of services that the administrator will consider is $S = \{S_1, \cdots, S_n\}$. We will assume that the weights of these services are values from 0 to 1 such that:*

$$\sum_{i=1}^{n} w_{S_i} = 1$$

Here also, we expect a service weight to reflect the importance of the service for the well functioning of the target system. The more essential the service, the greater its weight.

Naturally, a configuration could be required by one or many services. So, our idea consists of assigning a weight to each configuration regarding the number of constraints that requires it. The following definition describes the computation of the weight of each configuration in the target system.

Definition 8 (Configuration Weight). *Given a target system $\mathcal{I}$ having a set of services $\mathcal{S}_\mathcal{I} = \{S_1, \cdots, S_n\}$, each service S_i ($i \in [1, n]$) has a set of required configurations $\mathcal{C}_{S_i}$. The weight of each configuration $c_i \in \mathcal{I}$ is:*

$$
w_{c_i} = \frac{\displaystyle\sum_{c_i \in \mathcal{C}_{s_i}} w_{\mathcal{S}_i}}{\displaystyle\sum_{c_i \in \mathcal{I}} \left(\sum_{c_i \in \mathcal{C}_{S_i}} w_{\mathcal{S}_i} \right)}
$$

Where $\mathcal{C}_{S_i}$ is S_i-required configurations (Definition 6).

Using the previous definition we ensure that, more a configuration will be required by the services in the target system, more the weight of the configuration will be important. The reason behind the previous choice, is that, if a configuration that is required by many services in the target system is not satisfied after the application of an MTD technique, then we could end up with several functioning problems (several misconfigurations) in the target system. To illustrate, we give the following example.

Example 5. Let us consider an infrastructure $\mathcal{I}$ composed of the following services:

- S_{auth}: A single sign on authentication service. We suppose that the weight $w_{S_{auth}}$ is equal to $1/2$.
- S_{mail}: A mail service. We suppose that the weight $w_{S_{mail}}$ is equal to $1/4$.
- S_{web}: A web service with a weight $w_{S_{web}}$ equals to $1/4$.

We suppose that S_{auth} is used to authenticate the users aiming to access S_{web} and S_{mail}. These users are using the port 80 and 8080 to access S_{web} and S_{mail} respectively. The set of required configurations to be considered in this example are:

- c_1 : The Single Sign On server should be always accessible through the port 443 of the IP address ip_1.
- c_2 : Authentication service IP address ip_1 should be known to S_{web}.
- c_3 : Authentication service IP address ip_1 should be known to S_{mail}.
- c_4 : The port of S_{web} should be 80.
- c_5 : The port of S_{mail} should be 8080.

Table 2. Services' required configurations

Required configuration	Services
c_1	S_{auth}
c_2	S_{web}
c_3	S_{mail}
c_4	S_{web}
c_5	S_{mail}

Table 2 shows for each required configuration, the services that will require it. The weight of each configuration is as following:

$$w_{c_1} = 1/3$$
$$w_{c_2} = 1/6$$
$$w_{c_3} = 1/6$$
$$w_{c_4} = 1/6$$
$$w_{c_5} = 1/6$$

Once we assign a weight to each required configuration in the target system, the *functional impact* of the application of one (or many) MTD technique(s) over the target system represents the sum of weights of the required configuration that are violated by the application of MTD technique. The *functional impact* measurement is formalized as follows.

Definition 9 (Functional impact). *Given a target system $\mathcal{I}$ and an MTD-based technique $\mathcal{M}$. Let us denotes $\mathcal{C}_{\mathcal{I}}$ the set of required configurations needed for a correct functioning of the set of services hosted in $\mathcal{I}$. The functional impact $\mathcal{E}_{\mathcal{M}}^F$ of the application of $\mathcal{M}$ over $\mathcal{I}$ is:*

$$\mathcal{E}_{\mathcal{M}}^F = \sum_{c \in \mathcal{C}_{\mathcal{I}}^*} w_c$$

where $\mathcal{C}_{\mathcal{I}}$ is the set of required configuration in $\mathcal{C}_{\mathcal{I}}^*$ that are violated by the application of $\mathcal{M}$ over $\mathcal{I}$.

We illustrate functional impact measurement through the following example.

Example 6. Let us consider the same target system as the one used in Example 5. Let us suppose that the used diversification-based MTD mechanism changed randomly the port of S_{auth} and S_{web}. The functional impact of the application of the used MTD mechanism on the considered system is:

$$\mathcal{E}_{\mathcal{M}}^F = 1/3 + 1/6 = 1/2$$

Continuity of Service Impact. During the application of MTD techniques, target system services may become inaccessible for a while. A continuity of service impact is the duration on which the services hosted by the target system are inaccessible. This is formalized using the following definition.

Definition 10 (Continuity of service impact). *Given an infrastructure $\mathcal{I}$ hosting a set of services $\mathcal{S}$ and an MTD-based technique $\mathcal{M}$. The continuity of service impact $\mathcal{E}_{\mathcal{M}}^{CS}$ of the application of $\mathcal{M}$ over $\mathcal{I}$ is:*

$$\mathcal{E}_{\mathcal{M}}^{CS} = \sum_{S \in \mathcal{S}} t_S$$

where t_S is the time (in milliseconds) during which the service S is not accessible.

Optimal MTD Diversification. As we have seen, our previously presented model allows measuring the efficiency and the impacts (functional and continuity of service) of the application of an MTD-based diversification technique. Our model can be used to figure out the optimal MTD diversification for the target system. Informally, the optimal MTD diversification is the one that will maximize the MTD efficiency $\mathcal{E}_{\mathcal{M}}^{+}$ (Definition 5) and minimize $\mathcal{E}_{\mathcal{M}}^{F}$ (Definition 9) and $\mathcal{E}_{\mathcal{M}}^{CS}$ (Definition 10). Obviously, finding the optimal diversification is then to find the optimal solution to a Multi-Objective Optimization Problem. It is known that, if some objective functions are conflicting, no single solution exists that simultaneously optimizes each objective. Unfortunately, our problem of finding the optimal diversification involves two conflicting objective functions: maximize the MTD efficiency $\mathcal{E}_{\mathcal{M}}^{+}$ and minimize $\mathcal{E}_{\mathcal{M}}^{F}$. Clearly more the used diversification-based MTD mechanism diversifies the target system, more $\mathcal{E}_{\mathcal{M}}^{+}$ will be high and more $\mathcal{E}_{\mathcal{M}}^{F}$ will be (probably) high (since more we will diversify the target system, more we are likely to modify services required configurations). One way to overcome this difficulty is to use the ϵ-method [7]. That is, we will suppose that the administrator of the target system will specify two maximum thresholds ϵ_F and ϵ_{CS}. ϵ_F will be used to denote the maximum acceptable functional impact that could be occur when using the MTD mechanism. ϵ_{CS} denotes the maximum acceptable discontinuity time of the services running in the target system. Then the optimal diversification can be defined as follows.

Definition 11 (Optimal diversification). *Given an infrastructure $\mathcal{I}$ and a diversification-based MTD mechanism $\mathcal{M}$. Let us denote $\mathcal{P}_\mathcal{I}$ the set of properties of $\mathcal{I}$ to be considered and $\mathcal{D}_p$ the diversification domain of a property $p \in \mathcal{P}_\mathcal{I}$. An optimal diversification is the solution to the following multi-objective optimization problem:*

$$\text{maximize} \quad \mathcal{E}_{\mathcal{M}}^{+}$$
$$\text{s.t.} \quad \mathcal{E}_{\mathcal{M}}^{F} < \epsilon_F$$
$$\mathcal{E}_{\mathcal{M}}^{CS} < \epsilon_{CS}$$
$$\forall p \in \mathcal{P}_\mathcal{I} : v(p) \in \mathcal{D}_p.$$

where $v(p)$ denotes the value of the property p in $\mathcal{I}$.

4   Conclusion

This paper proposes a new model to quantify the effectiveness and the impact of the diversification-based MTD approaches. The proposed model relies on three metrics: (1) the efficiency metric that quantifies how good a diversification-based MTD mechanism is preventing a set of considered attacks, (2) the functional impact metric that measures the magnitude by which system services may deviate from their correct functioning, and (3), the continuity of service impact which measures the period of inaccessibility of the target system services during the application of the MTD-based technique. We showed also how our model can be used to find an optimal diversification that maximizes the efficiency of the MTD mechanism while respecting a fixed function and continuity of service budget. Our proposed model can be used to quantify the impact of any diversification-based MTD mechanism regardless the kind of the considered target system. Currently, some experimentations are in progress to test the quantification of several MTD mechanisms on the different levels of an OpenStack IaaS cloud platform.

References

1. National Cyber Leap Year Summit 2009 Participants' Ideas Report (2009). https://www.qinetiq-na.com/wp-content/uploads/2011/12/National_Cyber_Leap_Year_Summit_2009_Participants_Ideas_Report.pdf. Accessed 19 Apr 2018
2. National Cyber Leap Year Summit Cochair's Report (2009). https://www.qinetiq-na.com/wp-content/uploads/2011/12/National_Cyber_Leap_Year_Summit_2009_CoChairs_Report.pdf. Accessed 19 Apr 2018
3. Collins, M.P.: A cost-based mechanism for evaluating the effectiveness of moving target defenses. In: Grossklags, J., Walrand, J. (eds.) GameSec 2012. LNCS, vol. 7638, pp. 221–233. Springer, Heidelberg (2012). https://doi.org/10.1007/978-3-642-34266-0_13
4. Collins, M., RedJack, L.: Payoff based ids evaluation. In: CSET (2009)
5. Connell, W.J.: A quantitative framework for cyber moving target defenses. Ph.D. thesis, George Mason University (2017)
6. Gaffney, J.E., Ulvila, J.W.: Evaluation of intrusion detectors: a decision theory approach. In: Proceedings of 2001 IEEE Symposium on Security and Privacy, S&P 2001, pp. 50–61. IEEE (2001)
7. Haimes, Y.: On a bicriterion formulation of the problems of integrated system identification and system optimization. IEEE Trans. Syst. Man Cybern. 1(3), 296–297 (1971)
8. Jafarian, J.H.H., Al-Shaer, E., Duan, Q.: Spatio-temporal address mutation for proactive cyber agility against sophisticated attackers. In: Proceedings of the First ACM Workshop on Moving Target Defense, MTD 2014, pp. 69–78. ACM, New York (2014). https://doi.acm.org/10.1145/2663474.2663483
9. Peng, W., Li, F., Huang, C.T., Zou, X.: A moving-target defense strategy for cloud-based services with heterogeneous and dynamic attack surfaces. In: 2014 IEEE International Conference on Communications (ICC), pp. 804–809. IEEE (2014)
10. Stolfo, S.J., Fan, W., Lee, W., Prodromidis, A., Chan, P.K.: Cost-based modeling for fraud and intrusion detection: results from the jam project. Technical report, Department of Computer Science, Columbia University, New York (2000)

11. Zaffarano, K., Taylor, J., Hamilton, S.: A quantitative framework for moving target defense effectiveness evaluation. In: Proceedings of the Second ACM Workshop on Moving Target Defense, MTD 2015, pp. 3–10. ACM, New York (2015). https://doi.acm.org/10.1145/2808475.2808476
12. Zhuang, R., Zhang, S., Bardas, A., DeLoach, S.A., Ou, X., Singhal, A.: Investigating the application of moving target defenses to network security. In: 2013 6th International Symposium on Resilient Control Systems (ISRCS), pp. 162–169. IEEE (2013)

Practical Security Exploits of the FlexRay In-Vehicle Communication Protocol

Pal-Stefan Murvay[(⊠)] and Bogdan Groza

Department of Automation and Applied Informatics,
Politehnica University of Timisoara, Timisoara, Romania
{pal-stefan.murvay,bogdan.groza}@aut.upt.ro

Abstract. The ever increasing number of electronic control units inside a car demanded more complex buses with higher bandwidth capacities. But even the more recently designed in-vehicle network protocols, e.g., FlexRay, were engineered in thse absence of security concerns and thus they are highly vulnerable to adversarial interventions. In this work, we study the FlexRay protocol specification to identify features that can be used to mount various attacks. The attacks exploit both the physical layer and the data-link layer of the protocol to discard messages from the bus, i.e., DoS attacks, or to spoof messages by inserting adversarial frames and later discarding the genuine frames. We illustrate the feasibility of these attacks on an experimental setup composed of several FlexRay nodes implemented on automotive-grade controllers. While these attacks may not be a surprise, recognizing them may be relevant in preventing potential future exploits.

Keywords: Security · FlexRay · Attacks · DoS · Automotive

1   Introduction and Motivation

Modern vehicles are complex systems integrating an ever increasing number of electronic control units (ECUs) interconnected via dedicated communication lines. While the most widely used in-vehicle communication bus is still the decades old CAN (Controller Area Network), FlexRay was designed as the bus for future automotive applications. Indeed, FlexRay supports high data rates of up to 10 Mbit/s in contrast to the 1 Mbit/s of the regular CAN bus and is deterministic in nature which makes it suitable for hard real-time applications, e.g., x-by-wire technologies that are replacing regular mechanical interfaces.

Denial-of-service (DoS) attacks are a common concern for computer networks. For in-vehicle networks however, these were generally neglected from the same reasons as security was ignored: in-vehicle networks were perceived as isolated from outsiders. Today we are aware that this is not so as recent research demonstrated attacks that can be carried out from the outside over in-vehicle buses, e.g., [4,12].

In previous work we have already explored DoS attacks on the CAN protocol which were triggered by directly controlling the physical bus signaling from the

© Springer Nature Switzerland AG 2019
A. Zemmari et al. (Eds.): CRiSIS 2018, LNCS 11391, pp. 172–187, 2019.
https://doi.org/10.1007/978-3-030-12143-3_15

application layer [13]. Similar DoS attacks on the CAN bus were also shown in [15] while the work in [5] only focuses on targeted DoS attacks by placing specific CAN nodes in the bus-off state. All these attacks exploit the CAN error handling mechanism and may have severe consequences as a targeted DoS attack on a specific node may further facilitate impersonation attacks. Such attacks are easy to mount on the CAN bus since the error confinement mechanism is built to isolate faulty nodes and reacts on malformed frames. Even at the time of our previous work it was apparent to us that similar attacks can be mounted on FlexRay but the denser protocol specification made it less obvious how easy is to deploy the attacks. As we later discuss in the related work section, attacks on the FlexRay network were suggested as early as the work in [16] and even demonstrated almost a decade ago by the authors in [14] via a FlexRay simulation in CANoe. But since then, these attacks appear to be somewhat neglected. We were able to find more recent results only in [7] where a man-in-the-middle adversary for FlexRay is discussed. We contribute to these by giving more practical insights and experimental results on DoS attacks and frame spoofing on FlexRay by using a Freescale (NXP) evaluation board. In Table 1 we give a summary of the attacks that are tested in our work, more details will be given in the forthcoming sections.

Table 1. Summary of potential attacks on FlexRay (tested on the Freescale (NXP) evaluation board)

Attack	Static Segment	Dynamic Segment
DoS-full	Yes, required adversary actions: i) place the bus in a dominant state (physical layer) or, ii) break synchronization by sending frames in occupied slots (data-link layer)	
DoS-targeted	Yes, required adversary actions: same as full DoS i) or ii) for specific frames	Yes* *only if frame occurrence is predictable
Msg. spoof	No* *collisions lead to unpredictable bus state	Yes*, required adversary actions: redefine messages in own comm. cycle * may result in collisions, i.e., targeted DoS

1.1 Related Work

Security in automotive networks was intensely studied in recent years. Most of the research done in this area had CAN as the main focus since it is the most widely used communication technology for in-vehicle networks. CAN was proved to be vulnerable to replay and spoofing attacks which are easy to mount once access is gained to the in-vehicle network [4,11,12]. Moreover, due to its arbitration and fault confinement mechanisms CAN is susceptible to denial of service attacks (DoS) [13].

One of the first mentions of security issues regarding the FlexRay protocol were made by Wolf et al. which briefly mentions several potential attacks

[16]. The first requires the exploitation of the bus guardian for disabling targeted nodes by sending faked error messages. This is not an immediate threat since the bus guardian specification is still preliminary and, to the best of our knowledge, there exists no bus guardian implementation in use. The second mentioned attack, which we investigate in more detail in our work, refers to impeding communication by causing loss of synchronization. Finally, the third proposed attack involves disabling nodes with power saving capabilities by sending malicious messages to force them enter sleep mode. No experiments are provided to demonstrate the attacks, but outlining them is valuable.

In the work done by Nilsson et al. [14] the FlexRay protocol specification is analysed in search of security mechanisms for providing basic security objectives. Such mechanisms are clearly not present in FlexRay since security was not considered when designing this protocol. Furthermore, they employ a simulated environment in CANoe to prove that mounting read and spoofing attacks on FlexRay is an easy task. As we discuss in Sect. 3, this kind of attack is only possible in certain situations since otherwise it may result in collisions on the bus.

A more recent study [7] shows how an adversary listening to a FlexRay network can estimate communication parameters having only the bit rate as a priori knowledge. The same work investigates the possibility of man-in-the-middle attacks on FlexRay nodes by interposing a malicious device between the network and the target node. Although efficient, this type of attack requires more complex equipments and physical access that is not always available. Our attacks are simply implemented at the software layer of automotive-grade controllers.

1.2 Paper Organization

Section 2 introduces the theoretical concepts behind the FlexRay protocol focusing on general aspects of the specification. Particular FlexRay behaviour and features enabling attacks are presented and discussed in Sect. 3 which is dedicated to the protocol security analysis for a better understanding of the attacks they make possible. The attacks presented in Sect. 3 are put into practice and analysed in terms of feasibility in the experimental Sect. 4. Finally, Sect. 5 presents the conclusions of our work.

2 FlexRay Protocol Fundamentals

The FlexRay protocol was developed by the FlexRay consortium founded by several major automotive OEMs (Original Equipment Manufacturers) later joined by electronics manufacturers. The latest specification version published by the consortium in 2010, before being transferred to an ISO standard, is 3.0.1. and includes information on the physical layer [1] and the actual protocol specification [2]. Currently the FlexRay protocol specification is provided as the multi-part standard ISO 17458. Part 1 [8] of the standard covers general aspects of the protocol like use case scenarios and terminology, while parts 2 [9] and 4 [10] cover the FlexRay data link layer and physical layer respectively.

Given its intended use for high performance and safety-critical applications FlexRay was designed to provide deterministic, fault tolerant and high-speed data transmission. Deterministic communication is assured by employing a time-triggered communication model while fault tolerance is provided through communication channel redundancy as two independent channels are supported. Each of the two channels available on FlexRay capable nodes can achieve bit rates of up to 10 Mbit/s. When communication redundancy is not required, the two channels can be used for simultaneous data transmission increasing the bit rate up to 20 Mbit/s.

2.1   Communication Architecture

By specification FlexRay is not limited to a certain network topology. It can be used to implement point-to-point communication as well as bus, passive or active star and even hybrid network topologies. The active star topology is implemented by the use of an active star coupler which improves protection against error propagation, allowing the disconnection of faulty nodes.

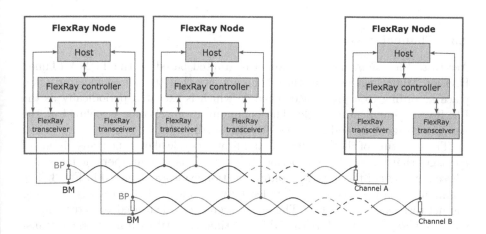

Fig. 1. FlexRay nodes connected in a bus topology

As illustrated in Fig. 1, each FlexRay node consists of a transceiver, controller and host. The transceiver or bus driver is responsible with the physical layer signaling part of the FlexRay communication stack while the controller implements the protocol logic corresponding to the data link layer. All higher level logic has to be implemented in the host application.

2.2 Physical Signaling

FlexRay uses a two line differential interface to implement the physical signaling. The FlexRay transmission medium consist of a pair of twisted lines denoted as *BP* (bus plus) and *BM* (bus minus) which must be fitted with proper termination at its ends. The FlexRay physical signaling is based on four line levels, as illustrated in Fig. 2, two recessive levels to signal low power or idle mode and two dominant levels representing the two logical line levels: *Data_0* (logical zero) and *Data_1* (logical one).

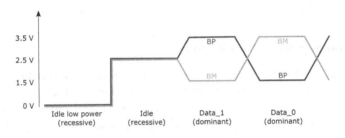

Fig. 2. FlexRay physical bus levels

2.3 Channel Access

Access to the communication channel is granted based on the TDMA (Timed Division Multiple Access) method. This implies that the communication takes place according to a predefined schedule which is executed periodically as the FlexRay communication cycle. The communication schedule is defined at the network design time and must be followed by all nodes.

The structure of the FlexRay communication cycle allows the transmission of messages that have to be sent periodically as well as sending sporadic messages. These segments of the FlexRay communication cycle are depicted in Fig. 3. The communication cycle consists of at least two segments, the static segment and the network idle time (NIT). The static segment is dedicated to deterministic message transmission, while the NIT is a time interval with no message transmission required for clock synchronization. Two other optional segments can be also present in the communication cycle, the dynamic segment and the symbol window. The dynamic segment is used for event-triggered message transmission and must always follow the static segment. The symbol window is used to signal specific FlexRay activities such as communication wake-up or a node joining the communication by the use of special bit sequences called symbols.

The bulk of the FlexRay communication occurs during the static and dynamic (if present) segments. The static segment consists of a number of static slots equal in length that can be assigned to periodic messages. The static segment can hold at most 1023 static slots and must be configured to accommodate at least 2 slots. The messages that must be transmitted in the dynamic segment

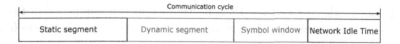

Fig. 3. Components of the FlexRay communication cycle

also have to be defined in the communication schedule. They will only be transmitted if the event triggering their transmission occurs in this segment. The dynamic segment always has the same length. Therefore, if the allocated time interval is not enough to accommodate all dynamic messages marked for sending in the current cycle then the unsent messages will be deferred to the next cycle. Transmission priority in the dynamic segment is based on the message schedule such that messages with lower ID values will be sent first.

2.4 Frame Format

FlexRay data transmission is done using dedicated frames which, as depicted in Fig. 4, are composed of three main segments: header, payload and trailer. The frame header consists of 5 bytes carrying a set of indicator bits, the frame identifier (ID), payload length, header CRC and cycle count. The five indicator bits are to be interpreted as follows: (a) *Reserved bit* - reserved for future protocol use and should be always set to 0 when transmitting, (b) *Payload preamble indicator* - when set to one it indicates that the payload segment contains specific optional information depending on the segment used to transmit the frame, (c) *Null frame indicator* - when set to zero indicates that the payload segment contains no valid data, (d)*Sync frame indicator* - when set to one it indicates that all receiving nodes should use the frame for synchronization purposes, and (e)*Startup frame indicator* - when set to one it indicates that the current frame is a startup frame which is used by the startup mechanism.

			Header segment				Payload segment			Trailer segment
Indicators	ID	Payload length	Header CRC	Cycle count	Data byte 0	Data byte 0	Data byte n-1	Data byte n	CRC
5 bit	11 bit	7 bit	11 bit	6 bit		0-254 bytes			24 bit

Fig. 4. The FlexRay frame format

The ID defines the slot in which the frame should be sent, hence it will be sent at most one time during a communication cycle. The payload length field indicates the size of the payload as a multiple of 16 bit words. The header CRC value is computed over the last two indicator bits, frame ID and payload length fields. The cycle count represents the current value of the cycle count from the sender's perspective.

The payload segment contains the actual data transmitted and can hold between 0 and 254 bytes. It will always contain an even number of bytes as a consequence of the payload length indicating its size as a multiple of two byte words. The trailer segment contains the CRC computed over the entire frame.

2.5   Error Handling

The FlexRay error handling mechanisms uses three states to achieve error confinement: *normal active*, *normal passive* and *halt*. Normal active is the normal operation state in which it is assumed that the node can perform all its activities. In the normal passive state the node is not allowed to transmit as it is assumed that collisions may occur on transmission attempts due to existing synchronization errors. The halt state is entered when detected errors are considered severe enough that proper protocol operation can only be re-established by reinitializing the node.

There are two main mechanisms for handling errors. The first is used for significant errors and causes transitions directly into the halt state. The second mechanism employs a degradation model based on switching between the three operation states to avoid immediate transitions to the halt state in case of transient errors. The degradation model handles synchronization related errors. Direct transitions to the halt state are made on product-specific errors, fatal errors during frame and symbol processing or direct host command.

3   Specification Analysis

We will next present elements of the FlexRay protocol specification that can be exploited to mount various attacks. Each vulnerability is introduced considering a passive network topology. We also discuss the identified vulnerabilities from the perspective of an active star network topology in a dedicated section.

3.1   Attacker Model

The vulnerabilities discussed in this section are considered as seen from the perspective of an attacker with the intent of disrupting or faking FlexRay communication. This attacker has reasonable to good knowledge of the FlexRay protocol or the ability to gain the knowledge by studying the publicly available specification. The attacker has the ability to compromise the firmware of an in-vehicle FlexRay network node either by updating the firmware through available channels (e.g. OBD port or OTA mechanisms) or by providing an already compromised node to be fitted as a replacement or after-market component. We also assume that the attacker is capable of controlling HW components of the compromised node through SW but not able to effect any HW changes. The attacker can not make any changes to the target FlexRay network topology such as interposing a malicious node between an existing one and the rest of the network.

3.2   Physical Layer

The functionality of the FlexRay protocol primarily relies on the ability of generating the basic physical line signals corresponding to the logical bus states Idle, Data_0 and Data_1, depicted in Fig. 2. The FlexRay electrical physical layer specification [1,10] defines differential voltage thresholds for the detection of the logical bus states. Since FlexRay has no integrated means of resolving collisions, during normal operation it is only allowed for one node to generate a dominant signal (i.e. Data_0 or Data_1) at a moment in time while all other nodes have to generate an Idle (recessive) signal. In case of colliding dominant signals the detected line level cannot be predicted as the resulting line voltage level will depend on the voltage levels of the generated dominant signals. Therefore, generating collisions will lead to perturbations of the FlexRay communication. This can be easily achieved on a FlexRay node by directly interacting with the FlexRay transceiver which is responsible of generating physical bus levels based on logical input data coming from the host microcontroller. Normally the transceiver input lines are controlled through the communication controller but this can also be done by using the microcontroller's I/O ports. This approach could be used to implement several variants of DoS attacks as presented in what follows depending on the intended effect.

Full DoS Attack. The FlexRay communication could be completely blocked by generating a continuous dominant level on the bus. For this, the attacker should assure corresponding high, or low constant levels on the transceiver's transmit data (TxD) pin and enable the transmitter circuit by setting the transmit enable (TxEN) pin to low. Due to protection circuitry in the transceiver it may be required to periodically assure short high level pulses on the TxEN.

While, the effect of this attack is to prevent any FlexRay communication, the reasons for achieving this depend on the moment of the attack launch. If the attack is initiated at system startup before initiating the FlexRay communication, the nodes will not be able to successfully perform wakeup and startup activities preventing any data transmission. Starting the attack after the communication has been successfully initiated will lead to all nodes being unable to interpret any sent messages. As a result the resynchronization tasks performed on each node will fail for all subsequent communication cycles. After a configurable number of failed resynchronization attempts all nodes will enter the normal passive followed by the halt state.

Targeted DoS Attack. The attacker may intend to only prevent a certain node from sending messages or just certain messages from being sent. To achieve this the attacker node needs to generate a continuous dominant level during the transmission of the target message that leads to failure on the receiver side in correctly interpreting the message. Any failure in verifying correct frame encoding or frame content integrity (i.e. CRC verification) will result in the frame being ignored by the receiver. Knowledge about the network and schedule configuration is needed in order to mount this type of attack but this might be automatically achieved by analysing network traffic as demonstrated in [3,6,7].

While static frames have a clearly defined slot allocated for their transmission, the transmission slot of dynamic frames within the dynamic segment cannot be predicted. Therefore, employing this attack approach for preventing the transmission of certain dynamic frames might prove to be more difficult as it would require additional real-time traffic analysis.

3.3 Data-Link Layer

The FlexRay communication controller implements the data link layer part of the protocol. The correct functioning of the FlexRay communication relies on using the communication controller along with a proper configuration of FlexRay protocol parameters and common knowledge of the communication cycle on each network node. However, this configurability makes it possible to misuse protocol parameters and communication cycle settings directly from the application layer. We will discuss specific elements of the FlexRay protocol and the attacks they can enable in the following sections.

Full DoS Attack. Improper configuration of the FlexRay communication cycle on one network node can generate protocol errors on all other nodes and can potentially lead to a suspended communication if synchronization is lost. This issue can be exploited to mount a full DoS attack on the network by purposely affecting node synchronization.

A way to achieve this is for the attacker node to send messages in all slots of the communication cycle causing collisions with messages from any of the other nodes. This will result in a loss of synchronization due to the inability of legit nodes to correctly receive synchronization frames. The loss of synchronization occurs after a configurable number of resynchronization attempts. In this version of the attack it is not necessary for the attacker to know detailed information about the communication schedule of the target network. It is enough to know the communication cycle length and bit rate on which to build a setup that will allow integration in the existing communication to enable sending messages in all slots so that collisions are guaranteed.

A more targeted approach would be to only generate collisions on synchronization frames. When defining the communication schedule it is specified which frames should be used for synchronization. As presented in the FlexRay frame description, these frames can be identified by the Sync frame indicator bit in the frame header. This makes it easy for the attacker to identify the slots used for synchronization. It would be enough for the attacker to generate collisions by sending messages in the slots allocated for these frames to force loss of synchronization. Based on its implementation methodology this attack could be considered a special case of the targeted DoS attack which we detail next. Here the target messages are all synchronization frames but the intended end result is complete communication halt.

Targeted DoS Attack. Similar to the case of transceiver-based attacks, mounting targeted DoS attacks using the FlexRay communication controller aims to prevent certain network traffic for being correctly received. This can be easily achieved by adding target messages to the attacker node's own communication schedule setup and transmitting them in the appropriate slots. This will cause collisions on the target messages and decoding errors on the receivers side leading to the message being rejected. FlexRay does not provide any means of signaling failed transmissions to the sender node, these are only reported to the hosts of the receiver nodes.

While mounting this attack on static messages is straight forward, targeting dynamic frames will require sending the target frame in each communication cycle since the attacker has no knowledge on the occurrence of message transmission trigger event on the legitimate message sender side. This results in a combined DoS and spoof attack efficient in feeding receiving nodes false data while preventing the legit node from intervening.

Message Spoofing. The methodology behind message spoofing is similar to the one employed for the targeted DoS attack. The attacker node has to define the target messages in its own communication schedule. To assure its correct transmission the spoofed message has to be sent inside communication cycles which do not contain the message transmitted by the legit node. To increase attack efficiency the legit message transmission could be prevented by generating a collision.

Messages sent in the static segment are cyclic messages which are sent with a certain periodicity that is a multiple of the communication cycle period. According to the FlexRay specification, a node should always transmit a frame in a static slot assigned to it regardless of data availability for the particular communication cycle. The node should transmit a null frame in the static slots for which there is no data ready to send. This behaviour makes it impossible to spoof messages in a static slot as long as it is assigned to an active legit node since any attempt to do so will result in a collision.

Spoofing messages assigned to the dynamic segment is possible since their corresponding slots will only be occupied if there is data to transmit. Spoofing dynamic frames might result in collisions as it is impossible to know when the legit node will send a message in the same slot. Similar to the case of targeted DoS attacks this effect works to the advantage of the attacker rendering the legit node unable to send correct data while the attacker transmits faked frames.

3.4 Feasibility of Attacks in Networks Based on Active Star

Given their nature, networks built on an active star topology could be used to prevent attacks.

We discuss the feasibility of the previously proposed attacks on active star-based FlexRay network topologies by strictly referring to the effect of the attacks on the nodes connected to the attacker node through the active star coupler. It is obvious that the behaviour of the proposed attacks on the direct link between the active star coupler and the attacker node will be as already described.

According to the FlexRay physical layer specification [1,10] the star coupler can set a branch (i.e. physical link) in one of two states for preventing the propagation of communication misbehaviour from it to other branches, i.e., *Branch_FailSilent* and *Branch_Disabled*. The *Branch_FailSilent* state is entered as a result of a bus error detection which is specific to particular transceiver implementations. A transition to the *Branch_Disabled* state is done on host control and depends on specific implementations of the host. Therefore, the star coupler could implement the ability to detect and block any misbehaving traffic from reaching other network branches. The FlexRay specification does not include specific requirements or recommendations for misbehaviour detection and handling for the active star coupler besides switching the transmitter state to off after exceeding the maximum allowed length of transmitter activation. This protection mechanism can be overcome by periodically toggling the attacker transmitter state as discussed in the section dedicated to physical layer based attacks. In this context, it may be possible to implement all previously presented attacks on active star based FlexRay networks if proper user-defined protection mechanisms are not implemented.

Compromising the active coupler node would make it possible to spoof and DoS any traffic (including static segment frames) from directly connected nodes since all message routing would be under the control of the attacker. Without introducing additional security mechanisms it would be virtually impossible for the other nodes to detect any attack launched by the active star coupler node.

4 Experimental Analysis

4.1 Experimental Setup

To evaluate the feasibility of the proposed attacks we built a FlexRay network containing 4 nodes connected according to a bus topology. One of the 4 nodes is always used as the attacker node. Each node of our test network is built on an EVB9S12XF512E development board equipped with a Freescale (NXP) S12XF512 microcontroller two TJA1080A FlexRay transceivers (dedicated to the two FlexRay channels). The employed microcontrollers are equipped with 32 Kbytes of RAM and 512 Kbytes of Flash and can operate at a top frequency of 50 MHz. They are intended for automotive applications that require low to medium performance. Figure 5 illustrates our experimental setup with the cluster of 4 FlexRay nodes and a PicoScope used to analyse network traffic. In particular, the FlexRay protocol decoder provided by the PicoScope application was used to identify malformed frames resulted from the tested attacks.

For the legit nodes we defined a communication schedule that includes transmissions both in the static and dynamic segment. Each communication cycle uses the same slot assignment for both the static and dynamic segments as shown in Table 2 where A_i, B_i, and C_i are messages sent by nodes A, B and C respectively. To simplify the attack implementations we considered that, where

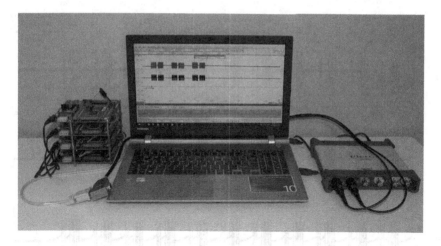

Fig. 5. Experimental FlexRay network setup used for testing proposed attacks

required, knowledge about communication parameters are already at hand. This is a realistic assumption as past research has shown it is possible to extract FlexRay communication parameters by listening to existing traffic [3,6].

Table 2. Slot assignment within the test communication cycle.

	Static segment															Dynamic segment							
Slot	1	2	3	4	5	6	7	8	9	10	11	12	13	14	15	16	17	18	19	20	21	22	23
Message	A_1	A_2		B_1	B_2		A_3	B_3	C_1	C_2			C_3							C_4		A_4	B_4

4.2 Full DoS Attack Evaluation

Transceiver-Based Full DoS. We tested this attack by using it to prevent the start of FlexRay communication as well as force the end of an already established communication. In the first case, legit nodes attempted to establish communication in the presence of the attacker generated signal but are not able to do so as neither node is able to receive correct data. The second attack scenario resulted in the nodes attempting to achieve resynchronization for a configurable number of consecutive odd cycles before entering the passive state and stop transmitting. Figure 6(a) exemplifies the result of the attack on already established communication by generating a permanent Data_1 level on the communication channel. The number of resynchronization attempts parameter was set to 5 in our case, hence the 10 additional cycles following the attack start. The nodes eventually enter the halt state which can only be exited if the host restarts the FlexRay controller. We investigated both generating permanent Data_0 and permanent Data_1 for the attack and achieved the same end effect in both cases.

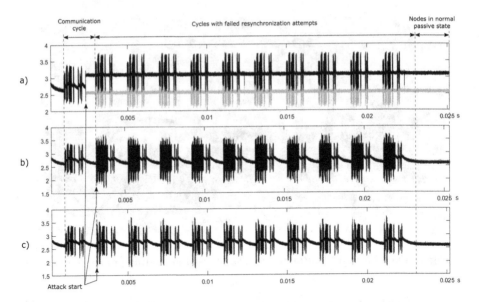

Fig. 6. Full DoS attacks: (a) transceiver-based version, (b) controller-based version targeting all static frames, (c) controller-based version targeting only synchronization frames

Controller-Based Full DoS. For the implementation of this type of attack and the subsequent controller-based attacks we configured the FlexRay controller on the attacker side with the same communication parameters employed by the other nodes. We tested several variants of the full DoS attack first by creating collisions on the entire communication schedule, then only on the static segment frames and finally by targeting only the synchronization frames. In all cases, the implementation is straight forward as it only requires including messages targeted for collision in the communication schedule of the attacker and making sure they are sent in the defined slot. The result in all cases was, as expected, the termination of FlexRay communication once all nodes lost synchronization and entered the normal passive state in which a node is not allowed to transmit. From this state all nodes will then transition to the halt state since in this case there is no method of regaining synchronization in the absence of traffic containing synchronization frames. Figure 6(b) and (c) illustrate the effect of the attack on all static segment frames and all synchronization frames respectively. The attack should persist long enough for all the nodes to enter the halt state. This is achieved by setting the maximum allowed cycles without clock correction on the attacker side to the maximum value used within the network or maximum allowed value according to the specification which is 15.

Collisions occur when sending frames in a slot allocated to another node regardless of the frame content. If the attack frame is other than the legit frame the result of distinct dominant levels colliding is undefined and cannot be interpreted. Even if the attack frame is identical to the legit one the resulting physical levels are still in violation of protocol specification making the frame non-decodable.

Comparing Attack Variants. As illustrated in Fig. 6 all variants of the full DoS attack lead to the same end result, i.e. the transitioning of all legit nodes in the halt state and the end of message transmission. In terms of attack complexity, the transceiver-based attack requires less knowledge on the FlexRay protocol and communication schedule configuration.

4.3 Targeted DoS Attack Evaluation

Transceiver-Based Targeted DoS. We implemented this type of attack by using the timer module to identify the start of a communication cycle by detecting the appearance of the NIT and then measure the offset from the cycle start to the target frame. Once the target frame slot is detected, the attacker node starts generating the continuous dominant bus level ending the attack no later than the frame slot end. The result, as shown in Fig. 7(a), is that collisions will be generated on transmitted target frames making the receiver side unable to correctly decode the frame. All other traffic passes unaffected. Both targeted nodes and other communication participants continue fulfilling the communication cycle as the attack does not generate any transitions in the error confinement mechanism. Receiver nodes could detect the missing frame in the expected slot and implement a special handling for this case at the application layer.

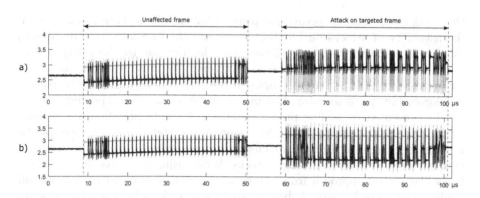

Fig. 7. Targeted DoS attacks: (a) transceiver-based version, (b) controller-based version

Controller-Based Targeted DoS. The approach for mounting the targeted DoS attack using the FlexRay controller was similar to the case of the full DoS attack. Target messages were added in the attacker's communication schedule end transmitted in the corresponding slot. As a result, like in the previous attack version, nodes are unable to receive targeted frames but communication continues as long as unaffected synchronization frames are still sent to maintain synchronization. This effect of this attack on the physical line levels is depicted in Fig. 7(b).

Comparing Attack Variants. While the end result of the targeted DoS attack is the same in both attack variants, the effort of implementing the transceiver-based version is higher in contrast with the controller-based approach which only requires adding the target slot in the attacker's communication schedule.

4.4   Message Spoofing Attack Evaluation

We checked the behaviour of the FlexRay controller on our S12XF platform when configuring message transmission periods for the static slots to be greater than the communication cycle period. As specified, all unused occurrences of allocated slots were filled by the communication controller with a null frame transmission making it impossible to mount a spoofing attack on the static segment messages.

On the dynamic segment side we were able to implement message spoofing by assuring periodic transmission of the injected frame. As expected, some of the spoof transmissions collided with the legit on-event frame stopping it from being correctly received.

5   Conclusions

Our work brings more experimental insights but also theoretical discussions on the feasibility of attacks on FlexRay networks. The DoS and spoofing attacks that we experiment with are relevant for FlexRay due to the safety-critical nature of in-vehicle communications. In terms of countermeasures, the possible approaches depend on the employed network topology. In case of passive topologies (i.e. point-to-point, bus or passive star), message spoofing attacks can be prevented by adding proper cryptographic authentication mechanisms while DoS remains a more demanding issue. Active star topologies with specific message filtering mechanisms implemented in the active star couplers can circumvent both DoS and spoofing attacks. While using an active star topology looks like a good approach from the security point of view it may not suit all applications. In such cases a hybrid topology approach could be used to separate parts of the FlexRay network through an active star coupler. It is good news that FlexRay supports such topologies and given the safety-critical nature of in-vehicle devices, more efforts in this direction may be desirable.

Acknowledgements. This work was supported by a grant of the Romanian Ministry of Research and Innovation, CNCS - UEFISCDI, project number PN-III-P1-1.1-PD-2016-1198, within PNCDI III.

References

1. FlexRay Communications System - Electrical Physical Layer Specification, Version 3.0.1. Standard, FlexRay Consortium (2010)
2. FlexRay Communications System - Protocol Specification, Version 3.0.1. Standard, FlexRay Consortium (2010)
3. Armengaud, E., Steininger, A., Horauer, M.: Automatic parameter identification in FlexRay based automotive communication networks. In: IEEE Conference on Emerging Technologies and Factory Automation, ETFA 2006, pp. 897–904. IEEE (2006)
4. Checkoway, S., McCoy, D., Kantor, B., et al.: Comprehensive experimental analyses of automotive attack surfaces. In: USENIX Security Symposium (2011)
5. Cho, K.T., Shin, K.G.: Error handling of in-vehicle networks makes them vulnerable. In: Proceedings of the 2016 ACM SIGSAC Conference on Computer and Communications Security, pp. 1044–1055. ACM (2016)
6. Heinz, M., Höss, V., Müller-Glaser, K.D.: Physical layer extraction of FlexRay configuration parameters. In: IEEE/IFIP International Symposium on Rapid System Prototyping, RSP 2009, pp. 173–180. IEEE (2009)
7. Huse, M.I.: FlexRay analysis, configuration parameter estimation, and adversaries. Master's thesis, NTNU (2017)
8. ISO: 17458-1, Road vehicles - FlexRay communications system - part 1: general information and use case definition. Standard, International Organization for Standardization (2013)
9. ISO: 17458-2, Road vehicles - FlexRay communications system - part 2: data link layer specification. Standard, International Organization for Standardization (2013)
10. ISO: 17458-4, Road vehicles - FlexRay communications system - part 4: electrical physical layer specification. Standard, International Organization for Standardization (2013)
11. Koscher, K., Czeskis, A., Roesner, F., et al.: Experimental security analysis of a modern automobile. In: 2010 IEEE Symposium on Security and Privacy (SP), pp. 447–462. IEEE (2010)
12. Miller, C., Valasek, C.: Adventures in automotive networks and control units. DEF CON **21**, 260–264 (2013)
13. Murvay, P.S., Groza, B.: DoS attacks on controller area networks by fault injections from the software layer. In: Proceedings of the 12th International Conference on Availability, Reliability and Security (ARES 2017), 3rd International Workshop on Secure Software Engineering (2017)
14. Nilsson, D.K., Larson, U.E., Picasso, F., Jonsson, E.: A first simulation of attacks in the automotive network communications protocol FlexRay. In: Corchado, E., Zunino, R., Gastaldo, P., Herrero, Á. (eds.) Proceedings of the International Workshop on Computational Intelligence in Security for Information Systems CISIS'08. ASC, vol. 53. Springer, Heidelberg (2009). https://doi.org/10.1007/978-3-540-88181-0_11
15. Palanca, A., Evenchick, E., Maggi, F., Zanero, S.: A stealth, selective, link-layer denial-of-service attack against automotive networks. In: Polychronakis, M., Meier, M. (eds.) DIMVA 2017. LNCS, vol. 10327, pp. 185–206. Springer, Cham (2017). https://doi.org/10.1007/978-3-319-60876-1_9
16. Wolf, M., Weimerskirch, A., Paar, C.: Security in automotive bus systems. In: Workshop on Embedded Security in Cars (2004)

Connection Dumping Vulnerability Affecting Bluetooth Availability

Karim Lounis[✉] and Mohammad Zulkernine[✉]

Queen's Reliable Software Technology Lab, School of Computing, Queen's University,
Kingston, ON, Canada
{lounis,mzulker}@cs.queensu.ca

Abstract. Over the last few years, Bluetooth technology has been deployed in millions of devices including laptops, watches, mobile phones, cars, printer, and many other devices. It has been rapidly adopted as a short-range wireless communication technology for different IoT applications such as smart cities, smart healthcare, and smart grids. Yet, little attention has been paid to Bluetooth security. In this paper, we report a new Bluetooth vulnerability, named connection dumping. We show that this vulnerability can be exploited to affect Bluetooth availability. We generate three attack scenarios which exploit the vulnerability to cause disconnection between Bluetooth devices. We also generate attack scenarios for Bluetooth role switching and connection deprivation. We demonstrate the occurrences of the attacks on Bluetooth devices made by various manufacturers, running different Bluetooth versions and operating systems, and recommend possible mitigations for them.

Keywords: Bluetooth security · Bluetooth threats · Bluetooth pairing

1 Introduction

Bluetooth is a wireless communication technology based on the IEEE 802.15.1 standard. It is used for exchanging data between fixed and mobile wireless devices within a short range and building WPANs (Wireless Personal Area Networks). It uses the free unlicensed ISM (Industrial, Scientific, and Medical) radio band at 2.4 GHz and adopts the FHSS (Frequency Hopping Spread Spectrum) transmission technique to send packets while reducing interferences. Bluetooth has evolved for the last twenty years, from Bluetooth v1.0 (1999) to Bluetooth 5 (2017), coming out with better power consumption, stronger security, higher data rate and longer range. These improved features made Bluetooth a substantial technology for different IoT applications [1–3].

In order to communicate, Bluetooth devices have to be associated and authenticated to each other. This is performed during an authentication procedure called pairing. The Bluetooth device which initiates the pairing procedure is assigned the role of a master, whereas the other devices which accept the pairing

© Springer Nature Switzerland AG 2019
A. Zemmari et al. (Eds.): CRiSIS 2018, LNCS 11391, pp. 188–204, 2019.
https://doi.org/10.1007/978-3-030-12143-3_16

are assigned the role of slaves. When a certain number of slave devices are connected to the same master device, they form a network structure called piconet. The interconnection of at least two piconets, forms a scaternet. The pairing procedure allows Bluetooth devices to get authenticated by proving to each other the knowledge of a secret key. It also allows to negotiate security parameters to derive cryptographic keys that will be used further for establishing a secure communication. This pairing mechanism has evolved along with Bluetooth providing Bluetooth devices with robust security services, mainly, authentication, encryption, and data integrity. This made Bluetooth more and more resilient against multiple attacks discovered during Bluetooth evolution cycle [4–13]. Most of these attacks exploit vulnerabilities in either the implementation of the Bluetooth protocol stack or the specification itself, or in both. Some of these attacks are easy to perform, whereas others need important resources, additional effort and time to successfully conduct them. For example, to eavesdrop a Bluetooth communication, an attacker needs to determine the frequency hopping sequence being used in the Bluetooth communication [11] and use dedicated hardware such as Ubertooth One [14] which costs around $150.

In this paper, we identify a new vulnerability which we call connection dumping vulnerability. It is mainly due to the Bluetooth specification and the wrong implementation of the Bluetooth stack by different manufacturers. This vulnerability can be exploited to generate different attacks which aim to abuse the availability of Bluetooth. We generate three Bluetooth attack scenarios which cause disconnection between Bluetooth devices, regardless of which Bluetooth versions and operating systems are being used. We also generate attack scenarios for Bluetooth roles switching and connection deprivation. We demonstrate that an attacker with a very low budget[1] can negatively affect Bluetooth networks availability even if these networks are connecting the latest sophisticated devices. Finally, we propose possible mitigations to thwart those attacks.

Contributions: To summarize, the contributions of this paper are threefold.

– We identify a vulnerability in Bluetooth technology.
– By exploiting the vulnerability, we demonstrate different attack scenarios that affect Bluetooth availability.
– Finally, we propose possible mitigations to defend against those attacks.

The remainder of the paper is organized as follows. In Sect. 2, we briefly discuss the Bluetooth stack architecture and in Sect. 3, we review the existing Bluetooth pairing mechanisms and security modes. In Sect. 4, we introduce the new connection dumping vulnerability and show different attack scenarios that affect Bluetooth availability in Sect. 5. In Sect. 6, we discuss the implementation and experimentations and recommend possible countermeasures for the vulnerability. We conclude the paper in Sect. 7.

---

[1] The attacker only needs a Bluetooth USB dongle which may cost less than $4.

2   Bluetooth Stack Architecture

In this section, we briefly discuss the Bluetooth protocol stack following the commonly used model [15–18]. This will help the reader understand the attacks generated over the Bluetooth stack. Broadly speaking, Bluetooth stack architecture can be divided into two main components: the Bluetooth controller (hardware) and the Bluetooth host (software). These two components are separated by an intermediary standardized layer called HCI (Host Controller Interface) that transports commands and events between them.

The Bluetooth Controller: The controller is classically composed of three layers, the radio layer, the baseband and link control layer, and the link management layer. The radio layer is responsible for receiving and transmitting radio signals and adapting the power strength. The baseband and link control layer handles channel hopping, error correction, and channel access control. It provides two physical link types: ACL (Asynchronous Connectionless Link) for general data traffic and SCO (Synchronous Connection Oriented) for speech traffic. It is also responsible for performing inquiry procedures for detecting nearby devices. Finally, the link management layer is responsible for establishing, securing, and controlling logical links [19].

The Bluetooth Host: The Bluetooth host is essentially composed of four layers, the logical link control and adaptation protocol a.k.a. L2CAP, the upper level core protocols, the adopted protocols layer, and the application layer. The L2CAP layer provides upper layer protocols such as SDP (Service Discovery Protocol), RFCOMM (Radio Frequency Communication), and TCS (Telephony Control Service) with connection-oriented and connectionless data services. It has four main functions: protocol multiplexing, packets segmentation and reassembly, quality of service, and group abstractions [20]. The upper level core protocols, which is classically made of three upper level protocols, namely, RFCOMM which is a replacement for serial cable used to emulate serial ports over L2CAP, the SDP used by applications to discover the available Bluetooth services in remote Bluetooth devices, and TCS for telephony services between Bluetooth devices. Then, the adopted protocol layer which is made of protocols that are already defined by other standard stacks such as OBEX (OBject Exchange) used for exchanging objects, AT-commands which controls phone operations using legacy Hayes AT command set, and WAP (Wireless Application Protocol) used for browsing web-pages on mobile devices [15,21]. Finally, the application layer gathers all end-user Bluetooth applications and profiles.

3   Bluetooth Pairing Mechanims and Security Modes

In order to use the Bluetooth technology, Bluetooth capable devices have to pair with each other to get securely connected. This process known as pairing, allows two Bluetooth devices to authenticate each other and negotiate on a set of security parameters to derive a master key called link key. This link key is derived further to generate other keys that will be used to guarantee a secure communication. In the following, we present the different pairing mechanisms used in Bluetooth. Currently, there are three Bluetooth pairing mechanisms, the legacy pairing used in Bluetooth versions v1.0 to v2.0+EDR, the SSP (Secure Simple Pairing) pairing used in v2.1+EDR to v4.1+LE, and the Secure Connections, used in Bluetooth v4.2+LE to Bluetooth 5.

Legacy Pairing: This mechanism is conceptually composed of 3 to 4 steps, where the master device, known as the prover, initiates the connection and generates a PIN code or a passkey. The same PIN code or passkey must then be introduced into the other device, known as the verifier, which takes the role of a slave device. Once correctly entered, an initialization key is derived in both devices using the E_{22} algorithm. This key is then used to generate a link key for each new session using the E_{21} algorithm. The link key is used by the E_1 algorithm to provide mutual authentication. The final step, which is optional, consists of using the E_3 algorithm to derive the encryption key[2] [23].

SSP (Secure Simple Pairing): In Bluetooth versions 2.1+EDR up to 4.1+LE, the pairing procedure has been considerably improved. It uses the SSP paring, which instead of using a PIN code to derive the link key, uses the ECDH (Elliptic Curve Diffie-Hellman) key establishment protocol along with the public-private key pairs of both devices, a number of nonces, and their Bluetooth device addresses. In this way, the SSP improves the security of Bluetooth pairing by providing protection against passive eavesdropping and MITM attacks. SSP provides four possible association modes that are flexible in terms of device input/output capabilities, namely, the numeric comparison mode, the passkey entry mode, the just work mode, and finally, the out of band mode [21].

Secure Connections: It is also known as FIPS-pairing. This mode was introduced in Bluetooth v4.2+LE. It merely upgrades the SSP to utilize longer key sizes and stronger algorithms. For examples, the SSP uses E_3 for encryption, SAFER+ for authentication, and P-192-ECDH with HMAC-SHA256 for key generation. Secure connections however, uses AES-CTR for encryption, HMAC-SHA256 for authentication, P-256-ECDH with HMAC-SHA256 for key generation and guarantees message integrity service using AES-CCM algorithm [23].

In addition to the pairing process, a Bluetooth device can be set on a security mode to get access to security services. These security modes define when and where security procedures such as authentication and encryption shall be initiated. There are four different security modes [21], security mode 1, 2, 3 and 4. Security mode 1, a.k.a. unprotected mode, provides no security procedures. The security mode 2, a.k.a. service-level enforced security mode, allows the initialization of security procedures after link establishment but before logical channel establishment. Security mode 3, a.k.a. link-level enforced security mode, initiates security procedures before the physical link is fully established. Finally, the security mode 4 allows security procedures to be initiated after physical and

---

[2] All algorithms used in legacy paring are based on the SAFER+ (Secure And Fast Encryption Routine +) block cipher algorithm [22].

logical link setup. Security modes 1, 2, and 3, use the legacy pairing and are only supported in Bluetooth versions v2.0+EDR and earlier. The security mode 4, uses the SSP pairing and it is supported in Bluetooth versions v2.1+EDR to Bluetooth 5. This last mode is supposed to be the most secure mode, however, we have discovered a vulnerability in this mode which can be exploited to generate attacks that affect Bluetooth availability as described in the next section.

4   Connection Dumping Vulnerability

In this section, we present the vulnerability that we have discovered in Bluetooth devices. This vulnerability can be exploited to generate devastating attacks on Bluetooth network availability. In fact, if the vulnerability is correctly exploited, an attacker will be able to realize different attack scenarios which mainly cause disconnection between legitimate Bluetooth devices in a Bluetooth network or deprive legitimate Bluetooth devices from establishing usual paired connections.

Connection Establishment in Bluetooth: The pairing process allows two devices to get connected and authenticated to each other to start a secure communication. Bluetooth secure communications are mainly related to application level. That is to say, in such type of communications, Bluetooth devices use Bluetooth applications running on top of the protocol stack. These applications use adopted protocols such as OBEX and AT Commands, and transport their messages over the RFCOMM or TSC transport protocol. However, there are other service protocols such as SDP (Service Discovery Protocol) and Echo-Request/Reply which do not require Bluetooth devices to be paired in order to use the services. Only, a simple and non-secured ACL (Asynchronous Connectionless Link) connection is needed. Therefore, we can state that there are two types of Bluetooth connections, a *pairing-based* and a *pairing-free connection*.

Observation: Conceptually, most Bluetooth devices are designed to accept more than one ACL-connection from different remote Bluetooth devices. This basically, allows the construction of Bluetooth networks such as scaternets. However, we have observed that some Bluetooth devices accept more than one ACL-connection from the same remote Bluetooth device, regardless of whether the connections are pairing-free or pairing-based connections. This appears to be practical since two paired devices, in addition to sending files to each other, send pings and/or request for service discovery from each other as well. Unfortunately, we have discovered that, by allowing the establishment of more than one connection at a time from the same remote Bluetooth device, the ordinary termination of one connection, automatically terminates the other ones. This seems to be an implementation flaw. However, we rather perceive it to be a serious vulnerability that can be exploited by attackers to abuse Bluetooth networks availability. We consider this flaw to be related to the specification of Bluetooth security mode 4, which allows two types of ACL-connections, namely, the pairing-based ACL-connection and the pairing-free ACL-connection.

Vulnerability Exploitation: Consider a Bluetooth device which accepts the establishment of more than one ACL-connection from the same remote Bluetooth device. An attacker exploits the vulnerability by spoofing any Bluetooth device which is paired with the Bluetooth device that accepts multiple connections, and establishes a pairing-free ACL-connection (since it does not know any credentials) with the later Bluetooth device. Then, by terminating the pairing-free ACL-connection, the impersonated device gets automatically disconnected as illustrated in Fig. 1, where the prover is the impersonated Bluetooth device and the verifier being the Bluetooth device to exploit. We call this vulnerability *connection dumping vulnerability* or simply CDV, since it can mainly be exploited to dump and cut down legitimate Bluetooth connections between Bluetooth devices without performing any hard cryptanalysis or other difficult tasks such as determining the frequency hopping sequence [11] used in the connection or breaking the SSP encryption and authentication mechanism [5,6]. The attacker needs just to impersonate its target and legitimately request services.

CDV Formal Semantics: Let $D = \{d_1, \ldots, d_n\}$ be the set of nearby discovered Bluetooth devices[3], and let *Paired* denotes a predicate for a couple of devices $(d_i, d_j) \in D \times D$ indicating whether the two devices are connected through a pairing-based connection or not. If two devices d_i and d_j are paired, we write $Paired(d_i, d_j) = True$. Let *Master* denotes a predicate for a given Bluetooth device indicating whether that device is a *master* or a *slave* device. Hence, if device $d_i \in D$ is a *slave* device and $Paired(d_i, d_j) = True$ then $Master(d_i) = False$ and $Master(d_j) = True$. Finally, let *Accpt* denotes a predicate indicating whether a given Bluetooth device $d_i \in D$ accepts more than one ACL-connection (paring-based and/or pairing-free) at the same time from the same remote Bluetooth device. If that is the case, we write $Accpt(d_i) = True$. Hence, a Bluetooth connection between two devices $d_i \in D$ and $d_j \in D$ is vulnerable to the CDV if at least $Accpt(d_i) = True$ or $Accpt(d_j) = True$. Conversely, a Bluetooth network connecting several devices $d_i \in \{d_1, \ldots, d_n\}$ is secure from the CDV if $\forall d_i \in D : Accpt(d_i) = False$.

Besides detecting at least two paired Bluetooth devices i.e., $(d_i, d_j) \in D \times D$ such that $Paired(d_i, d_j) = True$, the attacker has to target Bluetooth devices satisfying the following assumption Γ:

If $(Paired(d_i, d_j) = True)$ **and** $(Accpt(d_j) = False)$ **then** $(Accpt(d_i) = True)$

or

If $(Paired(d_i, d_j) = True)$ **and** $(Accpt(d_i) = False)$ **then** $(Accpt(d_j) = True)$

It simply means that if both devices d_i and d_j are paired together, at least one of them should accept more than one connection from the other Bluetooth device. Thus, if $Accpt(d_i) = Accpt(d_j) = False$, the vulnerability cannot be exploited. At the same time, we emphasize that the attacker assumes that these devices are

---

[3] Note that after the invention of the Bluegun [7], the attacker does not need to be within the short range of its target Bluetooth devices.

not set on non-discoverable[4] mode which make it easy for the attacker to perform the spoofing. Otherwise, the attacker should perform brute-forcing attacks [11] to detect the presence of nearby devices that are set on non-discoverable mode.

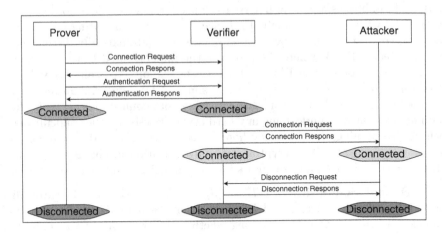

Fig. 1. Connection dumping vulnerability exploitation

5   Attack Scenarios on Bluetooth Availability

In this section, we generate three attack scenarios on Bluetooth security mode 4. These attack scenarios exploit the CDV (Connection Dumping Vulnerability) presented in the previous section to affect the availability of Bluetooth networks in general, and Bluetooth devices in particular. Note that we only generate three attack scenarios in this paper, but there may be other attack scenarios that may be generated by exploiting this vulnerability.

5.1   Attack Scenario 1 (SDP Connection Dump)

This attack scenario exploits the CDV using the SDP (Service Discovery Protocol) protocol to affect the availability of a Bluetooth network. Bluetooth devices use the SDP protocol to discover available services (e.g., printing service) running on remote Bluetooth devices. It is based on client/server communication concept where a SDP client requests (via a SDP-request) the SDP server for service records. The SDP server which maintains a list of service records that describe the characteristics of particular services associated to the server, replies back to the client via SDP-response containing the requested records. To that

---

[4] Bluetooth technology allows Bluetooth devices to be set on non-discoverable mode in order to hide their presence to nearby Bluetooth devices.

end, a pairing-free ACL (Asynchronous Connectionless Link) connection is established between the client and the server. Once all service records are received, the connection is ordinarily terminated by the SDP-client.

To exploit the vulnerability, the attacker follows the steps described in Algorithm 1. Basically, the attacker scans and inquiries the neighborhood to discover nearby Bluetooth devices (Line 1 and 2). Assuming the attacker has discovered two paired Bluetooth devices where at least one of them accepts more than one ACL-connection at a time from the same source. The attacker spoofs one of the Bluetooth device's MAC address[5], user-friendly name, and optionally the device class (Line 4) and then continuously sends SDP requests to the device that accepts multiple ACL-connections (Line 5). This will consequently disconnect the spoofed device. In fact, when a SDP request is sent to the device that accepts multiple connections, a pairing-free ACL-connection is established without any authentication. This connection is then normally terminated by the attacker after all service records are retrieved by sending an ACL-disconnect request. The remote server disconnects upon receiving the disconnection request and replies back with a disconnection response. After a short time of inactivity from the SDP server, the spoofed device disconnects.

Algorithm 1. SDP Connection Dump

---
1. Scan for nearby Bluetooth devices;
2. Identify a set of target Bluetooth devices $D \in \{d_1, \ldots, d_n\}$;
3. Assuming Γ, select a couple of Bluetooth devices $(d_i, d_j) \in D \times D$;
4. **If** $(Accpt(d_i)$ **and** $Accpt(d_j) = True)$ **then** spoof device $d_s \in \{d_i, d_j\}$;
   (a) Spoof BD_ADDR address of device d_s;
   (b) Spoof user-friendly name of device d_s;
   (c) Spoof class of device d_s;
   Else if $(Accpt(d_i)$ **or** $Accpt(d_j) = True)$ **then** spoof device $d_s \in \{d_i, d_j\}$ such that $Accpt(d_s) = False$;
   (a) Spoof BD_ADDR address of device d_s;
   (b) Spoof user-friendly name of device d_s;
   (c) Spoof class of device d_s;
   Else Abort;
5. **While** (1): Send one SDP-Request to target Bluetooth device $d_t \in \{d_i, d_j\} - \{d_s\}$;

5.2   Attack Scenario 2 (Ping Connection Dump)

The second attack scenario is quite similar to the previous one but uses the echo-request and echo-reply protocol instead of SDP to disconnect legitimate Bluetooth devices. The echo-request and echo-reply L2CAP (Logical Link Control

---

[5] In a Bluetooth network, each Bluetooth device is uniquely identified by a 48-bit Bluetooth device MAC address denoted by BD_ADDR.

and Adaptation Protocol) layer protocol is used by Bluetooth devices to test the round-trip time of their ACL-connection with remote Bluetooth devices. To that end, it initiates a pairing-free ACL-connection with the remote Bluetooth device, then sends echo-requests over that connection. The remote device responds back with an echo-reply. Once the desired number of echo-requests is achieved, the connection is normally terminated by the device which initiated the connection. Similar to SDP connection dump, an attacker performs the steps described in Algorithm 1, where this time it uses Ping requests instead of SDP request.

5.3   Attack Scenario 3 (RFCOMM Connection Dump)

The third attack scenario is somehow different from the previous scenarios. It uses a pairing-based ACL-connection instead of a pairing-free ACL-connection. Basically, almost all application-based connections use the RFCOMM protocol as their transport protocol. Therefore, any application (e.g., obexftp or minicom) that uses any of the adopted protocols (e.g., OBEX or AT-Commands) built on top of the RFCOMM transport protocol can be used to generate this attack scenario. As illustrated in Algorithm 2, the attacker discovers two paired Bluetooth devices where at least one of them accepts multiple ACL-connections from the same source (Line 1–3). Then, it establishes a spoofed ACL-connection with the device that accepts multiple connections, using an application that runs an adopted protocol over RFCOMM (Line 4–5a). For example, obexftp is used to transfer files. Finally, the attacker aborts the connection just before the authentication procedure starts (Line 5b). This will consequently disconnect the spoofed Bluetooth device in the same way as it did in the previous scenarios.

Algorithm 2. RFCOMM Connection Dump

1. Scan for nearby Bluetooth devices;
2. Identify a set of target Bluetooth devices $D \in \{d_1, \ldots, d_n\}$;
3. Assuming Γ, select a couple of Bluetooth devices $(d_i, d_j) \in D \times D$;
4. **If** $(Accpt(d_i)$ **and** $Accpt(d_j) = True)$ **then** spoof device $d_s \in \{d_i, d_j\}$;
   (a) Spoof BD_ADDR address of device d_s;
   (b) Spoof user-friendly name of device d_s;
   (c) Spoof class of device d_s;
   Else if $(Accpt(d_i)$ **or** $Accpt(d_j) = True)$ **then** spoof device $d_s \in \{d_i, d_j\}$ such that $Accpt(d_s) = False$;
   (a) Spoof BD_ADDR address of device d_s;
   (b) Spoof user-friendly name of device d_s;
   (c) Spoof class of device d_s;
   Else Abort;
5. **While** (1):
   (a) Establish an RFCOMM connection with the target device $d_t \in \{d_i, d_j\} - \{d_s\}$;
   (b) Abort spoofed connection before authentication.

5.4 Role Switching Attack

The role switching attack is actually a consequence of the previous attack scenarios. As we mentioned in the beginning, Bluetooth technology adopts a master-salve communication mode. In this mode, the Bluetooth device which initiates a connection is assigned the role of a master whereas the device which accepts the connection is assigned the role of a slave. Therefore, if an attacker manages to initiate a pairing-free ACL-connection with a remote Bluetooth device that accepts multiple ACL-connections, the Bluetooth device roles may be switched depending on the current device configurations. In fact, when the attacker discovers two paired Bluetooth devices d_i and d_j satisfying assumption Γ, and spoofs one of the devices $d_s \in \{d_i, \ldots, d_j\}$, it performs one time, a connection dumping to cause a disconnection. Thus, if the spoofed device was a master device i.e., $Master(d_s) = True$, the roles will change and the master becomes the salve and vice-versa. Indeed, upon disconnection, the slave will try to reconnect as a master, which will change the roles. Another scenario to switch the roles consists of just spoofing the slave device and establishing a pairing-free ACL-connection with the master device without terminating the connection.

6 Implementation and Experimental Evaluation

In this section, we present our implementation of the attack scenarios presented in the previous section. We describe our testbed configuration with respect to the target Bluetooth devices and Bluetooth attacker. Since all presented attack scenarios exploit the same vulnerability and aim for the same purpose, we only consider reporting the experience related to the SDP connection dump by providing the attack code and performing a dynamic analysis during the attack using $hcidump^6$ and $Wireshark^7$.

6.1 Evaluation Environment

We consider a set of Bluetooth devices, namely, smartphones, laptops, handsfree, cars, and smartwatches. These devices run different types of operating systems or firmwares and implement different versions of Bluetooth protocol stack. Concretely, we consider Android, iOS, MacOS X, Windows, Linux, and other operating systems and Bluetooth versions from v2.0+EDR to 5. For the attacker profile, we use a laptop HP ProBook 6560b (Intel Core i5 CPU and 4GB of RAM) operating on Linux Ubuntu 16.04, Kernel 4.13.0-45-generic and running the Bluez 5.37 Linux Bluetooth host implementation. We also use a ORICO BTA-403 Bluetooth dongle (which costs around $4) and a set of Linux-based software tools such as *hciconfig, hcitool, sdptool, l2ping, spooftooph, obexftp, minicom* and *rfcomm*. Finally, in order to follow what is happening during the attacks, we use some

---

[6] hcidump is a Linux utility which allows the monitoring of Bluetooth activity. It reads raw HCI data coming from and going to a Bluetooth device.

[7] Wireshark is a free and open source packet analyzer: www.wireshark.org..

Linux software utilities such as *hcidump* and *Wireshark*. The *hcidump* tool allows us to capture all messages being sent and received by the attacker's Bluetooth controller and store them into files in PCAP-format. These PCAP-files are then read using *Wireshark* to visualize and analyze the packets that were exchanged between the attacker and target Bluetooth devices.

```
1.  #! /bin/bash
2.  hciconfig -a
3.  hciconfig hci0 up
4.  hciconfig -i hci0 scan
5.  spooftooph -i hci0 -a spoofed_device_BDADDR
6.  hciconfig -i hci0 name 'spoofed_device_name'
7.  SDP_Num=0
8.  while $one
9.  do
10. sdptool browse $target_BDADDR >> /dev/null
11. let SDP_Num++
12. echo $(date + "%T")': Disconnection'(''$SDP_Num)'
13. done
```

Fig. 2. Bash script for SDP connection dumping attack

6.2   Attack Scenario Implementation

We develop a Linux bash script in order to launch the presented attacks, namely, SDP connection dump, Ping connection dump, and RFCOMM connection dump. Figure 2 illustrates a snippet of the bash script used to launch the SDP connection dump attack, where the *target_BDADDR* variable refers to the MAC address of the target device. To run the attack, the attacker performs the following steps: By executing Line 2, the attacker displays all available Bluetooth controllers physically connected to its device along with other related information such as the name of the controller, status (up or down), BD_AADR address, device class, manufacturer, and Bluetooth version. In our case, the ORICO BTA-403 Bluetooth dongle has the pseudonym *hci0*. This interface is set up in Line 3. Next, the attacker scans for nearby available Bluetooth devices (Line 4). This inquiries nearby devices and grab useful information about these devices such as devices BD_ADDR addresses, names, and classes. Then, considering $D = \{d_1, \ldots, d_n\}$, the set of discovered devices, the attacker is assumed to know that at least two devices are paired i.e., $\exists (d_i, d_j) \in D^2$ s.t. $Paired(d_i, d_j) = True$. If the attacker knows this information, he can try to impersonate one of the two paired devices, let us say d_i, by changing its Bluetooth controller's user-friendly name as well as his Bluetooth controller's BD_ADDR address into the d_i's user-friendly name and BD_ADDR address (Line 5 and 6). Finally, the attacker sends SDP-requests to the target Bluetooth device d_j (Line 8 to 13). This repeatedly initiates and terminates pairing-free ACL-connections with the target device d_j, which results in a permanent disconnection of the legitimate Bluetooth device d_i.

6.3   Experimentation

To experiment the attack scenarios presented in Sect. 5, we launch the attack scenarios on various Bluetooth devices. These devices were made by different manufacturers and operate different Bluetooth versions and operating systems.

Table 1. Connection dumping attack results with respect to our Bluetooth devices testbed (✓ : vulnerable, ×: not vulnerable, and •: not concerned).

Devices name	Devices type	Firmwares or operating systems	Bluetooth Versions	Evaluation
Hewlett-Packard ProBook 6560b	Laptop	Ubuntu 16.04.1 Kernel 4.13.0-45	v2.1+EDR	×
Lenovo Yoga 720	Laptop	Windows 10	v4.1+LE	✓
ACER Aspire E15	Laptop	Windows 10	v4.0+LE	✓
ASUS N43S	Laptop	Windows 7 SP1	v3.0+HS	✓
Apple MacBook Air	Laptop	MacOS High Sierra 10.13.4	v4.0+LE	×
Apple iPad Air 2	Tablet	iOS 9.3.5	v4.2+LE	×
Apple iPhone 8	Smartphone	iOS 11.4	5	×
Apple iPhone 7	Smartphone	iOS 11.3	v4.2+LE	×
Apple iPhone 4	Smartphone	iOS 7.1.2	v2.1+EDR	×
Sony Xperia Z2	Smartphone	Android 6.0.1	v4.0+LE	×
Samsung Galaxy S8	Smartphone	Android 8.0	5	×
Samsung Galaxy S7	Smartphone	Android 8.0	v4.2+LE	×
Samsung Galaxy A5	Smartphone	Android 7.0	v4.2+LE	×
Samsung Galaxy J5	Smartphone	Android 7.1.1	v4.1+LE	✓
Samsung Galaxy J7	Smartphone	Android 7.0	v4.1+LE	✓
Samsung Galaxy S4	Smartphone	Android 5.0.1	v4.0+LE	✓
Samsung Grand Prime	Smartphone	Android 5.1.1	v4.0+LE	✓
LG Nexus 5X	Smartphone	Android 8.0.0	v4.2+LE	✓
Huawei Nexus 6P	Smartphone	Android 8.1.0	v4.2+LE	✓
HTC One M8	Smartphone	Android 4.4	v4.0+LE	✓
BLU Studio G2	Smartphone	Android 6.0	v4.0+LE	✓
Motorola Moto Z2	Smartphone	Android 7.1.1	v4.2+LE	✓
Xiaomi Redmi Nt3	Smartphone	Android 6.0	v4.1+LE	✓
Xiaomi Redmi Nt2	Smartphone	Android 5.0.2	v4.0+LE	✓
OnePlus X	Smartphone	Android 6.0.1	v4.0+LE	✓
EDIMAX EW-7611ULB	BL USB dongle + Computer	Linux Kernel 4.15.0-23-generic	v4.0+LE	✓
Raspberry Pi 3 Model B+	Single Board Computer	Linux raspberrypi 4.14.42-v7	v4.1+LE	×
Kivors DZ09	Smartwatch	Nucleus RTOS 3.x	v3.0+HS	•
Unknown	Handfree	Unknown	v4.1+LE	•
Lexus ES350 (2009)	Car Handfree	Unknown	v2.0+EDR	•
Mercedes-Benz C300 (2010)	Car Handfree	Unknown	v2.0+EDR	•
Kia Sedona (2010)	Car Handfree	Unknown	v2.0+EDR	•
Mini Cooper JCW (2017)	Car Handfree	Unknown	v2.0+EDR	•

We have discovered that some modern Bluetooth devices are vulnerable to these attacks and can be easily disconnected from a Bluetooth network, whereas other devices seem to be "unintentionally secure" from the CDV. Table 1 shows different Bluetooth devices used in our testbed, with respect to their names, types, operating systems, Bluetooth versions, and whether they are affected by the CDV or not. Actually, we have identified three classes of Bluetooth devices:

1. Bluetooth devices marked with (•) in Table 1 are not affected by this vulnerability. This is mainly because these Bluetooth devices are designed to establish one and only one connection at a time. Once a connection is established, these devices do not accept or respond to any other connection. In fact, when these devices are already paired and connected with other Bluetooth devices, our attacking Bluetooth device displays a *"Host is down"* message when we try to establish a new pairing-free connection with them. In the experimentations, we have considered pairing the Kirvos DZ09 smartwatch with the Samsung J7 smartphone. Then, by impersonating the smartphone, we have sent a SDP-request to the smartwatch which did not respond back.

2. Bluetooth devices marked with (✓) in Table 1 are not safe from the CDV. We have successfully conducted the attack scenarios on those devices. In fact, those Bluetooth devices accept more than one ACL-connection at a time from the same source. In the experimentations, we have considered pairing the Kirvos DZ09 smartwatch with the Samsung J7 smartphone. Then, by impersonating the smartwatch, we have sent a SDP-request to the smartphone, captured the exchanged messages using *hcidump* tool and visualized the messages using *Wireshark*. By analyzing the exchanged packets, we notice that the new pairing-free ACL-connection was successfully initiated by the attacker with the smartphone followed by a certain number of packets related to the SDP. At the end, the connection was terminated by the attacker using a disconnect request. The smartphone replied back with a disconnect response before disconnecting. This resulted in a successful disconnection of the legitimate smartwatch the Kirvos DZ09 after a short time.

For the role switching, we have performed the attack by first running the SDP dump attack scenario which caused a spontaneous disconnection of the smartphone. After its disconnection, the smartphone tried a reconnection which was successful. This made the smartphone to become the master and the smartwatch became the salve. In fact, by impersonating the smartwatch, which is in slave role and by initiating a pairing-free ACL-connection with the smartphone, the roles were changed. We have noticed that a "role change" packet has been exchanged during the attack. The packet indicated that the roles were changed upon the establishment of the spoofed ACL-connection.

3. The third category marked with (×) in Table 1 seems to be "unintentionally secure" from the CDV. We have failed to successfully conduct the attack scenarios on those devices. In fact, the Bluetooth implementations in those devices seem to restrict the number of connections coming from the same remote device to one connection only. When conducting the attack scenario, we have cap-

tured the packets that were exchanged during the attack and visualized them using *Wireshark*. The number of packets captured when attacking this category of devices was considerably fewer (precisely 3 packets) compared to the previous category (55 packets) where the attack succeeded. By analyzing these three packets, we have noticed that those devices reply to the attacker with an "ACL Connection Already Exists (0 × 0b)" message when the attacker tries to establish a new spoofed connection with those devices. This message indicates that those devices do not accept a new connection from a Bluetooth device as long as a current connection is running with the same Bluetooth device. In the experimentations, we have paired the smartwatch Kirvos DZ09 with the Apple iPad Air 2, then spoofed the smartwatch to launch the SDP dumping attack scenario which failed.

As a first hypothesis, we have assumed that the third category of Bluetooth devices seems to be unintentionally secure. Yet, we have confirmed our assumption to be true after running other experiments. In fact, we have discovered that those Bluetooth devices are vulnerable to an other type of attack which also affect the Bluetooth availability if the CDV vulnerability is exploited in a different way. In the case of the connection dumping attacks, those devices reply with an "ACL Connection Already Exists (0 × 0b)" message. By observing this indication of an ongoing connection, we have asked ourselves the following question: "*What could happen if the attacker establishes a spoofed pairing-free ACL-connection with those devices before the spoofed device does?*". To answer this question, we have conducted two experiments. In the first experiment, we have spoofed the smartwatch Kirvos DZ09 and established a pairing-free connection with two of the those devices (Samsung S8 and Apple iPhone 8). Then, we have tried to connect the legitimate smartwatch to the smartphones, which resulted in a complete connection failure. The smartwatch was not able to connect to the smartphones since the attacker has already established a connection. This constitutes another threat on availability w.r.t. this category of devices. The second experiment was conducted on the devices of the first category, specifically the handfree and the smartwatch. We have spoofed the smartphone Samsung J7 and established a pairing-free connection with those devices. Then, we have tried to connect the legitimate smartphone Samsung J7 with those devices. This resulted in a complete connection failure since the attacker is already connected to them.

6.4 Countermeasures

According to the experimental results, we believe that this security flaw is strongly related to following causes:

1. The Bluetooth security mode 4: In this mode, security procedures are initiated after the physical and logical link establishment. This allows to establish two types of connections, namely, the pairing-based and the pairing-free connection which creates the CDV.

2. The Bluetooth host implementation by different manufacturers: For instance, the original and main core of the Android mobile operating system is designed and built by Google with the source code released publicly when a new version of Android is released. Yet, when device manufacturers such as Samsung, Sony, HTC, Motorola, and LG use the operating system, the manufacturers bring some modifications to it and adapt the system to their device architectures. Hence, we would not be surprised if two devices, from different manufacturers, running the same version of the operating system and Bluetooth stack, do not behave in the same way against the attacks.

Therefore, we recommend that connection handling mechanism in Bluetooth, should be seriously reviewed in the specification and should be correctly implemented by the manufacturers. We recommend a combination of two solutions to mitigate against the CDV vulnerability: (1) require an authentication before physical and logical connection as it is performed in security mode 3 used in Bluetooth versions v2.0+EDR and earlier, and (2) restrict the number of connections coming from the same remote device to one connection at a time. In this way, we believe that the attack scenarios presented earlier will fail to succeed.

7   Conclusion

Bluetooth technology provides substantial features such as mobility, range, data rate, power consumption and security. It has been adopted as a short-range wireless communication technology in different IoT critical applications. Therefore, Bluetooth security is a major research concern. In this paper, we have presented a new Bluetooth vulnerability that we have discovered in the Bluetooth security mode 4, called connection dumping vulnerability (CDV). This vulnerability can be exploited to generate attacks that compromise Bluetooth availability. We have generated three attack scenarios and demonstrated the existence of the vulnerability on modern Bluetooth devices. We have assumed that the target Bluetooth devices are set on discoverable mode and can be easily spoofed. We have also demonstrated that by exploiting the CVD, an attacker is able to perform Bluetooth connection deprivation and role switching. We claim that this vulnerability is due to both Bluetooth host implementation by different manufacturers and the Bluetooth specification. We also claim that this vulnerability can be exploited further to launch more sophisticated attacks. Finally, we highlight that the implementation of connection handling must be seriously reviewed. Finally, we have discussed possible countermeasures to address the CDV.

Acknowledgment. This work is partially supported by the Natural Sciences and Engineering Research Council of Canada (NSERC) and the Canada Research Chairs (CRC) program. At the same time, we would like to give special thanks to all QRST (Queen's Reliable Software Technology) lab members for providing their Bluetooth devices: smartphones, laptops, and cars, to run the experimentations.

References

1. CTV-Calgary-News: Wireless waves used to track travel times. https://calgary. ctvnews.ca/wireless-waves-used-to-track-travel-times-1.1054731 (2012). Accessed 15 Sept 2018
2. Orthogonal: The growing significance of Bluetooth BTLE in healthcare. http:// orthogonal.io/medical-softtware/the-growing-significance-of-bluetooth-btle-in-healthcare-html/ (2018). Accessed 15 Sept 2018
3. EECatalog: Bluetooth 5 expands into the smart grid. http://eecatalog.com/ wireless/2017/09/07/bluetooth-5-expands-into-the-smart-grid/ (2017). Accessed 15 Sept 2018
4. Laurie, A., Holtmann, M., Herfurt, M.: Hacking Bluetooth enabled mobile phones and beyond. http://www.blackhat.com/html/bh-europe-05/bh-eu-05-speakers. html (2007). Accessed 15 Sept 2018
5. Barnickel, J., Wang, J., Meyer, U.: Implementing an attack on Bluetooth 2.1+ secure simple pairing in Passkey entry mode. In: The proceedings of the 11th IEEE International Conference on Trust, Security and Privacy in Computing and Communications, pp. 17–24 (2012)
6. Sun, D.Z., Mu, Y., Susilo, W.: Man-in-the-middle attacks on secure simple pairing in Bluetooth standard V5.0 and its countermeasure. Pers. Ubiquit. Comput. J. **22**, 55–67 (2018)
7. Flexilis-Hackers-Group: Bluetooth-cracking gun: BlueSniper. https://www. defcon.org/html/links/dc_press/archives/12/esato_bluetoothcracking.htm (2004). Accessed 15 Sept 2018
8. Jakobsson, M., Wetzel, S.: Security weaknesses in Bluetooth. In: Naccache, D. (ed.) CT-RSA 2001. LNCS, vol. 2020, pp. 176–191. Springer, Heidelberg (2001). https:// doi.org/10.1007/3-540-45353-9_14
9. Armis: BlueBorne cyber threat impacts Amazon Echo and Google Home. https:// www.armis.com/blueborne/ (2017). Accessed 15 Sept 2018
10. Herfurt, M.: Introducing the car whisperer at what the hack. https://trifinite.org/ trifinite_stuff_carwhisperer.html (2005). Accessed 15 Sept 2018
11. Spill, D., Bittau, A.: BlueSniff: Eve meets Alice and Bluetooth. In: T1st USENIX Workshop on Offensive Technologies (2007)
12. Mulliner, C., BlueSpam. http://www.mulliner.org/palm/bluespam.php (2013). Accessed 15 Sept 2018
13. Laurie, A.: HeloMoto Bluetooth device planter. https://trifinite.org/trifinite_stuff_ helomoto.html (2013). Accessed 15 Sept 2018
14. Project-Ubertooth: An open source 2.4GHz wireless development platform suitable for Bluetooth experimentation. http://ubertooth.sourceforge.net/ (2015). Accessed 15 Sept 2018
15. Prabhu, C.S.R., Prathap, R.A.: Bluetooth Technology and its Applications with JAVA and J2ME. Prentice-Hall of India Pvt Ltd., Delhi (2006)
16. Zheng, P., Ni, L.: Smart Phone and Next Generation Mobile Computing. Morgan Kaufmann Series in Networking. Elsevier Science, New York (2005)
17. Pendli, P.K.: Contribution of Modelling and Analysis of Wireless Communication for Safety related Systems with Bluetooth Technology. Kassel University Press, Kassel (2014)
18. Aftab, M.U.B.: Building Bluetooth Low Energy Systems. Packt Publishing, Birmingham (2017)

19. Thompson, T.J., Kumar, C.B., Kline, P.J.: Bluetooth Application Programming with the Java APIs Essentials Edition. The Morgan Kaufmann Series in Networking. Elsevier Science, New York (2008)
20. Antony, R., Hopkins, B.: Bluetooth For Java. Apress, New York (2008)
21. NIST: Advanced Encryption Standard (AES). http://csrc.nist.gov/publications/fips/fips197/fips-197.pdf (2001). Accessed 15 Sept 2018
22. Massey, J., Khachatrian, G., Kuregian, M.: Secure and fast encryption routine+. In: The 1st NIST Advanced Encryption Standard Candidate (1998)
23. Bluetooth-SIG: Bluetooth Core Specification Version 5.0. Bluetooth Spec document (2018)

A Systematic Method to Describe and Identify Security Threats Based on Functional Requirements

Roman Wirtz[✉] and Maritta Heisel

University of Duisburg-Essen, Duisburg, Germany
{roman.wirtz,maritta.heisel}@uni-due.de

Abstract. Scenarios in which the security of software-based systems is harmed become more and more frequent. Such scenarios can lead to substantial damage, not only financially, but also in terms of loss of reputation. Hence, it is important to consider those threats to security already in the early stages of software development. However, it is non-trivial to identify all of them in a systematic manner. In particular, the knowledge about threats is not documented in a consistent manner. The *Common Vulnerability Scoring System* is a well known way to characterize vulnerabilities in a structured way. Our idea is to document threats in a similar way, using a template. A distinguishing feature of our approach is that we relate the threats to the envisaged functionality of the software. Our contribution is two-fold: first, we propose a general template to describe security threats that can be used in the early stages of software development. Second, we define a systematic and semi-automatic procedure to identify relevant threats for a software development project, taking the functionality of the software-to-be into account.

1 Introduction

In the last few years, the number of documented security incidents highly increased. Such an incident causes value and reputation loss. Additionally, fixing vulnerabilities leading to those incidents is cost intensive. A risk for a software can be defined as the combination of the likelihood of incidents and the consequence for an asset due to that incident. A risk management process defines different steps for coordinating activities to reduce the risk. The challenge for software engineers is to identify and control risks as early as possible. Following the principle of security-by-design, software is built from the beginning with regard to security.

Most knowledge about threats that might lead to a harm for assets exists for already running software. An example of such a knowledge base is the *National Vulnerability Database (NVD)*[1]. In these knowledge bases, it is possible to search for vulnerabilities based on component names like *MySQL Server*. In the analysis

---

[1] NVD - https://nvd.nist.gov/ (accessed on 2018-02-01).

© Springer Nature Switzerland AG 2019
A. Zemmari et al. (Eds.): CRiSIS 2018, LNCS 11391, pp. 205–221, 2019.
https://doi.org/10.1007/978-3-030-12143-3_17

phase of a software development project, however, we need a more abstract view on vulnerabilities, which is for example provided by the *Open Web Application Security Project* [1]. Such abstract resources, like OWASP, are focused on specific domains, e.g. web applications, and often do not provide a common structure to characterize possible threats. We aim to assist software engineers in managing risks based on the functional requirements of software systems.

In this paper, we contribute to the identification of risks. Our first contribution is a template to describe threats independently of the application domain, specific design decisions, or implementation details. The template is based on the *Common Vulnerability Scoring System* [2]. To integrate threats into models of functional requirements, we propose a new diagram type based on *Problem Frames* [3]. The extended model later supports security engineers in defining security requirements for the software to be developed. A method to identify relevant threats based on the template is our second contribution. The method is semi-automatic, which means, that we want to minimize the manual interaction for security engineers to perform the method as most as possible. Both, the template and the method are applied in the early stages of software development to ensure security-by-design.

The paper is structured as follows: In Sect. 2, we briefly summarize the concepts on which our work is based. A conceptual model describing the used terminology is given in Sect. 3. Section 4 introduces a general template to describe threats. The template is exemplified by an instantiation for a sample threat. The identification method for relevant threats is explained in Sect. 5. Related work is discussed in Sect. 6. We conclude our work with a discussion and future work in Sect. 7.

2   Background

In this section, we introduce the fundamentals on which our work is based. First, we present Michael Jackson's problem frames approach [3] to model functional requirements. Afterwards, we introduce the ProCOR method [4] which is a problem-based risk management process.

2.1   Problem Frames

To model requirements, we make use of Michael Jackson's problem frames approach [3]. Problem frames are patterns to characterize subproblems of a complex software development problem. These patterns are used in the early stages of the software development life-cycle. An instance of such a pattern is called problem diagram (examples are given in Figs. 3, 4 and 5). It contains a functional requirement **FR** (dashed ovals) for the system-to-be. A requirement is an optative statement which describes how the environment should behave when the software is installed. The entities related to a requirement are represented as domains (gray rectangles). There are different types of domains: biddable domains **B** (e.g., persons), causal domains **C** (e.g., technical equipment), machine domains **M** (representing the piece of software to be developed), lexical domains **X** (data representations) and display domains **D** (visual output devices). There are symbolic phenomena, representing some kind of information or a state, and causal phenomena, representing events, actions and so on. Each phenomenon is controlled by exactly one domain and can be observed by other domains. A phenomenon controlled by one domain and observed by another is called a shared phenomenon between these two domains. Interfaces (solid lines) contain sets of shared phenomena. Such a set contains phenomena controlled by the same domain (indicated by $A!\{...\}$, where A is an abbreviation for the controlling domain). Some phenomena are *referred to* by a requirement (dashed line to the controlling domain), and at least one phenomenon is *constrained* by a requirement (dashed lines with arrowhead to the controlling domain). The domains and their phenomena that are referred to by a requirement are not influenced by the machine, whereas we build the machine to influence the constrained domain's phenomena in such a way that the requirement is fulfilled.

Faßbender et al. [5] describe a method to combine aspects with problem frames. Aspects are considered as cross-cutting concerns for different requirements. To integrate aspects into problem frames, join points are defined. A join point, is a placeholder in an aspect diagram. We mark those join points in white, whereas normal domains are given in gray (cf. Table 2). By mapping the join points to domains of the problem frame, the aspects are integrated into the problem frame. Mapping means that a join point is replaced by the corresponding domain contained in the problem diagram in which the aspect shall be integrated.

2.2   ProCOR

Wirtz et al. [4] propose a risk- and problem-based method to identify security requirements in the early stages of a software development process. According to the principles of risk management described in ISO 31000 [6], the ProCOR method contains steps for risk identification, risk evaluation and risk treatment. The step for risk identification is described as a structured brainstorming with experts. The template to describe threats and the identification method we propose in this paper assists the security engineer in risk identification step.

In ProCOR, an asset is defined as some kind of information to be protected with regard to a security goal (confidentiality, integrity or availability). A piece of information is described as a phenomenon used in a problem diagram. The set of assets is the focus of the analysis. As the scope of the analysis we consider all domains at which some information to be protected is available. Available means that a domain controls or observes phenomena in which the information is contained. ProCOR defines a so-called information flow graph to derive these domains automatically, based on a set of problem diagrams. The identification of relevant threats described in this paper is based on this scope definition.

3   Conceptual Model

We first introduce a conceptual model, we developed in previous work based on the ISO 27005 standard [7]. The model is shown in Fig. 1 and describes the terminology we make use of in this paper. The ISO 27005 standard [8] has a special focus on security and is based on the ISO 31000 standard.

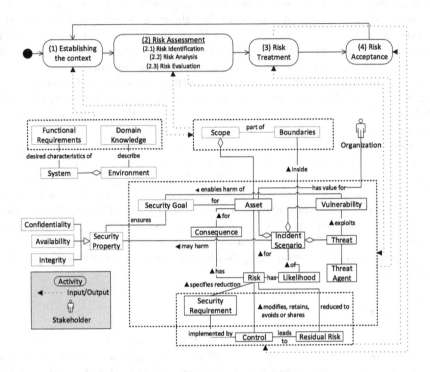

Fig. 1. Conceptual model [7]

According to the standard, a risk management process consists of four steps: (1) Establishing the context, (2) Risk Assessment, (3) Risk Treatment, and (4) Risk Acceptance. Risk Assessment contains three sub activities: (2.1) Risk Identification, (2.2) Risk Analysis and (2.3) Risk Evaluation. In this paper, we contribute to the identification of risks. The initial input is a set of *Functional Requirements* which describe the desired characteristics of the *System*. The system is part of the *Environment* which is described by *Domain Knowledge*. An *Asset* is part of the *Scope* and the scope is inside the *Boundaries* of the analysis. An asset has some value for an *Organization*. In the following, we consider a piece of information as an asset. For an asset, there is a *Security Goal* which ensures a *Security Property* for an asset. We consider the following types of properties: (1) *Confidentiality*: Some piece of information shall not be disclosed to unauthorized third parties. (2) *Integrity*: Some piece of information shall not be altered by unauthorized third parties. (3) *Availability*: Some piece of information shall be available for authorized parties. A security goal might be harmed when a *Threat* exploits a *Vulnerability*. According to ISO 27005, a threat might be human or natural (for instance a thunderstorm), and deliberate or accidental. In the Common Criteria [9], a *Threat Agent* is explicitly mentioned. A threat is the action which has a negative influence on assets, and a threat agent performs that action. An *Incident Scenario* includes a threat, a vulnerability and an asset that might be harmed. Such a scenario has a likelihood which is further used to evaluate risks. A *Risk* is related to that likelihood and the specific consequence for the asset. A risk can be treated (e.g. modified, retained, avoided or shared) by some *Controls*. After applying controls, there is still a *Residual Risk*, because usually, a risk cannot be eliminated. The risk reduction is specified by a *Security Requirement* which is implemented by some controls. In the following, we focus on the description of threats. A detailed description of threats is essential for the risk evaluation and the treatment of risks by selecting appropriate treatments.

4 Threat Description

In this section, we introduce a template to describe threats. We also describe how to integrate these threats into the model of functional requirements. This enables developers to consider threats along with functional requirements during the software development life-cycle.

4.1 Template Format

The structure of the template is inspired by the *Common Vulnerability Scoring System (CVSS)* [2]. The CVSS is used to score known vulnerabilities. This scoring system enables the security engineers to calculate the severity of a discovered vulnerability based on attacker information, information about the consequences and how the vulnerability can be used. Usually, the CVSS is used to classify vulnerabilities according to the CVSS User Guide [10].

In Tables 1 and 2, we show the structure of the template for an example threat. A threat is characterized by different attributes. The left-hand column states the name of an attribute, and the right-hand column shows its corresponding value. We extend the structure of the CVSS with new attributes (marked gray). There are four sections: *Basic Information, Threat Information, Relevant Problem Diagrams* and *Integration*.

Basic Information. The attributes contained in the section *Basic Information* are used to provide an overview of the described threat. There is a *name*, a *context* in which the threat might occur, a *reference* to the original document that describes the threat, a list of *keywords*, and an informal *description* of the threat. The *Vulnerability* that enables the harm of the security goal and the *Consequences* are described informally.

Table 1. Threat description: injection part 1

Basic Information	
Name	*Injection*
Context	*Application that provides some user input to select or edit some data.*
Reference	*OWASP Top Ten 2017 [1]*
Keywords	*injection, database, untrusted data*
Description	*Data entered by users is not validated and used in queries to read or modify data, e.g. SQL queries. An attacker needs to be able to input data which is then used to query or modify data.*
Vulnerability	*User input is not validated before execution.*
Consequences	*Data is manipulated, deleted or disclosed by unauthorized persons.*
Threat Information	
Threat Type	☐ Accidental ☑ Deliberate
Threat Agent	☑ Human ☐ Technical ☐ Natural
Threat Vector	☑ Network ☑ Adjacent ☑ Local ☐ Physical ☐ Personal (Social Engineering)
Type of affected domain	☐ causal ☑ machine ☐ lexical ☐ biddable ☐ display
Type of target domains	☐ causal ☐ machine ☑ lexical ☐ biddable ☐ Display
Complexity	☑ Low ☐ High
Privileges Required	☐ None ☑ Low ☐ High
User Interaction	☑ None ☐ Required
Threat Scope	☐ Unchanged ☑ Changed
Confidentiality Impact	☐ None ☐ Low ☑ High
Integrity Impact	☐ None ☐ Low ☑ High
Availability Impact	☐ None ☐ Low ☑ High

Threat Information. The section *Threat information* is divided into several attributes describing the characteristics of the threat. The CVSS concentrates on attacks, but we consider threats in general. The attribute *Threat Type* indicates whether a threat is accidental or deliberate. A *Threat Agent* might be human, technical or natural.

The *Threat Vector* describes the possible ways of accessing the piece of software to realize the threat. In the CVSS specification, it is called Attack Vector. *Network* describes threats that can be realized from any network, for example a wide area network, *adjacent* stands for local network access, *local* means that the threat agent needs direct access to the computer, and *physical* describes physical access to components such as a hard disk. To describe the communication between humans, for example by bribing an employee, we add the value *Personal (Social Engineering)*.

To map the threat description to the initial set of functional requirements, we also document the types of related domains. The *type of affected domain* documents the type of the domain on which the threat takes place. This domain might differ from the domains on which the harmed asset is available. For instance, attacking software (machine domain) might be necessary to get access to some data (lexical domain). Hence, we need to document the *type of the target domains*, as well.

The *Complexity* has two qualitative values: *low* and *high*. A low complexity means that a threat agent can expect repeatable success when realizing the threat without specialized access conditions or preparations. In contrast to that, a high complexity is considered when the threat agent has to invest some measurable effort in preparing the action that might harm the asset. For instance, an attacker needs local access to the server by breaking into the server room.

There are three possible values to state whether privileges are required. *None* means that no special privileges are required, *low* stands for a user account, and *high* means that administrator rights are necessary to realize the threat.

In some cases, an additional user interaction is necessary to realize the threat, for example an end-user has to confirm the installation of additional software. This is indicated by the corresponding attribute.

The initial *Scope* of a threat is the domain on which the threat is realized. In case that the attacker gets only access to this domain, the scope remains *unchanged*. If the threat affects additional domains, the scope is considered as *changed*, i.e. the target domain differs from the affected domain.

For the security goals confidentiality, integrity and availability, a qualitative scale for the impact on the security goal is defined. *None* means that there is no impact on this security goal, *Low* means access or manipulation only to parts of the information to be protected and *High* means full access or at least major impact to the information to be protected. However, it is hard to define the impact independently of the concrete application. Hence, the given scale can only be considered as a minor indicator for the risk evaluation.

Relevant Problem Diagrams. It does not suffice to consider the aforementioned attributes to decide whether a threat is relevant or not. Some threats require a specific functionality to be realized. For example, to perform an injection, user input is required. Without such an input, the threat is not relevant. The functional requirements of a software system can be described with problem diagrams. To relate threats to functional requirements, we introduce the section *Relevant Problem Diagrams* as shown in Table 2. The given diagrams describe the minimal set of elements to be contained in a problem diagram for which the threat might be relevant. In the left-hand column, we annotate the corresponding consequence. The graphical representation is shown in the right-hand column.

Integration. The section *Integration* describes how the threat can be integrated into the model of functional requirements. We follow an aspect-oriented approach (see Sect. 2.1) to consider threats along with functional requirements. Lin et al. [11] introduce the notion of an anti-requirement (**AR**) to describe the undesired behavior of software due to an attack. We make use of anti-requirements to describe the system's behavior when a threat becomes effective. We consider an anti-requirement as a special type of aspect, because the relevance of a threat is not limited to one specific functional requirement. We introduce a new kind of aspect diagram, called *Threat diagram*. Such a diagram is part of the threat description. It is used to identify the interfaces and domains that are related to the described threat. The anti-requirement constrains the undesired phenomena, for example the information flow from a domain to a threat agent. It refers to the phenomena which enable the threat, for example the injection performed by an attacker. In the further steps of a risk management process, security engineers have to ensure that the anti-requirement cannot be fulfilled by choosing appropriate controls. Such controls have to be selected with regard to the functional requirements, which means that treatments shall not interfere with the functionality. By combining threats and functional requirements in one model, we provide a global view for security engineers on the functionalities and threats and help to investigate both aspects in a whole.

Table 2. Threat description: injection part 2

4.2   Application Example

In 2017, the Open Web Application Security Project (OWASP) published a list of the ten most critical security risks for web applications [1]. We created a threat description with our template for all entries of that list. Tables 1 and 2 show the instance for the entry *Injection*. An injection as described by OWASP can be used to inject malicious code. Since there are different types of injections, we focus on the case of malicious database queries via the user input. There is no validation of the user input and the input is forwarded directly to the database. It is a deliberate threat performed by a human threat agent and can be performed via a wide area network, via a local network or locally. The domain to be affected is the machine, because the injection takes place on the software level where the user input is not validated. The target domain representing the database is a lexical domain. The complexity of the described threat is high, because an attacker needs deeper knowledge about the table structure of the database. Since the attacker acts as a user, only low privileges are required without any additional user interaction. The scope is changed because attacking the machine leads to an impact on the lexical domain. For all security goals, the impact is defined as high. The corresponding problem diagrams are given in Table 2. They have in common that an input by a user is possible. Using the provided input, a threat agent is able to inject malicious code. To integrate the threat into the initial set of problem diagrams, we define three join points. First, the lexical domain representing the database (target domain) needs to be mapped, as well as the machine domain (affected domain). Since the threat agent takes the role of user, the biddable domain of the the threat agent is a join point, too. The anti-requirement refers to the event of injection (phenomenon *inject*) and constrains the manipulated data at the target domain. The information that the threat agent might disclose by performing an injection is indicated by the constrained phenomena *knowledge*.

In the next section, we introduce a method to identify relevant threats based on elements of ProCOR (see Sect. 2.2) and the presented template. In the application example of the method, we make use of the instantiated template.

5   Threat Identification

In this section, we describe a semi-automatic procedure to identify relevant threats based on the previously described template. As input, we consider the domains in scope of the analysis that are derived with ProCOR (see Sect. 2.2). The procedure has five steps. Figure 2 shows an overview of the steps to be carried out. Steps that can be carried out automatically are shown in gray. Manual steps are shown in white. In the following, we first describe the steps of the procedure, and then we exemplify the procedure with a case study.

5.1   Procedure Steps

In the first step of ProCOR, we define the focus and scope of the security analysis based on problem diagrams. The scope can be described as shown in Table 3.

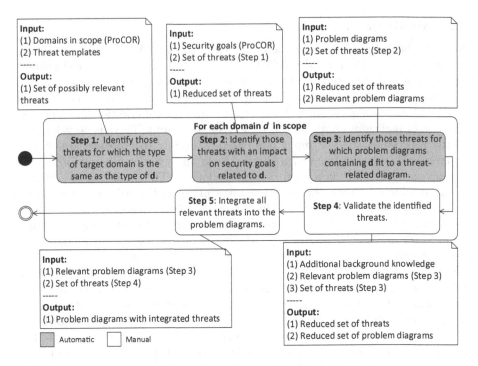

Fig. 2. Procedure description

For each domain in scope, we document the piece of information that is in the focus of the analysis and that is available at this domain. For each piece of information, we also document the related security goals. Each step of our procedure has to be carried out for each domain **d** that is considered to be in scope.

*Step 1: Identify those threats for which the type of target domain is the same as the type of **d**.*

For this step, it is necessary to compare the type of **d** with the documented type of the target domain. The step can be realized automatically when using a model for the domains and when the template is encoded in a machine-readable way, for example XML.

*Step 2: Identify those threats with an impact on security goals related to **d**.*

All information in focus of the analysis that is available at **d** is documented along with the related security goals. We compare these security goals with the impact for confidentiality, integrity and availability documented in the template. Only those threats remain in the reduced set of threats which have such an impact. In this step, we do not distinguish between low and high impact for a security goal. The impact scales are used for calculating the risk level.

*Step 3: Identify those threats for which problem diagrams containing **d** fit to a threat-related diagram.*

As already mentioned, it does not suffice to consider the domain type and the security goal to decide whether a threat is relevant or not. In this step, we also take the functional requirements into account, which are expressed with problem diagrams. For each problem diagram in which **d** is contained, it has to be checked whether it is comparable with the diagrams given in the threat description. Comparable means that the domains, interfaces and dependencies mentioned in the threat description are also contained in the problem diagram under investigation. The relevant problem diagrams are collected to integrate the threats in the fifth step of the method.

Step 4: Validate the identified threats.

The previously mentioned steps can be performed automatically, based on the requirements model and threat templates. A manual validation of the identified threats is still necessary. For example, a threat might only be relevant for wireless connections. The type of connection is not given in the requirements model, and hence has to be evaluated by security engineers.

Step 5: Integrate all relevant threats into the problem diagrams.

The identified threats are integrated into the problem diagrams as described in Sect. 4 using the integration section of the underlying templates.

5.2 Application Example

Our case study is inspired by the OPEN meter project [12]. It describes a smart grid scenario in which an energy supplier is able to control the grid and to retrieve information such as the power consumption of customers. We performed our procedure for eight requirements, but in this paper we only show its application for the requirements *Setup*, *Measuring* and *Change Personal Data*. The communication hub is the piece of software to be developed and serves as the interface between customer's home and the energy supplier. The energy supplier has to perform an initial setup of the communication hub by entering the customer data and necessary tariff parameters, which are stored in the configuration. The corresponding problem diagram for this requirement is shown in Fig. 3. The communication hub can be used for automatic measuring and storing of the power consumption. The measuring component is called *SmartMeter* and measures the consumption in regular intervals to forward it to the communication hub. The measured data is stored as *MeterData*. Figure 4 shows the problem diagram for the requirement *Measuring*. A user is able to change his/her personal data using an interface provided by the communication hub. The personal data is stored in the configuration. The corresponding problem diagram is shown in Fig. 5. We limit our application example to the following assets: (1) Integrity of tariffParameters, (2) Availability of measuredData and (3) Integrity of measuredData.

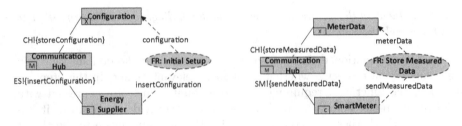

Fig. 3. Problem diagram *Setup*   **Fig. 4.** Problem diagram *Measuring*

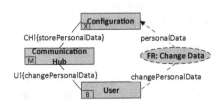

Fig. 5. Problem diagram *Change Personal Data*

Following the ProCOR method, we obtain the domains to be considered for the threat identification. The list of domains is shown in Table 3.

For all domains in scope (see Table 3), we perform the steps of the introduced procedure. We use the threat *Injection* described in Tables 1 and 2 as the input for the procedure.

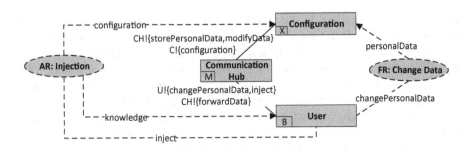

Fig. 6. Problem diagram with integration

Configuration (X). *Step 1:* The domain *Configuration* is a lexical domain. Comparing the domain type with the type of target domain documented for the threat, we consider the threat as relevant. *Step 2:* The security goal related to this domain is integrity. There is a high impact for integrity documented in the template. Hence, the threat remains relevant. *Step 3:* The domain is contained in the problem diagrams shown in Figs. 3 and 5. Both are comparable to the diagrams mentioned in the threat description. Hence, the threat is considered for the next step. *Step 4:* Considering the informal description of the threat, the problem diagram for *Setup* is not relevant. The input is only available for employees of the energy supplier. The threat agent acts as a user, but not as the energy supplier. The problem diagram *Change Personal Data* is relevant because the threat agent takes the role of a user. He/She can use the user interface to inject malicious code, which violates the security goal integrity. *Step 5:* The threat needs to be integrated into the problem diagram *Change Personal Data*. The join point for the machine is mapped to the communication hub, and the join point for the lexical domain is mapped to the configuration. The anti-requirement for injection is added to the problem diagram. All phenomena described in the threat diagram are added to the interfaces. The extended problem diagram is shown in Fig. 6.

CommunicationHub (M). *Step 1:* There is no threat mentioned with a machine as type of target domain. The other steps do not need to be carried out.

EnergySupplier (B). *Step 1:* There is no threat mentioned with a biddable domain as type of target domain. The other steps do not need to be carried out.

Table 3. Domains in scope

Domain (Type)	Information	Security goal
Configuration (X)	tariffParameters	Integrity
CommunicationHub (M)	measuredData	Availability
	measuredData	Integrity
	tariffParameters	Integrity
EnergySupplier (B)	tariffParameters	Integrity
MeterData (X)	measuredData	Availability
	measuredData	Integrity
SmartMeter (C)	measuredData	Availability
	measuredData	Integrity

MeterData (X). *Step 1:* The type of target domain of the threat *Injection* is the same as of *MeterData*. *Step 2:* The threat violates the security goals availability and integrity. Hence, the threat needs further consideration. *Step 3:* The domain *MeterData* is contained in the problem diagram shown in Fig. 4. The problem diagram is not comparable to the diagrams which are relevant for the threat *Injection*, because there is no user. Hence, the threat is not relevant for this domain, and the following steps do not need to be carried out.

SmartMeter (C). *Step 1:* There is no threat mentioned with a causal domain as type of target domain. The other steps do not need to be carried out.

As a result, we have determined that the threat *Injection* is relevant for the requirement *Change personal data*.

6 Related Work

There are numerous resources for threats, most of them focusing on attacks without using a common description format. There is also a lack of automatic identification methods for these resources. Moreover, some resources are restricted to a specific application context, such as web applications. In the following discussion, we use the terminology described in Sect. 3.

Lin et al. [11] propose abuse frames to analyze security requirements from an attacker's point of view. An anti-requirement is fulfilled when a threat initiated by an attacker is realized. Domains are considered as assets. The malicious machine of an abuse frame acts as the interface between attacker and asset domain. Comparable to problem frames, abuse frames are patterns to describe a typical attacker behavior. To use an abuse frame, it is composed with a base problem which is represented by a problem frame. Composing means to map domains from the base problem into the abuse frame. Based on the composed abuse frame, the attacker's behavior can then be further analyzed. In contrast, we consider some piece of information as an asset and our contribution is not restricted to attacks.

The Open Source Web Application Project [1] provides a list of the ten most severe security risks for web applications. The described risks have been used to evaluate our description template. A method to identify threats or to incorporate them with functional requirement is not given.

The Cloud Security Alliance (CSA) [13] provides a list of top threats for cloud computing. Threats are grouped in so called security concerns. To define such security concerns, the CSA makes use of articles about documented security incidents. The articles are determined using search engines, and the identified incidents are categorized to build a set of security concerns. The description format is informal, and the application context is restricted to cloud computing.

Uzunov and Fernandez [14] propose an extensible threat library. The library is based on a pattern for an abstract threat description. The definition of threat is similar to attack. The focus for this library is on distributed systems, but the pattern can be adapted for other needs. There is a strong relation to software architectures, whereas we focus on the relation to functional requirements.

Microsoft developed a method called STRIDE [15]. It is a popular security framework which is used to identify security threats. Using data flow diagrams for modeling the system and its behavior, threats are elicited based on existing threat categories: Spoofing, Tampering, Repudiation, Information Disclosure, Denial of Service and Elevation of privilege. Each of these categories is a negative counterpart to a security goal. Using STRIDE, threats are identified based on data flow diagrams, whereas our approach is domain-based and considers functional requirements.

The *Bundesamt für Sicherheit in der Informationstechnik* [16] provides a catalogue describing incidents that might harm IT security. Incidents are not restricted to attacks. General aspects as fire harming the hardware are considered, too. The descriptions in this catalogues are informal and textual.

Lund et al. [17] propose a model driven risk management method, called CORAS. The terminology used in this work differs from the one we use. The identification of relevant threats is performed as a structured brainstorming where analysts meet experts with a specific domain knowledge. To document the results of the discussion, a specific graphical language has been developed. A common description format for threats is not used, and there is no relation to functional requirements.

Jürjens [18] describes an extension for UML to integrate security related information into UML diagrams. To model problem diagrams with UML, Côté et al. [19] provide a UML profile, called UML4PF to model problem frames. The consideration of UMLSec and UML4PF for our template might support the consistency between the requirement model and the security model.

Opdahl and Sindre [20] introduce misuse cases as an extension of use cases. A misuse case is related to the notion of an anti-requirement (cf. Sect. 4). We provide a more detailed view based on the software level and information flow.

7   Conclusion and Future Work

In the present paper, we propose a template to describe security threats for software-based systems. Our template follows the principle of security-by-design and is applicable during requirements engineering. A systematic risk identification requires a catalogue of threats. Using our template, security engineers can describe threats in a structured manner and a threat catalogue can be set up as needed. We do not restrict the approach to any specific domain.

By making technical decisions, new and more concrete threats might arise. To describe and identify those new threats, one can adapt our template for other steps of the software development lifecycle.

The consideration of domains in the template allows the linking to a problem-based model for functional requirements. We also showed how threats can be identified based on functional requirements. The integration into the requirements model ensures the consideration of relevant threats in the further steps of the risk management and software development process.

Currently, we consider all threats in isolation. It is obvious that there are dependencies between different threats. For example, disclosing the credentials of an administrator by performing an injection may lead to new relevant threats. We plan to elaborate a way to add these relations between threats to the template. The method to identify threats will then be carried out iteratively until no new threats can be identified.

We extended the CVSS specification with some additional information such as the type of threat and the types of affected and target domains. As future work, we aim to make use of the CVSS scoring system to estimate the severity of a threat. This estimation then supports the derivation of the risk level. We will also elaborate how the provided scales can be improved with regard to the level of details, e.g. more values to define the impact of the threat.

We believe that the template can be used to capture most threats, for example social engineering, as well. Those threats may not be related to functional requirements but can be described using the first part of the template (see Table 1). In that case, the second part of the template needs to be replaced by diagrams representing domain knowledge. For the future, we plan to also consider domain knowledge diagrams as an input for the threat identification method. These diagrams describe for example an information flow between two persons, which is not related to any functional requirement, but can be used to realize a threat.

Based on our template, we defined a semi-automatic method to identify relevant threats. A limitation of that method is that only threats described by such a template can be identified. After applying the method, an additional manual validation to identify additional threats should be considered. We aim to assist the security engineer as best as possible in performing that validation. A possible starting point are questionnaires which guide through the validation process.

As already mentioned in Sect. 3, controls are used to reduce a risk. We plan to provide a comparable template to describe such controls. The selection of relevant controls will be based on the identified threats and their integration into the requirements model.

References

1. Open Web Application Security Project: OWASP Top 10 - The Ten Most Critical Web Application Security Risks (2017)
2. FIRST.org: Common Vulnerability Scoring System v3.0: Specification Document
3. Jackson, M.: Problem Frames. Analyzing and Structuring Software Development Problems. Addison-Wesley, Boston (2001)
4. Wirtz, R., Heisel, M., Meis, R., Omerovic, A., Stølen, K.: Problem-based elicitation of security requirements - the ProCOR method. In: Proceedings of the 13th International Conference on Evaluation of Novel Approaches to Software Engineering, vol. 1, pp. 26–38. ENASE, INSTICC, SciTePress (2018)
5. Faßbender, S., Heisel, M., Meis, R.: Aspect-oriented requirements engineering with problem frames. In: ICSOFT-PT 2014 - Proceedings of the 9th International Conference on Software Paradigm Trends. SciTePress (2014)
6. ISO: ISO 31000 Risk Management - Principles and Guidelines. International Organization for Standardization (2009)
7. Wirtz, R., Heisel, M., Borchert, A., Meis, R., Omerovic, A., Stølen, K.: Risk-based elicitation of security requirements according to the ISO 27005 standard. In: Evaluation of Novel Approaches to Software Engineering 13th International Conference, ENASE 2018. LNCS, Madeira, Portugal. Springer, Heidelberg (2018, submitted for publication)
8. International Organization for Standardization: ISO 27005:2011 Information technology - Security techniques - Information security risk management. Standard (2011)
9. Common Criteria: Common Criteria for Information Technology Security Evaluation v3.1. Release 5. Standard (2017)

10. FIRST.org: Common Vulnerability Scoring System v3.0: User Guide
11. Lin, L., Nuseibeh, B., Ince, D.C., Jackson, M., Moffett, J.D.: Analysing security threats and vulnerabilities using abuse frames (2003)
12. OPEN meter Consortium: Report on the identification and specification of functional, technical, economical and general requirements of advanced multi-metering infrastructure, including security requirements (2009)
13. Cloud Security Alliance: The treacherous 12 - cloud computing top threats in 2016
14. Uzunov, A., Fernandez, E.: An extensible pattern-based library and taxonomy of security threats for distributed systems. Comput. Stand. Interfaces **36**, 734–747 (2014)
15. Shostack, A.: Threat Modeling: Designing for Security. Wiley, Hoboken (2014)
16. BSI Germany: IT-Grundschutz-Katalog (2018)
17. Lund, M.S., Solhaug, B., Stølen, K.: Model-Driven Risk Analysis. The CORAS Approach. Springer, Heidelberg (2010). https://doi.org/10.1007/978-3-642-12323-8
18. Jürjens, J.: Model-based security engineering with UMLsec. In: Serenity Day: Establishing IT Security as a Full Engineering Discipline, Brussels (2009)
19. Côté, I., Hatebur, D., Heisel, M., Schmidt, H.: UML4PF - a tool for problem-oriented requirements analysis. In: Proceedings of the International Conference on Requirements Engineering (RE). IEEE Computer Society (2011)
20. Sindre, G., Opdahl, A.L.: Eliciting security requirements with misuse cases. Requir. Eng. **10**(1), 34–44 (2005)

Optimal Distribution of Privacy Budget in Differential Privacy

Anis Bkakria[1], Aimilia Tasidou[1(✉)], Nora Cuppens-Boulahia[1],
Frédéric Cuppens[1], Fatma Bouattour[2], and Feten Ben Fredj[2]

[1] IMT Atlantique, Cesson-Sévigné, France
{anis.bkakria,aimilia.tasidou}@imt-atlantique.fr
[2] Digital & Ethics, 15 rue rougemont, 75009 Paris, France

Abstract. Privacy budget management plays an important role when applying differential privacy, as it sets an upper limit in the ability to utilise the private database. In this paper, we explore the possibility of extending the total allocated privacy budget, taking into consideration the data consumer characteristics and the data utilisation context. To this end, we first study the problem of privacy budget distribution in adaptive multi-data consumer differential privacy use cases. Then, we present an extension of the classic differential privacy formal model that allows taking into consideration data consumers' information disclosure risk when distributing the privacy budget among them. Finally, we define a method that allows to optimally distribute a given privacy budget among a private database's data consumers.

Keywords: Differential privacy · Privacy budget distribution · Information disclosure risk

1 Introduction

In the last decade, a new paradigm called *differential privacy* has emerged as a new formal model that ensures more robust privacy guarantees, regardless of prior knowledge an adversary may possess [8]. The differential privacy model guarantees that given two databases which differ exactly in the information of a single individual *ind* (the two databases differ exactly on the record that contains the information of *ind*), a differential private data analysis mechanism will output, for the two databases, randomized results with almost identical probability distributions. Hence, regardless how much an adversary knows about the other records in the database, seeing the result of the performed private analysis will not allow guessing with high confidence the database over which the private analysis was performed. Therefore, the adversary cannot guess with high confidence whether *ind* is present in the database.

Differential privacy's strong privacy guarantee comes at the price of decreased precision for the query responses and analysis results delivered to data consumers (e.g., individuals or entities that are going to perform data analysis over the

A. Zemmari et al. (Eds.): CRiSIS 2018, LNCS 11391, pp. 222–236, 2019.
https://doi.org/10.1007/978-3-030-12143-3_18

private database). This trade-off between the level of ensured privacy and the precision of the query responses is represented in the differential privacy model through the parameter ϵ. A smaller value of ϵ means stronger privacy guarantees and lower precision of query responses.

In the last years several papers have been published [2,5,14,15,18,21,22] that study the trade-off between privacy and utility (precision) in differentially private mechanisms for different kinds of queries (e.g., counting queries [5,15,21], histogram queries [22], marginal queries [2], etc.). The aforementioned approaches tried to design new differential private mechanisms that allow either to enhance the precision of the responses for specific kinds of queries or to reduce the quantity of the privacy budget to be consumed for each query (i.e., increase the total number of queries that can be performed over the database).

Although the differential privacy model has drawn attention in quite a few areas and despite the over a hundred papers on differential privacy that are published from the security, database, machine learning, and statistics communities, some open problems remain untackled. The most obvious is how to optimally distribute among the set of data consumers the total privacy budget that can be consumed over the private database. To the best of our knowledge, all existing approaches and their developed solutions, such as PINQ [19] and Airavat [20], suppose that all data consumers who can query the private database share the same privacy budget (i.e., the total budget specified by the data owner). This configuration allows a data consumer to consume more privacy budget than other data consumers. In the case of a malicious data consumer who consumes the total privacy budget, other data consumers may be prevented from querying the private database.

In this paper, we present an approach that extends the classic differential private model to optimally distribute the total privacy budget to be consumed over a database among its data consumers that are allowed query the private database. The idea of our approach is to use the risk of publishing or disclosing the information learned from the private database for each data consumer, to optimally distribute the privacy budget.

The paper is organised as follows: In Sect. 2 we provide some useful background on differential privacy and in Sect. 3 we describe the problem statement that motivated our work. In Sect. 4 we propose an evaluation method for the contextual risk of the database and the data consumers. In Sect. 5 we present our proposed solution for optimal privacy budget allocation among data consumers. Finally, in Sect. 6 we discuss the conclusions drawn from this work.

2 Background on Differential Privacy

Informally, an algorithm is differentially private if a small change in its input does not considerably modify its output. Differential privacy is formalized as follows:

Definition 1 (ϵ-differential privacy [10]). *A mechanism $\mathcal{M}$ is ϵ-differentially private if for all input databases d, any $d' \in \mathcal{D}^d$ and any subset of outputs $S \in Range(\mathcal{M})$, the following condition holds:*

$$Pr[\mathcal{M}(d) \in S] \leq exp(\epsilon) \times Pr[\mathcal{M}(d') \in S]$$

where $\mathcal{D}^d$ is the set of d's neighboring databases, each differing from d by at most one record and the probability is taken over the randomness of the $\mathcal{M}$.

The previous definition states that any data consumer who will observe the result of the execution of $\mathcal{M}$ over d cannot guess the presence of an individual in d with more than $100 \times (|1 - 1/exp(\epsilon)|)\%$ of confidence.

The formal model of differential privacy allows computing the level of ensured privacy after performing a set of queries on the same database d.

Theorem 1 (Mechanism Composition [9]**).** *Given a set of k mechanisms $\mathcal{M}_1, \cdots, \mathcal{M}_k$ such that each $\mathcal{M}_i$ is ϵ_i-differential private, $i \in [1, k]$. Then, any mechanism $\mathcal{M}$ that is a composition of $\mathcal{M}_1, \cdots \mathcal{M}_k$ is $\sum_{i=1}^{k} \epsilon_i$-differentially private.*

Note that in the previous definition, each mechanism can be considered as the differential private execution of a query or analysis over database d. So, in order for d's data curator to allow a data consumer to execute a set of queries $q_1, \cdots, q_k$ using the mechanisms $\mathcal{M}_1, \cdots, \mathcal{M}_k$, a privacy budget greater or equal to $\sum_{i=1}^{k} \epsilon_i$ needs to be assigned to the data consumer.

3   Problem Statement

Let us consider that the total privacy budget for a medical database d specified by a hospital is ϵ_t. Let us also suppose that d will be used by three data consumers: a data scientist u_i working in an insurance company, a data scientist u_h working in the hospital, and a researcher u_r. The three data consumers want to perform interactively a set of queries. That is, the hospital does not know in advance the set of queries to be performed by each data consumer. So, the main question here is how to manage the usage of ϵ_t by the three data consumers?

One trivial solution is to share ϵ_t between the three data consumers. However, this solution will allow a data consumer to consume more privacy budget than others. In the worst case, one data consumer can prevent others to query the private database by consuming the total privacy budget (e.g., by performing sequentially a high-privacy-budget-consuming query many times).

To avoid the previous problem, the hospital can try to distribute the total privacy budget between the data consumers. In this case, due to the fact that the adversary model of differential privacy assumes that the risk/probability that each data consumer will disclose the information learned about d is equal to 1 (assumption (i)), ϵ_t should be distributed as follows:

$$\epsilon_{u_h} + \epsilon_{u_i} + \epsilon_{u_r} = \epsilon_t \tag{1}$$

Although the previous formula represents a privacy budget distribution condition, it does not specify how much privacy budget the hospital should give to each data consumer. Moreover, assumption (i) is too strong and probably not valid in our case, since, logically, the probability that u_i and u_h disclose the information they learned is less than 1. We strongly believe that by quantifying and taking into consideration the disclosure probability of data consumers' in the differential privacy model, we can achieve a better distribution of the privacy budget over the data consumers that are authorized to query d.

4   Contextual Risk Evaluation

In order to take into account the disclosure probability of data consumers for the allocation of the differential privacy budget, we define a model for identifying the parameters to be taken into account when assessing the disclosure risk of data consumers. Disclosure risk metrics need to take into account all contextual information surrounding the query. There are some attempts in the literature to model the contextual risk. In multimedia environments, Adams [1] built a model on users' perception of privacy, that proposes three elements affecting the user?s perception of privacy: the released information sensitivity, the level of trust of the user in the information receiver and the usage of the information. The author stresses the fact that information sensitivity perceptions would depend on the context of the data use, as argued by Dix [7].

The work by Lederer et al. [16] is based on Adams' model for conceptualizing privacy, in ubiquitous computing environments. In their privacy model the authors also introduce legal, normative, market and architectural forces from Lessig's societal-scale model [17]. Barker et al. [3] provide other factors to model data privacy: the purpose of data release, the visibility of data (who will be permitted to access and use the data) the granularity of the data, which refers to data characteristics, and the data retention (storage) period.

Working on data identifiability issues, El Emam [11,13] defined, in multiple consecutive studies, some criteria that affect the disclosure risk. These criteria include users' motives and capabilities and the level of security controls at the data recipient side. Recently, Dankar and Badgi [6] proposed a conceptual risk-aware data sharing system which proposes anonymisation solutions according to each context. To model the contextual privacy risk, the authors consider four factors: data sensitivity, data access purpose, the location of the user and the user risk.

According to the described literature, factors affecting privacy risk are mainly related to the data characteristics, the data recipient and the data usage. In this paper, based on the literature, we propose a new approach to model the contextual risk that can be used in the case of differential privacy.

In particular, we develop a three-dimensional framework to model the contextual risk. The three dimensions of the context considered in this work are: data characteristics, user profile and data access purpose. For each dimension, we define a number of representative criteria:

– Database Characteristics: This dimension encompasses several elements. We consider the presence of personal data and especially the presence of sensitive identifying attributes including those posing a legal risk (e.g. GDPR requirements), as well as those potentially presenting socio-cultural sensitivity.

– User profile: Inspired by the adversary's model proposed by El Emam [12], we consider that any database user can be viewed as a potential attacker. Thus, we consider the users' ability to re-identify the data (assessed through their core and technical competencies) and their trust level (through their history of incidents). We also consider the presence of confidentiality engagements and of the users' training on privacy issues as factors affecting user risk. The latter two criteria are two practices (among others) being used in the corporate sector, to address privacy issues while manipulating personal data.
– Purpose: We consider the possibility that the received data or the results obtained from this data would be published.

In order to assess the contextual risk, we propose a checklist containing several questions. In Table 1 we extract some representative questions, each one of which is associated with one dimension.

Table 1. Risk assessment checklist

Dimension	Question	Risk	
		Yes	No
Database characteristics	(Q1) Does the DB contain personal data?	1	0
	(Q2) How much the data stored in the DB are sensitive?	R_{Q_2}	
User	(Q3) Does the user have functional competencies that permit to understand the DB details?	R_{Q_3}	
	(Q4) Does the user have technical skills that permit to re-identify data?	R_{Q_4}	
	(Q5) Has not he received recent training on Privacy?	R_{Q_5}	
	(Q6) Has an engagement of confidentiality been signed?	R_{Q_6}	1
	(Q7) Does the history of the user contain breach incidents?	1	R_{Q_7}
Purpose	(Q8) Is there any aim of external publication of received data?	1	R_{Q_8}

For the questions Q_1, Q_6, Q_7 and Q_8 there are only two possible answers: Yes or No. For Q_1, Q_7 and Q_8, "Yes" means that the risk is 1, otherwise the risk is zero for Q_1[1], and R_{Q_7} and R_{Q_8} for Q_7 and Q_8 respectively. For questions Q_2, Q_3, Q_4 and Q_5 a value between zero and 1 is expected. For question Q_2 for example, one can consider databases containing legally sensitive data as riskier than those only containing socio-cultural sensitive attributes. For question Q_4, one can consider that the higher the expertise of the database user on computer or data science, the higher the value for R_{Q_4} is.

We then quantify the user disclosure risk as following:

$$p_u = \prod_{i=1}^{n} R_{Q_i} \tag{2}$$

5   Optimal Privacy Budget Allocation

Our solution extends the differential privacy model for optimal privacy budget assignment among data consumers. That is, instead of reasoning about the information leaked for all data consumers, our approach consists of modeling the leaked information for each data consumer separately. The following definition quantifies the amount of leaked information for each data consumer.

Definition 2. *Given a data consumer u of a private database D and the corresponding privacy budget ϵ_u, suppose that u queries D by using a differential private mechanism $\mathcal{M}$, then the following condition holds:*

$$Pr^u[\mathcal{Q}(x) \in S] \leq e^{\epsilon_u} Pr^u[\mathcal{Q}(y) \in S] \tag{3}$$

where D' and D are adjacent, $S \subseteq Range(\mathcal{M})$, and $Pr^u[c]$ denotes the probability that c holds from u's perspective.

By considering the risk/probability that all data consumers will share or disclose the information they learned about the private database, we can compute, as shown in the following theorem, the probability that an adversary will learn all the information that has been released to data consumers through their performed queries.

Theorem 2 (disclosure risk-based differential privacy). *Given a set of data consumers $\mathcal{U}$ of a private database D and p_u representing the risk/probability that the data consumers $u \in \mathcal{U}$ will share or disclose the information they are going to learn about D to other parties. If we assume that for each data consumer $u_i \in \mathcal{U}$ a privacy budget ϵ_{u_i} is attributed, then, in the worst case, the following condition holds:*

---

[1] The rationale behind that is that the anonymization would be less relevant when the dataset does not contain personal data.

$$Pr\left[\exists \mathcal{A}, \forall \mathcal{U}' \subseteq \mathcal{U} : Pr^{\mathcal{A}}[\mathcal{M}(D) \in S] = exp(\sum_{u \in \mathcal{U}'} \epsilon_u) Pr^{\mathcal{A}}[\mathcal{M}(D') \in S]\right] \leq \prod_{u \in \mathcal{U}'} p_u \tag{4}$$

where D and D' are adjacent databases, and $\mathcal{A}$ is an adversary.

Proof. Since each data consumer $u \in \mathcal{U}$ has a privacy budget ϵ_u, so in the worst case, we have:

$$\forall u \in \mathcal{U}' : Pr^u[\mathcal{M}(D) \in S] = e^{\epsilon_u} Pr^u[\mathcal{M}(D') \in S] \tag{5}$$

Let us suppose that each data consumer $u_i \in \mathcal{U}'$ performed the set of queries $\mathcal{Q}_{u_i} = \{q_1^{u_i}, \cdots, q_{n_i}^{u_i}\}$ over the database D using a differential private mechanism $\mathcal{M}$ and got the set of outputs $\mathcal{Y}_{u_i} = \{y_1^{u_i}, \cdots, y_{n_i}^{u_i}\}$. Using the differential privacy composition theorem [9] we get:

$$\frac{Pr[\mathcal{M}(q_1^{u_i}(D)) = y_1^{u_i}] \times \cdots \times Pr[\mathcal{M}(q_{n_i}^{u_i}(D)) = y_{n_i}^{u_i}]}{Pr[\mathcal{M}(q_1^{u_i}(D')) = y_1^{u_i}] \times \cdots \times Pr[\mathcal{M}(q_{n_i}^{u_i}(D')) = y_{n_i}^{u_i}]} \leq \exp(\epsilon_{u_i}) \tag{6}$$

Then, in the worst case, the information learned by the data consumer u_i can be quantified as follows:

$$L_{u_i}^{D \to D'}(\mathcal{Y}_{u_i}) = \ln\left(\frac{Pr[\mathcal{M}(q_1^{u_i}(D)) = y_1^{u_i} \wedge \cdots \wedge \mathcal{M}(q_{n_i}^{u_i}(D)) = y_{n_i}^{u_i}]}{Pr[\mathcal{M}(q_1^{u_i}(D')) = y_1^{u_i} \wedge \cdots \wedge \mathcal{M}(q_{n_i}^{u_i}(D')) = y_{n_i}^{u_i}]}\right) = \epsilon_{u_i} \tag{7}$$

Let us now suppose that all data consumers in $\mathcal{U}'$ disclose the set of queries they performed and the set of responses they got to an adversary $\mathcal{A}$. Then, in the worst case, the information that can be learned by the adversary $\mathcal{A}$ can be quantified as follows:

$$
\begin{aligned}
L_{u_i}^{D \to D'}\left(\bigcup_{u \in \mathcal{U}'} \mathcal{Y}_u\right) &= \ln\left(\prod_{u_i \in \mathcal{U}}\left(\frac{\prod_{j=1}^{n_i} Pr[\mathcal{M}(q_j^{u_i}(D)) = y_j^{u_i}]}{\prod_{j=1}^{n_i} Pr[\mathcal{M}(q_j^{u_i}(D')) = y_j^{u_i}]}\right)\right) \\
&= \sum_{u_i \in \mathcal{U}'} \ln\left(\frac{\prod_{j=1}^{n_i} Pr[\mathcal{M}(q_j^{u_i}(D)) = y_j^{u_i}]}{\prod_{j=1}^{n_i} Pr[\mathcal{M}(q_j^{u_i}(D')) = y_j^{u_i}]}\right) \\
&= \sum_{u_i \in \mathcal{U}'} L_{u_i}^{D \to D'}(\mathcal{Y}_{u_i}) \\
&= \sum_{u_i \in \mathcal{U}'} \epsilon_{u_i}
\end{aligned}
\tag{8}
$$

Now, the probability that there exists an adversary who knows the set of queries performed by all data consumers in $\mathcal{U}'$ and the set of responses to those queries (an adversary who learns $\sum_{u_i \in \mathcal{U}'} \epsilon_{u_i}$ information about an individual in the database D) can be computed as follows:

$$Pr\left[\bigwedge_{u_i \in \mathcal{U}'}\left(\bigwedge_{j=1}^{n_i} disclose^{u_i}(q_j^{u_i}, y_j^{u_i})\right)\right] = \prod_{u_i \in \mathcal{U}} Pr\left[\bigwedge_{j=1}^{n_i} disclose^{u_i}(q_j^{u_i}, y_j^{u_i})\right]$$

$$(9)$$

$$= \prod_{u_i \in \mathcal{U}} p_{u_i}$$

where $disclose^u(q, y)$ means the disclosure of the query q and its response y by the data consumer u.

Finally, based on Eqs. 5, 8 and 9 we can deduce Eq. 4.

In our solution, we suppose that the data owner (or the data collector) will specify for each total privacy budget value (i.e., the value of disclosed information), the value of the maximum acceptable disclosure risk/probability level.

Definition 3 (α-risky privacy budget distribution). *Given a set of data consumers $\mathcal{U} = \{u_1, \cdots, u_n\}$ having each a disclosure probability p_{u_i}, we say that the privacy budget distribution function dist-budget: $\mathcal{U} \to \mathbb{R}$ is α-risky iff the following condition holds:*

$$\forall \mathcal{U}' \subseteq \mathcal{U} : \prod_{u \in \mathcal{U}'} p_u \le \alpha\left(\sum_{u \in \mathcal{U}'} dist\text{-}budget(u)\right)$$

$$(10)$$

where $\alpha : \mathbb{R} \to \mathbb{R}$.

The function α is going to be used by the data owner to indicate for each value of disclosed information, the value of the maximum acceptable disclosure risk/probability level. An example of the function definition could be:

$$\alpha(\epsilon^*) = \begin{cases} 1 & if \quad \epsilon^* \le \epsilon \\ e^{-\frac{\epsilon^* - \epsilon}{\epsilon}} & if \quad \epsilon^* > \epsilon \end{cases}$$

where ϵ is the quantity of information that an adversary can learn when the disclosure risk is 1 (i.e., the quantity of information that an adversary can learn in the classic differential privacy model). In this example, the data owner simply requires that the acceptable disclosure probability should decrease exponentially in relation to the amount of disclosed information. This function can be used for cases of not particularly sensitive data.

Other possibilities for the function α include:

- A logarithmic function for the disclosure probability, which could be selected in the case of very sensitive data, since the privacy budget is not increased significantly even for very small disclosure risk:

$$\alpha(\epsilon^*) = \begin{cases} 1 & if \quad \epsilon^* \le \epsilon \\ \frac{e^{\epsilon-1}-e^{\epsilon^*-1}}{e^{\epsilon-1}-1} & if \quad \epsilon^* > \epsilon \end{cases}$$

- A linear function for the disclosure probability, which could be selected in the case of moderately sensitive data, since the privacy budget is increased linearly in correspondence to the decrease of the disclosure risk.

$$\alpha(\epsilon^*) = \begin{cases} 1 & if \quad \epsilon^* \le \epsilon \\ \frac{\epsilon-\epsilon^*}{\epsilon-1} & if \quad \epsilon^* > \epsilon \end{cases}$$

In Fig. 1 the graphs of three possible functions (exponential, logarithmic and linear) for the budget allocation as a function of the disclosure risk are presented.

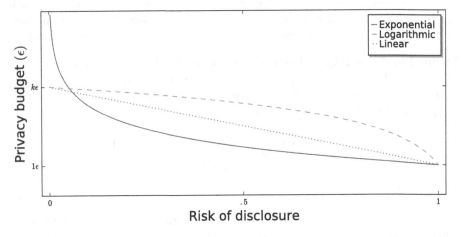

Fig. 1. Example functions for budget allocation as a function of risk

Note that Theorem 2 and Definition 3 are directly related through the right side of the inequality (4) and the left side of the inequality (10). Informally speaking, given a set of data consumers $\mathcal{U}'$ and a privacy budget distribution function *dist-budget* that assigns for each data consumer a privacy budget to use for querying the private database, *dist-budget* is alpha risky if the probability that there exists an adversary $\mathcal{A}$ who knows the information that has been released to data consumers in $\mathcal{U}'$ through their performed queries is less or equal to the maximum acceptable disclosure risk level defined by the data owner.

We now define our method for optimal privacy budget assignment among data consumers. This method is based mainly on the data owner's trade-off between the data consumers' disclosure probability/risk and the quantity of disclosed information, which we presented in Definition 3.

To meet the optimality in privacy budget sharing, we should maximize the privacy budget to be attributed to each data consumer while ensuring the satisfaction of the data owner's trade-off between data consumers' disclosure probability/risk and the quantity of disclosed information. This can be formalized as follows:

Definition 4. *Given a set of data consumers* $\mathcal{U} = \{u_1, \cdots, u_n\}$ *having each a disclosure probability* p_{u_i} *and a function* $\alpha : \mathbb{R} \to \mathbb{R}$ *that specifies for each value of disclosed information, the value of the acceptable disclosure probability. An optimal privacy budget assignment is the solution to the following maximization problem:*

$$\underset{u \in \mathcal{U}}{Maximize} \quad dist\text{-}budget(u)$$

$$s.t. \qquad \forall u \in \mathcal{U} : \epsilon_u > 0$$

$$\forall \mathcal{U}' \subseteq \mathcal{U} : \prod_{u \in \mathcal{U}'} p_u \leq \alpha \left(\sum_{u \in \mathcal{U}} dist\text{-}budget(u) \right) \tag{11}$$

$$\forall u_1, u_2 \in \mathcal{U} : (p_{u_1} - p_{u_2}) \times (\epsilon_{u_1} - \epsilon_{u_2}) \leq 0$$

In the previous definition, the first condition states that all data consumers of the private database should have a privacy budget greater than zero. The second condition ensures that given a set of data consumers in $\mathcal{U}$, the probability that all of them will disclose the information they learn is less or equal to the disclosure threshold specified by the function α. Finally, the last condition ensures that if a data consumer u_1 has a disclosure probability greater (respectively, lesser) than the disclosure probability of a data consumer u_2, then the privacy budget to be attributed to u_1 should be lesser or equal (respectively, greater or equal) than the privacy budget to be attributed to u_2.

Theorem 3. *Finding the optimal solution of a privacy budget assignment problem (Definition 4) is NP-hard.*

Proof. We prove the previous theorem by a reduction from the NP-hard problem of the profit maximization pricing problems [4], which is formulated as follows: *We consider profit maximization pricing problems, where we are given a set of m customers and a set of n items. Each customer c is associated with a subset $I_c \subseteq [n]$ of items of interest, together with a budget B_c, and we assume that there is an unlimited supply of each item. Once the prices are fixed for all items, each customer c buys a subset of items in Sc, according to its buying rule. The goal is to set the item prices so as to maximize the total profit.*

We define the correspondence between the problem of profit maximization pricing and our privacy budget assignment problem as follows: The privacy budget to be attributed to each user can be considered as the price of each item in the profit maximization pricing problem. The first constraint in our problem definition (Definition 4) is considered since, logically, the price of each item should be greater than zero. The second and the third constraints of our problem can be represented in the profit maximization pricing problem by the condition saying that each customer c wants to buy as much items as possible from I_c using the budget B_c. As a result, any algorithm that efficiently finds the optimal solution of a privacy budget assignment problem can be used to efficiently solve the profit maximization pricing problem optimality.

Since the problem of finding the optimal solution of a privacy budget assignment is NP-hard, we cannot expect to be able to solve an instance of arbitrary size of this problem to optimality. Thus, heuristic resolution strategies are widely exploited to solve such a problem with a reasonable computational effort.

Algorithm 1 shows our heuristic algorithm for finding a *near* optimal solution for privacy budget assignment among users. The algorithm starts by computing the probability that all users in $\mathcal{U}$ disclose the information they learn about the private database (lines 2 to 4). According to the computed probability and the function α, the algorithm computes the total privacy budget that can be shared between users ($\alpha(p_\mathcal{U})$), which will be initially shared equally between all users in $\mathcal{U}$ (lines 5 to 7). From line 11 to 13, for each user in $\mathcal{U}$, two variables are created and initialized to zero. The variable u_v will contains the number of user combinations to which u belongs and that violate the second constraint in the maximization problem (Definition 4), while variable e_w is going to be used to store the fraction of a user's privacy budget that should be removed to satisfy the violated constraints in the maximization problem. Then, for each combination c, we compute ϵ_c the privacy budget to be attributed to all users in the combination, and p_c, the probability that all users in c can disclose the information they learned about the private database (lines 17 to 20). After that, the algorithm checks for each combination whether the total privacy budget attributed to all users in the combination exceeds the threshold specified by the function α (lines 21 to 23). Then, the amount of privacy budget w that should be removed from each user's privacy budget to satisfy the violated constraints is computed (line 24). In the next step, the algorithm searches, in the set of users in $\mathcal{U}$, the one (*most_violater*) that belongs the most to the combinations that violated our maximization constraints (i.e., the one having the largest u_v) (lines 37 to 42).

Algorithm 1. Differential Privacy budget assignment algorithm

---

   input : $\mathcal{U} = \{u_1, \cdots, u_n\}$ /* A set of users */
              $\{p_{u_1}, \cdots, p_{u_n}\}$ /* the set of disclosure probabilities for the users in $\mathcal{U}$ */

        α /* A function that specifies for each value of disclosed information, the value of the disclosure probability */

   output: $\epsilon_u, \forall u \in \mathcal{U}$ /*The privacy budget to be attributed for each user */

1	**Begin**
2	**foreach** $u \in \mathcal{U}$ **do**
3	$\vert$ $p_\mathcal{U} = p_\mathcal{U} \times p_u$ /* Disclosure probability for $\mathcal{U}$ */
4	**endfch**
5	**foreach** $u \in \mathcal{U}$ **do**
6	$\vert$ $\epsilon_u = \frac{\alpha(p_\mathcal{U})}{card(\mathcal{U})}$ /* Privacy budget initialisation for each user */
7	**endfch**
8	$\mathcal{C} = all\_combination(\mathcal{U})$ /* compute all combination of users in $\mathcal{C}$ */
9	**do**
10	risky_assignment = **false**
11	**foreach** $u \in \mathcal{U}$ **do**
12	$\vert$ $u_v, u_w = 0$
13	**endfch**
14	**foreach** $c \in \mathcal{C}$ **do**
15	$p_c = 1, \epsilon_c = 0$
16	risky_combination = **false**
17	**foreach** $u \in c$ **do**
18	$\vert$ $p_c = p_u \times p_c$
19	$\vert$ $\epsilon_c = \epsilon_u + \epsilon_c$
20	**endfch**
21	**if** $(p_c > \alpha(\epsilon_c))$ **then**
22	$\vert$ risky_assignment, risky_combination = **true**
23	**end**
24	w $= \frac{\alpha^{-1}(p_c)}{\alpha(\epsilon_c)}$
25	**foreach** $u \in c$ **do**
26	$u_v {+}= 1$
27	**if** *(risky_combination **and** $u_w > w$)* **then**
28	$\vert$ $u_w = w$
29	**end**
30	**else if** *(!risky_combination **and** $u_w < w$ **and** $u_v = 0$)* **then**
31	$\vert$ $u_w = w$
32	**end**
33	**endfch**
34	**endfch**

```
35
36
37          most_violater = null
38          foreach u ∈ U do
39              if (most_violater = null or u_v > most_violater_v) then
40                  |   most_violater = u
41              end
42          endfch
43          available_budget = ε_{most_violater} − ε_{most_violater} × most_violater_w
44          ε_{most_violater} = ε_{most_violater} × most_violater_w
45          w_{total} = 0
46          foreach u ∈ U do
47              if (u_v = 0) then
48                  |   w_{total}+ = u_w
49              end
50          endfch
51          foreach u ∈ U do
52              if (u_v = 0) then
53                  |   ε_u+ = (available_budget × \frac{e_w}{w_{total}})
54              end
55          endfch
56      while risky_assignment;
57  end
```

Finally, the algorithm adds the privacy budget removed from the *most_violater*'s privacy budget to the users that belong less to the combinations that violated our maximization constraints (lines 43 to 55).

6   Conclusions

This paper proposes a solution for the problem of privacy budget distribution in adaptive multi-data consumers differential privacy use cases. The solution extends the classic differential privacy model to include data consumers' information disclosure risk, and define a maximization objective function that ensures an optimal privacy budget distribution among data consumers. As future work, we aim to define a method for quantifying the information disclosure risk of a data consumer, based on the criteria identified in this work, as well as to implement and evaluate our approach on a real use case.

References

1. Adams, A.: The implications of users' multimedia privacy perceptions on communication and information privacy policies. In: Proceedings of Telecommunications Policy Research Conference, Washington DC, p. 20 (1999)
2. Barak, B., Chaudhuri, K., Dwork, C., Kale, S., McSherry, F., Talwar, K.: Privacy, accuracy, and consistency too: a holistic solution to contingency table release. In: Proceedings of the Twenty-Sixth ACM SIGMOD-SIGACT-SIGART Symposium on Principles of Database Systems, pp. 273–282. ACM (2007)
3. Barker, K., et al.: A data privacy taxonomy. In: Sexton, A.P. (ed.) BNCOD 2009. LNCS, vol. 5588, pp. 42–54. Springer, Heidelberg (2009). https://doi.org/10.1007/978-3-642-02843-4_7
4. Chalermsook, P., Chuzhoy, J., Kannan, S., Khanna, S.: Improved hardness results for profit maximization pricing problems with unlimited supply. In: Gupta, A., Jansen, K., Rolim, J., Servedio, R. (eds.) APPROX/RANDOM -2012. LNCS, vol. 7408, pp. 73–84. Springer, Heidelberg (2012). https://doi.org/10.1007/978-3-642-32512-0_7
5. Cormode, G., Procopiuc, M., Srivastava, D., Tran, T.T.: Differentially private publication of sparse data. arXiv preprint arXiv:1103.0825 (2011)
6. Dankar, F.K., Badji, R.: A risk-based framework for biomedical data sharing. J. Biomed. Inform. **66**, 231–240 (2017)
7. Dix, A.J.: Information processing, context and privacy. In: INTERACT, pp. 15–20 (1990)
8. Dwork, C., McSherry, F., Nissim, K., Smith, A.: Calibrating noise to sensitivity in private data analysis. In: Halevi, S., Rabin, T. (eds.) TCC 2006. LNCS, vol. 3876, pp. 265–284. Springer, Heidelberg (2006). https://doi.org/10.1007/11681878_14
9. Dwork, C., McSherry, F., Nissim, K., Smith, A.: Calibrating noise to sensitivity in private data analysis. In: Halevi, S., Rabin, T. (eds.) TCC 2006. LNCS, vol. 3876, pp. 265–284. Springer, Heidelberg (2006). https://doi.org/10.1007/11681878_14
10. Dwork, C., Roth, A., et al.: The algorithmic foundations of differential privacy. Found. Trends® Theor. Comput. Sci. **9**(3–4), 211–407 (2014)
11. El Emam, K.: Risk-based de-identification of health data. IEEE Secur. Priv. **3**, 64–67 (2010)
12. El Emam, K.: Guide to the De-identification of Personal Health Information. Auerbach Publications, Boca Raton (2013)
13. El Emam, K., Dankar, F.K., Vaillancourt, R., Roffey, T., Lysyk, M.: Evaluating the risk of re-identification of patients from hospital prescription records. Can. J. Hosp. Pharm. **62**(4), 307 (2009)
14. Hardt, M., Talwar, K.: On the geometry of differential privacy. In: Proceedings of the Forty-Second ACM Symposium on Theory of Computing, pp. 705–714. ACM (2010)
15. Hay, M., Rastogi, V., Miklau, G., Suciu, D.: Boosting the accuracy of differentially private histograms through consistency. Proc. VLDB Endow. **3**(1–2), 1021–1032 (2010)
16. Lederer, S., Dey, A.K., Mankoff, J.: A conceptual model and a metaphor of everyday privacy in ubiquitous. Technical report, Berkeley, CA, USA (2002)
17. Lessig, L.: The architecture of privacy. Vand. J. Ent. L. Prac. **1**, 56 (1999)
18. Li, C., Hay, M., Rastogi, V., Miklau, G., McGregor, A.: Optimizing linear counting queries under differential privacy. In: Proceedings of the Twenty-Ninth ACM SIGMOD-SIGACT-SIGART Symposium on Principles of Database Systems, pp. 123–134. ACM (2010)

19. McSherry, F.D.: Privacy integrated queries: an extensible platform for privacy-preserving data analysis. In: Proceedings of the 2009 ACM SIGMOD International Conference on Management of data, pp. 19–30. ACM (2009)
20. Roy, I., Setty, S.T., Kilzer, A., Shmatikov, V., Witchel, E.: Airavat: security and privacy for mapreduce. NSDI **10**, 297–312 (2010)
21. Xiao, X., Wang, G., Gehrke, J.: Differential privacy via wavelet transforms. IEEE Trans. Knowl. Data Eng. **23**(8), 1200–1214 (2011)
22. Xu, J., Zhang, Z., Xiao, X., Yang, Y., Yu, G., Winslett, M.: Differentially private histogram publication. VLDB J. **22**(6), 797–822 (2013)

Author Index

Printed in the United States
By Bookmasters